Mastering AI for Healthcare

Revolutionizing Patient Care and Outcomes Through Hands-on AI-Driven Solutions

Nilashis Roy

Romita Ghosh

www.orangeava.com

First Published: April 2025

Published By: Orange Education Pvt Ltd, AVA®

Address: 9, Daryaganj, Delhi, 110002, India

275 New North Road Islington Suite 1314 London,
N1 7AA, United Kingdom

ISBN (PBK): 978-93-48107-64-0
ISBN (E-BOOK): 978-93-48107-06-0

Scan the QR code to explore our entire catalogue

www.orangeava.com

Dedicated To

My Beloved Parents,

Mr Snehashis Roy

Mrs Anjali Roy

and

My Uncle, Dr. Tushar Kanti Das

- Nilashis Roy

Papa

- Romita Ghosh

About the Authors

Nilashis Roy is a seasoned AI Scientist with a strong background in R&D, IT, Marketing, and Operations. He excels in leveraging the power of Data Analytics and Artificial Intelligence to lead digital transformation, especially in the healthcare sector. His expertise lies in analyzing trends and deriving valuable insights to enhance patient outcomes and revolutionize the healthcare industry.

An early adopter of AI technologies, Nilashis has had the distinct opportunity to collaborate with leading financial institutions such as HDFC, SBI, and ICICI. His contributions involve developing scalable machine learning models that have significantly improved their operational efficiency and service delivery.

Presently, Nilashis heads a dedicated team focused on improving healthcare quality for millions through advanced, data-driven AI solutions. His mission centers around making healthcare more accessible, efficient, and effective through the innovative application of technology.

Romita Ghosh is a passionate healthcare innovator on a mission to address unmet clinical needs and create lasting social impact. Her journey–rooted in personal resilience–began in 1998 after surviving a life-threatening illness. Since then, she has impacted over a million lives through her work at the intersection of health and technology, earning honors such as the Women Transforming India Award 2021.

A Public Health scholar at IIPHG, Romita is also an alumna of IIT Hyderabad and IIM Udaipur. She holds a double major in Biotechnology and Biochemistry, an MBA, and an ICMR Fellowship. Her AI-powered innovation, MAAP AI, is revolutionizing child nutrition in India.

Recognized by esteemed institutions such as the UN General Assembly, UN Women, and the Federal Foreign Office of Germany, Romita continues to shape the future of healthcare through empathy, expertise, and visionary leadership. She has been featured in prominent media outlets and programs such as Network18's *Jeetenge Hum*, and is a regular speaker at high-level forums and government events on AI, healthcare, and digital transformation.

About the Technical Reviewer

Nehaa Bansal is a trailblazing thought leader and data scientist with a strong passion for early innovation. Her extensive experience across diverse sectors including banking, finance, telecom, and insurance has honed her expertise in developing impactful predictive models. She graduated with top honors in Computer Science and holds a Master's in Data Science from BITS Pilani, which provided a strong foundation for her career.

Nehaa's professional life is guided by core values of ownership, prioritizing people, and understanding the "why" behind every action. She embraces an agile approach, acting quickly, learning from failures, iterating continuously, and prioritizing fairness. Driven by a passion for solving user problems, Nehaa combines her expertise in analytics, product strategy, and leadership to develop innovative solutions, consistently pushing boundaries and demonstrating unwavering dedication. Nehaa's commitment to continuous learning, inclusivity, and collaboration, combined with her dedication and empathy, makes her an inspiring leader driving positive change in technology and data science.

Acknowledgements

Writing this book has been a journey fueled by passion and purpose, made possible by the unwavering support of those around me.

Heartfelt thanks to my parents whose love, values, and sacrifices are the bedrock of who I am.

My deepest gratitude to my dearest friend and co-founder **Romita Ghosh**, and the team at Orange Education Pvt Ltd. Their vision and dedication have shaped this journey and its ideas.

I thank my friends whose patience, laughter, and belief added meaning to every step.

This book is not just a reflection of my work—it is a tribute to the collective strength, love, and brilliance of the people who walk beside me. Thank you for making this possible.

Warm regards,

Nilashis Roy

Artificial Intelligence reflects the humans who build it. At its heart, this book is a reminder that AI is a mirror of who we are.

Creating it has been personal—rooted in healing, purpose, and real-world public health, built alongside those who walked with us.

I would like to thank **Nilashis Roy**—co-founder, collaborator, and compass—for leading with vision.

To the teams at **iHeal HealthTech** and **Orange Education Pvt Ltd**—their dedication is the true source code.

To **friends** who became **family**—their love and laughter were the strength that carried me. Their presence, humor, and hope have been lifelines.

To the **shadow leaders**— who show up, work quietly, and lead without spotlight—this book is for them.

To **survivors**, whose resilience lights the way.

To **patients**, **caregivers**, and **healthcare workers** whose stories are the fuel for this journey.

This is not just my story. It's ours. Thank you for walking with me. Let's keep going.

With all my heart,

Romita Ghosh

Preface

Artificial Intelligence (AI) is no longer a futuristic concept–it is an essential component of modern healthcare. From streamlining clinical workflows to enhancing diagnostics, AI is revolutionizing how care is delivered, accessed, and experienced. As researchers, clinicians, and technologists come together to build smarter healthcare systems, the need to understand AI's potential and limitations becomes more urgent than ever.

This book, Leveraging AI in Healthcare, is a timely resource for healthcare professionals, researchers, students, and innovators seeking to explore the intersection of AI and medicine. Each chapter offers a structured exploration of AI's role across critical healthcare areas, grounded in real-world examples, practical use cases, and current challenges. We aim to simplify complex concepts while offering deep insights into how AI can be responsibly and effectively applied.

Whether you are a healthcare provider looking to improve patient outcomes or a policymaker planning to adopt AI-driven strategies, this book will serve as a trusted guide through the evolving landscape of intelligent healthcare.

Chapter 1. Introducing AI in Healthcare: This chapter sets the stage by defining AI, its origins, and its growing influence in healthcare. It provides an overview of the major areas where AI is making an impact and introduces key concepts readers will encounter throughout the book.

Chapter 2. AI Fundamentals for Healthcare: This chapter will cover the core AI technologies such as machine learning, deep learning, and natural language processing. The chapter explains these fundamentals in the context of healthcare applications, bridging the gap between technical jargon and medical utility.

Chapter 3. Predictive Analysis in Healthcare: This chapter explores how predictive analytics are used to forecast patient outcomes, disease outbreaks, and hospital resource needs. It includes case studies showing how data-driven predictions improve preventive care and operational efficiency.

Chapter 4. Artificial Intelligence in Telemedicine Remote Patient Monitoring: This chapter focuses on virtual care delivery, discussing how AI powers telemedicine platforms and supports continuous patient monitoring.

Readers will learn how wearable tech, chatbots, and remote diagnostics are redefining access to healthcare.

Chapter 5. AI in Clinical Decision Support and Electronic Health Record: This chapter dives into AI's role in assisting clinicians with diagnoses and treatment planning. It also highlights how AI improves the usability and intelligence of electronic health records, enabling more accurate and timely decisions.

Chapter 6. Imaging and Diagnosis Using AI: This chapter details how AI enhances diagnostic accuracy in radiology, pathology, and ophthalmology. It explores algorithmic interpretation of images, pattern recognition, and the integration of AI into existing diagnostic tools.

Chapter 7. Challenges and Limitations of AI in Healthcare: This chapter presents a balanced view by discussing data privacy, algorithmic bias, regulatory issues, and the need for ethical frameworks. It emphasizes the importance of transparency, inclusivity, and accountability in AI development and deployment.

Chapter 8. Future of AI in Healthcare: This chapter explores emerging trends such as personalized medicine, AI in genomics, and robotic surgeries. It also envisions how AI could reshape global health systems and the potential paths for inclusive and scalable AI adoption.

Get a Free eBook

We hope you are enjoying your recently purchased book! Your feedback is incredibly valuable to us, and to all other readers looking for great books.

If you found this book helpful or enjoyable, we would truly appreciate it, if you could take a moment to leave a short review with a 5 star rating on Amazon. It helps us grow, and lets other readers discover our books.

As a thank you, we would love to send you a free digital copy of this book, and a **30%** discount code on your next cart value on our official websites:

www.orangeava.com

www.orangeava.in (For Indian Subcontinent)

☑ **Here's how:**

Leave a review for the book on Amazon.

Take a screenshot of your review, and send an email to **info@orangeava.com** (it can be just the confirmation screen).

Once, we receive your screenshot, we will send you the digital file, within 24 hours.

Thank you so much for your support – it means a lot to us!

Downloading the code bundles and colored images

Please follow the links or scan the QR codes to download the
Code Bundles and Images of the book:

https://github.com/ava-orange-education/Mastering-AI-for-Healthcare

The code bundles and images of the book are also hosted on
https://rebrand.ly/5510fa

In case there's an update to the code, it will be updated on the existing GitHub repository.

Errata

We take immense pride in our work at **Orange Education Pvt Ltd,** and follow best practices to ensure the accuracy of our content to provide an indulging reading experience to our subscribers. Our readers are our mirrors, and we use their inputs to reflect and improve upon human errors, if any, that may have occurred during the publishing processes involved. To let us maintain the quality and help us reach out to any readers who might be having difficulties due to any unforeseen errors, please write to us at :

errata@orangeava.com

Your support, suggestions, and feedback are highly appreciated.

DID YOU KNOW

Did you know that Orange Education Pvt Ltd offers eBook versions of every book published, with PDF and ePub files available? You can upgrade to the eBook version at **www.orangeava.com** and as a print book customer, you are entitled to a discount on the eBook copy. Get in touch with us at: **info@orangeava.com** for more details.

At **www.orangeava.com**, you can also read a collection of free technical articles, sign up for a range of free newsletters, and receive exclusive discounts and offers on Print Books and eBooks.

PIRACY

If you come across any illegal copies of our works in any form on the internet, we would be grateful if you would provide us with the location address or website name. Please contact us at **info@orangeava.com** with a link to the material.

ARE YOU INTERESTED IN AUTHORING WITH US?

If there is a topic that you have expertise in, and you are interested in either writing or contributing to a book, please write to us at **business@orangeava.com**. We are on a journey to help developers and tech professionals to gain insights on the present technological advancements and innovations happening across the globe and build a community that believes Knowledge is best acquired by sharing and learning with others. Please reach out to us to learn what our audience demands and how you can be part of this educational reform. We also welcome ideas from tech experts and help them build learning and development content for their domains.

REVIEWS

Please leave a review. Once you have read and used this book, why not leave a review on the site that you purchased it from? Potential readers can then see and use your unbiased opinion to make purchase decisions. We at Orange Education would love to know what you think about our products, and our authors can learn from your feedback. Thank you!

For more information about Orange Education, please visit **www.orangeava.com**.

Table of Contents

Chapter 1
Introducing AI in Healthcare

Introduction

Artificial Intelligence (AI) is a field of computer science that focuses on creating machines and systems to perform tasks that typically require human intelligence. AI involves developing algorithms and models that allow machines to analyze and learn from data, recognize patterns, and make decisions based on that data. We can use AI in a variety of applications, such as natural language processing, computer vision, robotics, and data analysis. Artificial intelligence has the potential to transform many industries, from healthcare and finance to transportation and entertainment. However, there are also concerns about the ethical and social implications of AI, such as job displacement, bias, and privacy concerns. As AI continues to develop, it will be important to consider the benefits and risks associated with this powerful technology.

Structure

In this chapter, the following topics will be covered:

- Reason for Inventing AI
- Origin of Artificial Intelligence
- Building Blocks of AI
- AI in Healthcare
- Challenges of AI in Healthcare

Reason for Inventing AI

The invention of Artificial Intelligence (AI) was motivated by a desire to create machines and systems that could do tasks that typically required human intelligence. Recognizing speech, understanding natural language, making decisions, and identifying patterns in data are among these tasks.

In addition to the practical benefits of having machines that can perform intelligent tasks, there are also philosophical and scientific reasons for inventing AI. For example, some researchers are interested in studying the nature of intelligence itself, and building machines that can demonstrate intelligent behavior is one way to gain insight into how the human mind works. Others see AI as a way to automate tedious or dangerous tasks, freeing humans to focus on more interesting and creative work.

Overall, the invention of AI was driven by a combination of scientific curiosity, practical applications, and the ambition to develop new technologies that can improve our lives in numerous ways.

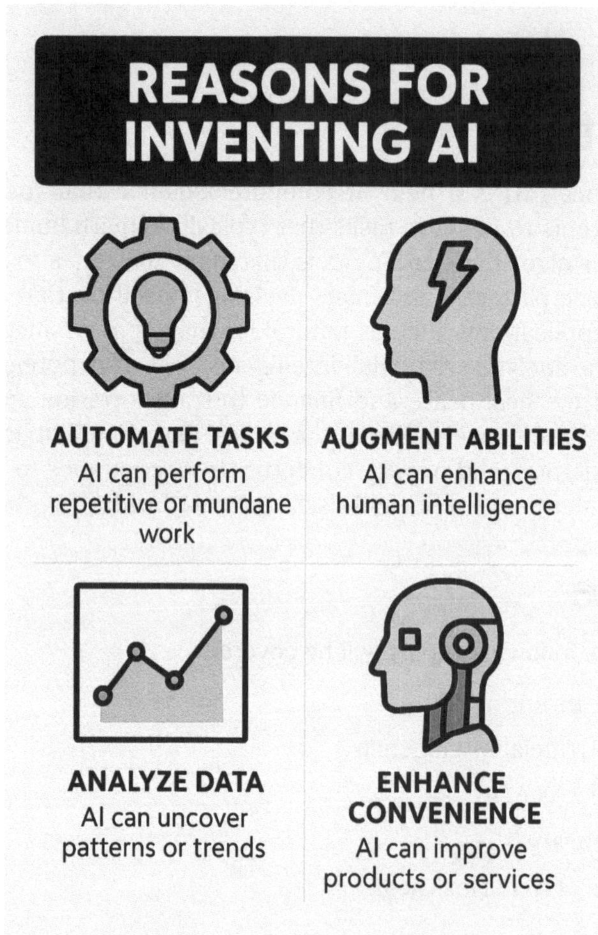

***Figure 1.1**: Reasons for Inventing AI*

Origin of Artificial Intelligence

The journey of AI in healthcare can be traced back to the 1950s when early AI programs were developed to simulate human reasoning. Over time, AI has advanced through several key milestones:

The 1950s-1970s: Foundations of AI in Healthcare

- The first AI programs, such as the Logic Theorist (1955) and General Problem Solver (1957), were designed to mimic human reasoning.
- In healthcare, AI applications were mostly theoretical, with a focus on knowledge representation and expert systems.

The 1980s: Rise of Expert Systems

- Expert systems such as MYCIN (for bacterial infections) and INTERNIST-I (for internal medicine) were developed to assist doctors in diagnosing diseases.
- These systems relied on rule-based logic and decision trees to suggest possible diagnoses and treatments.
- However, they were limited by their inability to learn from new data, requiring manual updates.

The 1990s-2000s: Emergence of Machine Learning in Healthcare

- Machine Learning (ML) algorithms began replacing rule-based systems, enabling AI to learn from data rather than relying solely on pre-programmed rules.
- AI applications expanded into medical imaging analysis, genomics, and predictive analytics.

The 2010s-Present: Deep Learning and AI Integration

- Deep learning (a subset of ML) enabled AI systems to analyze complex medical images, detect diseases, and assist in robotic surgeries.
- AI-powered Electronic Health Records (EHR) management streamlined administrative workflows.
- Google Health and IBM Watson Health began developing AI tools for diagnostics and personalized medicine.

The Future: AI-Powered Precision Medicine and Autonomous Healthcare

- AI is now being used for personalized treatment recommendations based on genetic data.
- Autonomous AI systems are being explored for robotic surgeries and real-time patient monitoring.
- AI-powered drug discovery platforms are accelerating the development of new medications.

Figure 1.2*: Origin of AI*

AI can be divided into several categories:

- **Narrow AI**, also known as Weak or Applied AI, is designed to perform specific tasks using predefined algorithms and rules, making it the most common form of AI in use today. In healthcare, AI models such as Google Health's diabetic retinopathy detection and IBM Watson for Oncology assist in diagnosing diseases but cannot generalize beyond their trained conditions. In finance, fraud detection systems and algorithmic trading AI analyze transactional data but lack decision-making capabilities beyond their scope. Customer service applications such as chatbots (Siri, Alexa, IBM Watson Assistant) efficiently handle predefined queries but cannot engage in deep reasoning. Retail platforms such as Amazon and Netflix's recommendation engines personalize user experiences but are limited to suggesting products or content based on past behavior. Autonomous systems, including Tesla's self-driving technology and industrial robotics, function within controlled environments but cannot adapt without retraining. In security, facial recognition software and AI-driven cybersecurity tools detect threats and authenticate users but do not understand the context. Entertainment AI, such as Deepfake technology, AlphaGo, and video game NPCs, enhances media experiences but remains task-specific. While these AI systems are highly effective at their respective functions, they lack the ability to generalize across different domains, distinguishing them from future advancements in Artificial General Intelligence (AGI).

- **General AI**, also known as Strong AI, is an advanced form of artificial intelligence that aspires to replicate human-like intelligence, reasoning, learning, and decision-making across multiple domains without being limited to specific tasks. Unlike Narrow AI, which excels in predefined areas, General AI would be capable of autonomous thinking, problem-solving, and adapting to new challenges without additional training. While no true General AI exists today, theoretical and fictional examples include HAL 9000 from 2001: A *Space Odyssey* and Jarvis from *Iron Man*—systems that understand complex human emotions, solve novel problems, and make independent decisions. In the real world, research initiatives such as OpenAI's work on advanced neural networks, DeepMind's progress in reinforcement learning, and GPT-based models aiming for broader intelligence are small steps toward this goal. However, significant technical and ethical barriers remain, and many experts debate whether General AI can ever be fully realized.
- **Super AI**, also known as Artificial Super Intelligence (ASI), refers to a hypothetical form of AI that would not only replicate human intelligence but surpass it in every aspect, including creativity, problem-solving, emotional intelligence, and even self-awareness. Unlike General AI, which aims to match human cognition, Super AI would have the ability to improve itself exponentially, leading to an intelligence explosion that could reshape civilization. While Super AI does not yet exist, it is a common theme in science fiction, often depicted as either a benevolent force or a potential existential threat. Examples from fiction include Skynet from *The Terminator*, the Machines from *The Matrix*, and Dr. Manhattan-like AI in *Ex Machina*, all of which demonstrate AI evolving beyond human control. Theoretical discussions around Singularity, a point where AI surpasses human intelligence and becomes uncontrollable, have been explored by researchers such as Ray Kurzweil and Nick Bostrom. While some argue that Super AI could solve humanity's greatest challenges, others warn of its risks, as an entity vastly superior to humans could have unpredictable motives or objectives. The feasibility of developing Super AI remains highly speculative, with ongoing debates about whether such intelligence is achievable or even desirable.

There is not always a clear distinction between these types of AI, which may overlap. For example, some researchers consider General AI to be a subset of Super AI, while others use the terms interchangeably.

Building Blocks of AI

Artificial Intelligence can be broken down into several subfields, which together form the building blocks of AI. Here are the main components of AI:

- **Machine Learning (ML):** ML is a subfield of AI that involves creating algorithms that can learn and improve from data without being explicitly programmed. It is the most common technique used in AI today and includes methods such as supervised learning, unsupervised learning, and reinforcement learning.
- **Deep Learning:** Deep learning is a subset of machine learning that uses neural networks with many layers to create more accurate models. It is particularly good at image and speech recognition and has been used to create chatbots and other conversational AI systems.
- **Natural Language Processing (NLP):** NLP is a subfield of AI that focuses on processing and analyzing human language. It involves tasks such as language translation, sentiment analysis, and speech recognition.
- **Computer Vision:** This is a subfield of AI that involves enabling computers to interpret and understand visual information from the world around them. This includes tasks such as image and video recognition, object detection, and facial recognition.
- **Robotics:** Robotics is the study of building robots that can perform tasks autonomously, using techniques from AI and other fields. Robotics involves hardware as well as software development and is used in manufacturing, healthcare, and other industries.
- **Expert Systems:** Expert systems are AI systems that mimic the decision-making ability of a human expert in a specific domain. They use rules and logic to make decisions and can be used in fields such as medicine, finance, and law.
- **AI Planning:** This involves creating algorithms that can plan and make decisions in complex and uncertain environments. This is useful in fields such as logistics, resource management, and game playing.
- **Knowledge Representation and Reasoning:** This area of AI assists in designing formal models of knowledge and reasoning about that knowledge. It is used in expert systems and other AI applications that require sophisticated reasoning abilities.

These parts of AI are often used in combination to create complex AI systems that can perform a wide range of tasks.

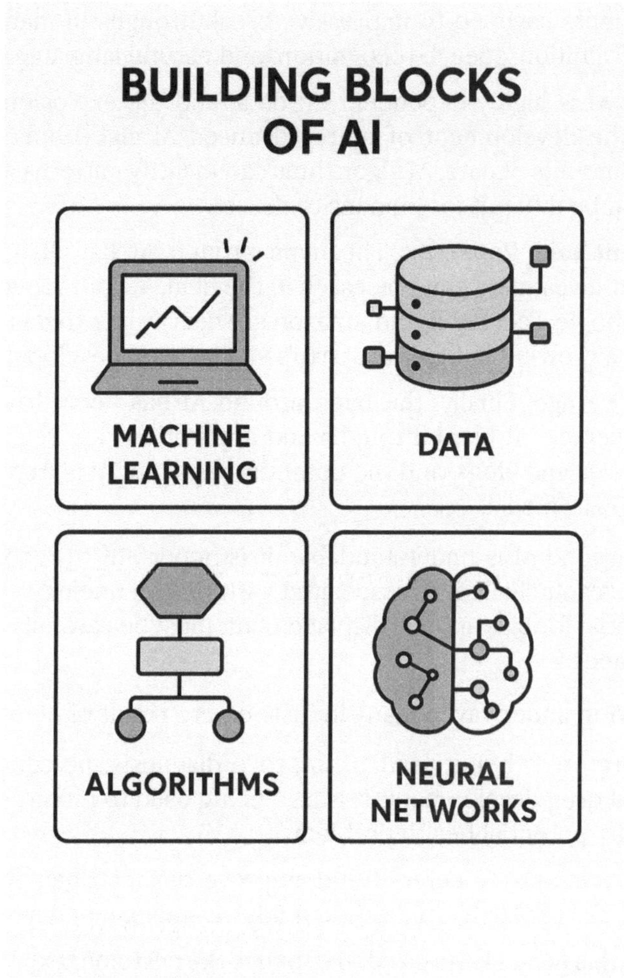

***Figure 1.3**: Building Blocks of AI*

AI Hype: So Popular!

The hype around Artificial Intelligence (AI) is driven by several factors, including the following:

- **Potential Benefits:** AI has the potential to revolutionize many industries, including healthcare, finance, and transportation. AI can help automate routine tasks, make more accurate predictions and decisions, and improve the efficiency of many processes. This potential for transformative benefits has generated a lot of excitement and interest in the field.
- **Rapid Advancements:** In recent years, there have been rapid advancements in AI, particularly in the areas of machine learning and deep learning. These

advancements have led to impressive breakthroughs in many areas, such as image recognition, speech recognition, and natural language processing.

- **Big Data:** AI is highly dependent on data, and the explosion of big data has enabled the development of more advanced AI algorithms. With access to massive amounts of data, AI algorithms can identify patterns and relationships that would be difficult for humans to detect.
- **Investment and Research:** The hype around AI has also been fueled by significant investments and research in the field. Major technology companies such as Google, Facebook, and Amazon are heavily invested in AI research, and there are a growing number of startups focused on developing AI solutions.
- **Media Coverage:** Finally, the hype around AI has been driven by extensive media coverage. AI breakthroughs and applications are regularly featured in news articles and blogs, and the potential impact of AI is frequently discussed in the popular media.

While the hype around AI is understandable, it is important to recognize that there are also limitations and challenges associated with this technology. Ethical concerns, such as the potential for bias and job displacement, must be carefully considered as AI continues to advance.

There is a revolution underway in many industries as a result of AI including:

- **Healthcare**: AI is being used to improve diagnosis, personalized treatment plans, and drug development. It is also being used to monitor patient's health and predict potential health problems.
- **Finance**: AI is used to detect fraud, improve risk management, and automate financial services such as investment advice and loan underwriting.
- **Retail**: In this field, AI is utilized to enhance the customer experience, automate inventory management, and optimize pricing and promotions.
- **Manufacturing**: AI helps in manufacturing to automate processes, optimize production, and reduce costs.
- **Transportation**: AI is being used to optimize routes, reduce traffic, and improve safety in autonomous vehicles.
- **Energy**: AI is being used to improve the efficiency of energy production and distribution, as well as to predict maintenance needs and prevent downtime.
- **Agriculture**: AI also supports agriculture to optimize crop yields, improve soil health, and detect plant diseases.
- **Education**: AI is being used to personalize learning and provide more effective feedback and assessment.

- **Media and Entertainment**: AI is used to personalize content recommendations, optimize advertising, and enhance user engagement.

These are just a few examples of how AI is transforming industries. As AI technology continues to advance, it has the potential to disrupt many other industries as well.

Funny Code Snippet

Here is a funny code snippet about why ai should be used:

```
print("Welcome to AI! Here are some reasons why you should learn
about it:")
print("- AI is transforming virtually every industry, from
healthcare to finance to transportation.")
print("- AI can help solve some of the world's most pressing
problems, such as climate change and livelihood.")
print("- AI is one of the fastest-growing fields, with many
exciting job opportunities and high salaries.")
print("- AI can be used to create intelligent machines that can
improve human lives and make our world a better place.")
print("- Learning about AI can also help you develop valuable
skills, such as problem-solving, critical thinking, and
creativity.")
```

AI in Healthcare

In the healthcare sector, AI refers to the use of advanced technologies such as machine learning, natural language processing, and computer vision to perform tasks that traditionally require human intelligence, such as diagnosis, treatment, and drug development. The objective of AI in healthcare is to improve patient outcomes by providing healthcare providers with more accurate diagnoses, personalized treatment plans, and proactive disease prevention.

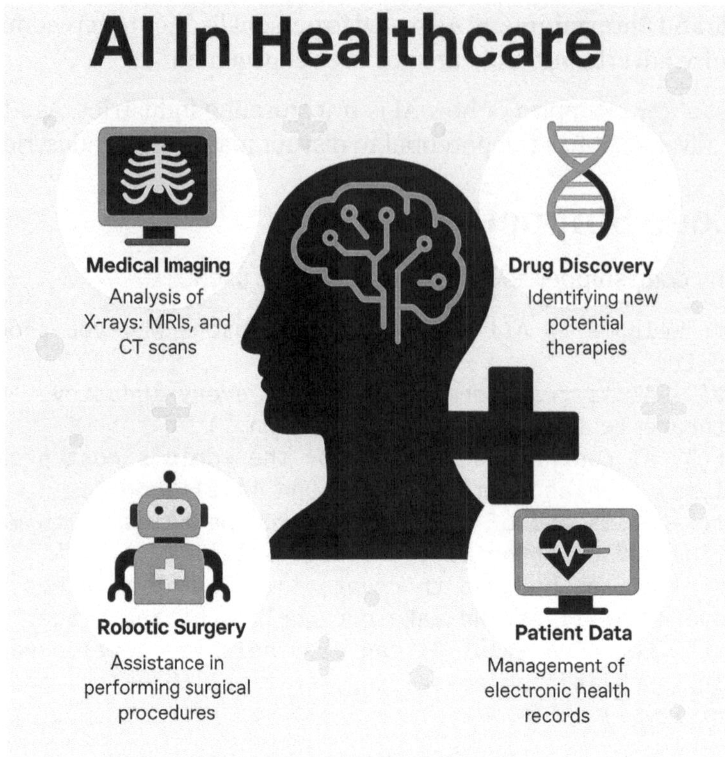

***Figure 1.4**: AI in Healthcare*

Artificial Intelligence (AI) is Transforming the Healthcare

Artificial Intelligence (AI) is transforming the healthcare industry in many ways, starting with:

- **Improved Diagnosis**: Using AI, healthcare providers can make more accurate diagnoses. AI algorithms can analyze medical images, such as X-rays and MRIs, to detect patterns and identify potential health issues. AI can also analyze patient data to help identify patients who are at high risk for certain health conditions.
- **Personalized Treatment**: AI is being used to develop personalized treatment plans for patients. AI algorithms can analyze patient data, including medical history, genetic data, and lifestyle factors, to identify the best treatment options for individual patients.
- **Drug Development**: AI is able to accelerate the drug development process. AI algorithms can analyze large amounts of data to identify potential drug targets, design new drugs, and predict the efficacy of new drugs.

- **Remote Patient Monitoring**: AI is used to monitor patient health remotely. AI algorithms can examine data from wearable devices and other sensors to detect changes in patient health and alert healthcare providers to potential health issues.
- **Administrative Tasks**: Even in administrative tasks, such as scheduling appointments, managing medical records, and processing insurance claims, AI is equally efficient. This can free up healthcare providers to spend more time with patients and focus on delivering high-quality care.
- **Medical Research**: To accelerate medical research, AI algorithms assist large amounts of medical data to identify patterns and relationships that would be difficult for humans to detect. This can lead to new discoveries and insights that can improve patient care.

These are just a few examples of how AI is transforming the healthcare industry. As AI technology continues to advance, it has the potential to revolutionize healthcare and improve patient outcomes.

AI has been making significant strides in the healthcare industry over the past few years. The integration of AI in healthcare has the potential to revolutionize the way healthcare providers deliver care and improve patient outcomes. This chapter will provide an overview of AI in healthcare and explore its potential benefits and challenges.

AI plays a significant role in digital therapeutics by enabling the development of more personalized and effective treatments.

Digital Therapeutics

Digital therapeutics (DTx) refers to a category of healthcare interventions that use digital technologies, such as mobile apps, software programs, wearable devices, and online platforms, to prevent, manage, or treat medical conditions. DTx interventions are designed to be evidence-based, clinically validated, and provide therapeutic benefits similar to traditional medical treatments.

Digital therapeutics are different from general health and wellness apps, as they are designed with a specific clinical purpose and are subject to rigorous clinical trials and regulatory oversight. DTx interventions can be used as standalone treatments or as part of a broader treatment plan, and they are often used in conjunction with traditional medical interventions.

DTx interventions can target a wide range of medical conditions, including chronic diseases such as diabetes, hypertension, and depression, as well as neurological disorders such as Parkinson's disease and multiple sclerosis. They can also be used for lifestyle interventions such as weight management, smoking cessation, and stress reduction.

Overall, digital therapeutics offer a promising approach to improving patient outcomes and expanding access to high-quality healthcare services, particularly for individuals who may have limited access to traditional healthcare services.

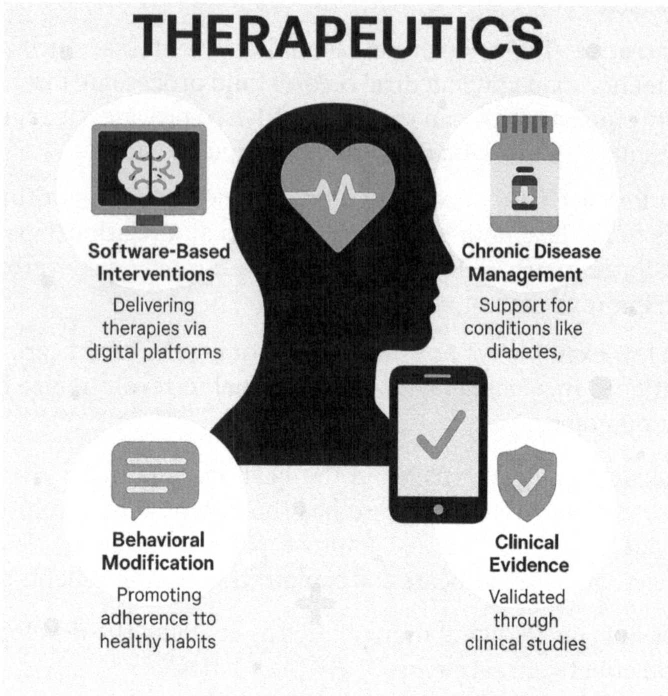

***Figure 1.5**: Digital Therapeutics*

Implementing AI in DTx

Now we will see how AI can be used in Digital therapeutics:

- **Personalized Treatment**: AI can be used to analyze large amounts of patient data, such as medical records, genetics, and lifestyle factors, to provide personalized treatment plans. For example, AI can be used to identify the most effective medication for an individual patient based on their genetic makeup and medical history.
- **Behavioral Modification**: AI helps patients modify their behavior to improve their health outcomes. For example, AI-powered chatbots can provide personalized support and coaching to patients with chronic conditions to help them make lifestyle changes, such as improving their diet and exercise habits.
- **Remote Patient Monitoring**: AI can be used to remotely monitor patients with chronic conditions and provide real-time feedback and interventions. For example, AI-powered wearables can track a patient's vital signs and alert healthcare providers if there are any significant changes that require attention.

- **Drug Discovery**: AI can be used to accelerate drug discovery by analyzing large amounts of medical data to identify potential drug candidates. For example, AI can be used to analyze genetic data to identify new drug targets for diseases that currently have no effective treatments.
- **Cognitive Behavioral Therapy**: AI can be used to provide Cognitive Behavioral Therapy (CBT) to patients with mental health conditions. For example, AI-powered chatbots can provide personalized CBT to patients with depression and anxiety, helping them manage their symptoms and improve their mental health.

Following are the new ways how AI is helping in healthcare:

- **Image Analysis**: AI algorithms can be trained to analyze medical images, such as X-rays, mammograms, and MRIs, to identify early signs of cancer that might be missed by human radiologists. These algorithms can identify subtle changes in the images that might not be apparent to the human eye, improving the accuracy of cancer detection.
- **Pathology**: AI algorithms can also be used to analyze tissue samples from biopsies to identify cancerous cells. This can be especially useful for identifying rare or difficult-to-diagnose types of cancer. AI can also help pathologists identify cancer in tissue samples more quickly and accurately, reducing the time it takes to get a diagnosis.
- **Risk Assessment**: AI algorithms can be trained to analyze large amounts of patient data, including medical records and genetic information, to identify patients who are at high risk of developing cancer. This can help doctors recommend early screening and surveillance for high-risk patients, improving the chances of early detection and treatment.
- **Treatment Planning**: AI can also help doctors to develop personalized treatment plans for cancer patients. By analyzing patient data, AI algorithms can identify the most effective treatments for individual patients based on their genetic makeup and other factors.

Overall, AI has the potential to revolutionize cancer detection and treatment by improving accuracy, speed, and personalized care.

AI Use Cases of Healthcare in Companies

Here are some AI use cases of healthcare in companies:

Google Health

- **Diabetic Retinopathy Detection**: In 2018, the U.S. Food and Drug Administration authorized the marketing of an AI-based device designed to detect diabetic retinopathy–a diabetes-related eye disease. This AI system analyzes retinal images to identify early signs of the condition, facilitating timely intervention and potentially preventing vision loss.

- **Breast Cancer Detection**: In January 2020, Google's DeepMind announced an AI algorithm capable of surpassing human experts in detecting breast cancer from screening mammograms. This development underscores AI's potential to enhance diagnostic accuracy in oncology.

IBM Watson Health

- **Oncology Treatment Recommendations**: IBM's Watson for Oncology has been utilized to assist oncologists in identifying personalized, evidence-based cancer treatment options. For instance, a study involving 1,000 challenging cancer cases revealed that Watson's recommendations aligned with those of human oncologists in 99% of the instances, highlighting its potential to support clinical decision-making.
- **Predictive Analytics for Patient Outcomes**: IBM Watson Health has developed AI models to predict patient readmissions and identify high-risk individuals. By analyzing extensive patient datasets, these models aim to improve clinical decision-making and optimize care management strategies.

Babylon Health

Babylon Health is using AI-powered chatbots to provide patients with personalized healthcare advice and support. Patients can ask the chatbot questions about their symptoms and receive recommendations for treatment or further medical attention.

Owkin

Owkin is using AI to improve drug development by analyzing large amounts of medical data. Their platform can identify patient subgroups that respond best to certain treatments and predict the efficacy and safety of new drugs.

Biofourmis

Biofourmis is using AI to develop personalized treatment plans for patients with chronic conditions such as heart failure. Their platform uses wearable sensors to monitor patient health and predict when patients are at risk of experiencing a health crisis, such as a heart attack.

These are just a few examples of how companies are using AI to transform healthcare. As AI technology continues to develop and mature, we can expect to see more and more applications of this technology in healthcare.

AI Use Cases of Healthcare in the Government

Following are some use cases of healthcare in Government:

- **NHS England**: The National Health Service (NHS) in England has implemented

AI tools to help improve patient care. For example, they have implemented an AI-powered chatbot called "*Ask A&E*" which provides patients with advice on when to seek medical attention and what type of care is needed.

- **Centers for Disease Control and Prevention (CDC)**: The CDC has implemented AI to help track and analyze infectious disease outbreaks. For example, they have used machine learning algorithms to predict the spread of the Zika virus and identify potential new outbreaks.
- **Veterans Affairs (VA)**: The VA has implemented AI tools to help improve patient outcomes and reduce costs. For example, they have implemented an AI-powered platform called "*Project HERO*" which helps identify high-risk patients and provide them with personalized treatment plans.
- **Health Research Authority (HRA)**: The HRA in the UK has implemented AI tools to help streamline the clinical trials process. For example, they have implemented an AI-powered platform that can identify patients who are eligible to participate in clinical trials based on their medical history.
- **National Institutes of Health (NIH)**: The NIH has implemented AI to help analyze medical images and improve disease diagnosis. For example, they have developed an AI algorithm that can analyze MRI scans to detect signs of Alzheimer's disease in patients.

These are just a few examples of how governments are using AI in healthcare. As AI technology continues to develop and mature, we can expect to see more and more applications of this technology in healthcare at both the national and local levels.

AI Use Cases of Healthcare in Startups Around the World

Here are some of the healthcare startups around the world:

- **K Health**: K Health is an AI-powered symptom checker that uses machine learning to provide patients with personalized medical advice. The platform can identify patterns in symptoms and medical histories to suggest possible diagnoses and treatment options.
- **Paige.AI**: Paige.AI is using AI to improve cancer diagnosis and treatment. The startup has developed an AI-powered platform that can analyze medical images, such as biopsies and pathology slides, to detect and classify cancer with high accuracy.
- **MAAP.AI:** MAAP.AI is an AI-powered platform designed to detect and combat malnutrition in children, particularly in underserved communities. By integrating Digital Public Infrastructure (DPI) with government systems, MAAP.AI enables real-time monitoring and assessment of nutrition

levels, helping policymakers and healthcare workers implement targeted interventions. Additionally, MAAP.AI is exploring state-wise nutritional food chart recommendations and height detection algorithms, making it a vital tool in addressing public health challenges.

- **PathAI**: PathAI is also using AI to improve cancer diagnosis and treatment. The startup has developed an AI-powered platform that can analyze digital pathology images to provide more accurate and efficient diagnoses.
- **Healx**: Healx is using AI to accelerate drug discovery for rare diseases. The startup has developed an AI-powered platform that can analyze large amounts of medical data to identify potential drug candidates for rare diseases.
- **Doc.ai**: Doc.ai is an AI-powered platform that uses natural language processing to provide patients with personalized health insights. The platform can analyze patient data, such as medical history and genetic information, to provide recommendations for improving health and preventing disease.

These are just a few examples of startups that are using AI to transform healthcare. As AI technology continues to develop and mature, we can expect to see more and more startups leveraging this technology to improve patient outcomes and reduce healthcare costs.

AI Use Cases of Healthcare in Startups in India

Some of the healthcare startups in India which use AI are as follows:

- **Niramai**: Niramai is a startup that is using AI-powered thermography to improve breast cancer detection. The startup has developed a non-invasive screening solution that uses thermal imaging and AI algorithms to detect breast cancer in its early stages.
- **Qure.ai**: Qure.ai is using AI to improve medical imaging analysis. The startup has developed an AI-powered platform that can analyze medical images, such as X-rays and CT scans, to detect diseases and abnormalities with high accuracy.
- **SigTuple**: SigTuple is using AI to improve diagnostic testing in India. The startup has developed an AI-powered platform that can analyze medical images and blood samples to provide accurate and efficient diagnoses.
- **Onward Assist**: Onward Assist is using AI to improve patient outcomes in critical care settings. The startup has developed an AI-powered platform that can analyze patient data, such as vital signs and medical history, to identify patients at risk of deterioration and provide early intervention.
- **MFine**: MFine is an AI-powered telemedicine platform that connects patients with doctors and healthcare providers. The platform uses AI algorithms

to provide patients with personalized medical advice and treatment recommendations.

- **Neurosynaptic**: Neurosynaptic is using AI to improve access to healthcare in remote and underserved areas of India. The startup has developed an AI-powered telemedicine platform that can connect patients with doctors and healthcare providers in real time, even in areas with limited internet connectivity.
- **Cognihealth**: Cognihealth is using AI to improve mental health diagnosis and treatment. The startup has developed an AI-powered chatbot that can provide personalized mental health support and guidance to patients.
- **Wellthy Therapeutics**: Wellthy Therapeutics is using AI to improve chronic disease management. The startup has developed an AI-powered platform that can provide personalized support and coaching to patients with chronic conditions, such as diabetes and hypertension.

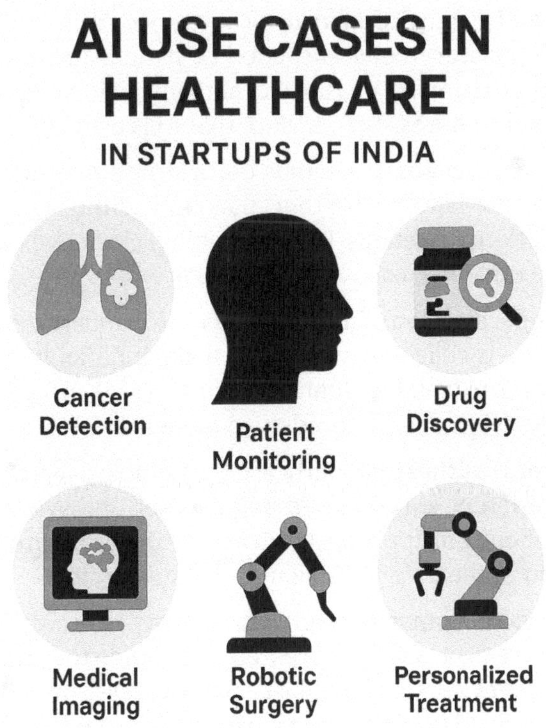

***Figure 1.6**: AI use in India*

These are just a few more examples of startups that are using AI to transform healthcare in India. As AI technology continues to develop and mature, we can expect to see more and more startups leveraging this technology to improve patient outcomes and reduce healthcare costs in India and around the world.

Challenges of AI in Healthcare

While the application of AI in healthcare has the potential to bring many benefits, there are also several challenges that need to be addressed to ensure that AI is used effectively and safely. Here are some of the key challenges facing the application of AI in healthcare:

- **Data Quality and Quantity**: AI relies on large amounts of high-quality data to train models and make accurate predictions. However, in healthcare, data is often incomplete, unstructured, and spread across many different systems, making it difficult to access and analyze.
- **Regulatory and Ethical Concerns**: The use of AI in healthcare raises many ethical and regulatory concerns, such as patient privacy, bias in algorithms, and the potential for AI to replace human healthcare professionals. These issues need to be addressed to ensure that AI is used ethically and responsibly.
- **Interoperability**: Healthcare data is often stored in disparate systems that do not communicate with each other, making it difficult to access and analyze data across different systems. Interoperability challenges need to be addressed to enable the effective use of AI in healthcare.
- **Lack of Standardization**: There is a lack of standardization in the way that healthcare data is collected, which can make it difficult to compare data from different sources. This can limit the worth of AI in healthcare and make it difficult to develop accurate predictive models.
- **Complexity of Healthcare**: Healthcare is a complex and rapidly changing field, with many different stakeholders, regulations, and systems. This complexity can cause difficulty in applying AI effectively in healthcare and requires careful consideration of the unique challenges facing the field.
- **Data Security**: The importance of data security in healthcare extends to every place that data can be used or accessed – including the endpoint. The endpoint refers to any device that could access, process, or store Personal Health Record (PHR), including mobile devices, tablets, laptops, desktop devices, or connected devices such as printers. The importance of data security is also directly related to the risk of liability, fines, and damage to an organization's reputation in the event of a data breach.

Addressing these challenges will require collaboration between healthcare professionals, AI researchers, regulators, and policymakers to ensure that AI is used effectively and safely to improve patient outcomes and the healthcare system as a whole.

Ethical Challenges in AI-Driven Healthcare

The integration of Artificial Intelligence (AI) into healthcare presents significant ethical concerns, particularly regarding transparency, accountability, and patient data protection. As AI systems increasingly influence medical decisions, ensuring ethical deployment becomes critical to maintaining trust and efficacy in healthcare delivery.

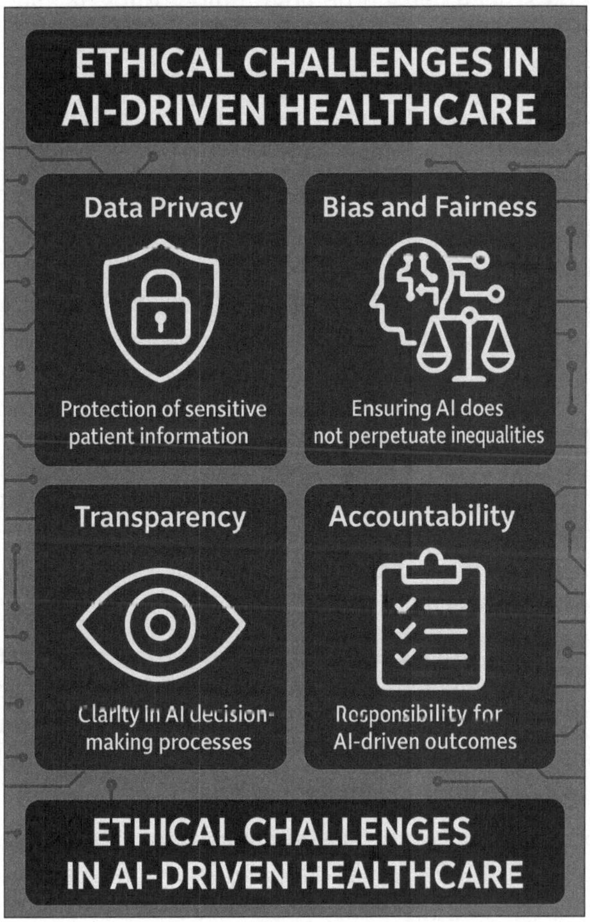

***Figure 1.7**: Ethical Challenges*

The Need for Transparent Algorithms

One of the most pressing ethical concerns is the opacity of AI algorithms, often described as the "*black box*" problem. Many AI models, particularly deep learning systems, operate in ways that are not easily interpretable by healthcare professionals, making it difficult to understand how they arrive at specific recommendations or diagnoses. This lack of transparency raises several ethical issues:

- **Accountability in Decision-Making**: When an AI system provides an incorrect diagnosis or recommendation, determining responsibility can be challenging. Should liability fall on the software developers, healthcare providers, or institutions deploying the AI?
- **Bias and Fairness**: AI models trained on biased datasets can reinforce or exacerbate existing healthcare disparities. If an algorithm is primarily trained on data from certain demographic groups, it may underperform for underrepresented populations, leading to unequal healthcare outcomes.
- **Explainability for Trust and Adoption**: Physicians and patients need to understand AI-driven recommendations to make informed decisions. Transparent algorithms—those designed with explainability in mind—are essential for fostering trust between AI systems and end-users.

To address these challenges, researchers and policymakers advocate for Explainable AI (XAI), which focuses on creating models that offer justifications for their outputs. Regulatory bodies such as the U.S. Food and Drug Administration (FDA) and the European Union's AI Act are pushing for more stringent guidelines requiring AI transparency in healthcare applications.

Patient Data Protection and Privacy

Another major ethical issue is the handling and security of patient data, as AI relies heavily on large-scale medical datasets for training and operation. Protecting sensitive health information is crucial to maintaining patient confidentiality and preventing data breaches. The key concerns include:

- **Informed Consent and Data Ownership**: Many AI systems rely on patient data collected through Electronic Health Records (EHRs), wearable devices, and genomics databases. However, patients may not always be aware of how their data is being used. Ensuring clear, informed consent and allowing patients to retain control over their health data is vital.
- **Data Anonymization and De-Identification**: To mitigate privacy risks, healthcare institutions must implement rigorous data anonymization techniques. However, research has shown that even de-identified data can sometimes be re-identified through advanced AI methods, posing a risk of privacy breaches.
- **Cybersecurity and Data Breaches**: With growing digitalization, cyberattacks on healthcare systems have become more frequent, exposing sensitive patient information. Hospitals and AI developers must adopt robust encryption methods, secure cloud storage solutions, and real-time monitoring systems to safeguard patient data from malicious threats.

- **Regulatory Compliance**: Compliance with health data protection laws, such as the Health Insurance Portability and Accountability Act (HIPAA) in the U.S. and the General Data Protection Regulation (GDPR) in the EU, is necessary for ethical AI deployment. These regulations emphasize data minimization, secure data processing, and strict consent policies to protect patient privacy.

Balancing Innovation with Ethical Responsibility

While AI has the potential to revolutionize healthcare, ethical considerations must be prioritized alongside technological advancements. Developers, healthcare providers, and policymakers must work together to establish guidelines that promote:

- **Human-in-the-Loop Systems**: Ensuring that AI supports, rather than replaces, human medical expertise.
- **Fair AI Practices**: Regular audits of AI models to identify and correct biases.
- **Patient-Centric Approaches**: Engaging patients in discussions about AI's role in their care and maintaining their right to opt out of AI-driven treatments if desired.

Conclusion

As we conclude this introductory chapter on the application of AI in healthcare, it is evident that AI has the potential to transform the industry by enhancing diagnostics, optimizing treatment plans, and improving operational efficiency. The use of machine learning, natural language processing, and computer vision has already demonstrated promising results in medical imaging, drug discovery, and personalized medicine. These advancements offer the potential to improve patient outcomes, reduce healthcare costs, and increase accessibility to medical services.

However, the integration of AI into healthcare is not without its complexities. Significant challenges remain, including issues related to data quality and availability, ethical concerns, regulatory compliance, interoperability, and the lack of standardization across healthcare systems. AI-driven solutions must also navigate the inherent complexities of clinical decision-making, ensuring that these technologies are not only accurate but also interpretable, fair, and trustworthy. Additionally, concerns about patient privacy, algorithmic biases, and the potential for over-reliance on AI require ongoing scrutiny and responsible governance.

While the promise of AI in healthcare is undeniable, its widespread adoption will depend on overcoming these barriers through continuous research, collaboration, and thoughtful policy frameworks. The road ahead is filled with both opportunities and uncertainties, requiring a balanced approach that embraces innovation while addressing the ethical, technical, and systemic challenges that come with it.

In the following chapters, we will explore AI's applications in various healthcare domains, examining both its transformative potential and the critical issues that must be navigated for responsible and effective implementation. It is our hope that this introduction has provided a solid foundation for understanding AI in healthcare, encouraging a nuanced exploration of this rapidly evolving field.

CHAPTER 2
AI Fundamentals for Healthcare

Introduction

Artificial Intelligence (AI) is rapidly transforming healthcare, offering the potential to improve patient outcomes, reduce costs, and enhance the efficiency of medical services. By leveraging machine learning, natural language processing, and computer vision, AI is being integrated into areas such as medical diagnostics, personalized treatment planning, drug discovery, and administrative automation. However, despite its potential, the implementation of AI in healthcare faces significant challenges that must be addressed to ensure its effectiveness, safety, and ethical use.

Structure

This chapter will cover the foundational principles of AI in healthcare, including:

- Basics of AI and Machine Learning
- Machine Learning Algorithms
- Convolutional Neural Networks (CNNs)
- Recurrent Neural Networks (RNNs)
- Generative Adversarial Networks (GANs)
- Haar Cascades

Basics of AI and Machine Learning

Machine learning, a key subfield of AI, is revolutionizing healthcare by improving diagnosis, treatment, and patient care through various techniques. Supervised learning enhances medical imaging and personalized treatment plans, as seen in Google's DeepMind AI, which outperforms radiologists in detecting breast cancer. Unsupervised learning identifies hidden disease patterns, such as discovering new diabetes subtypes for better-targeted treatments. Reinforcement Learning (RL) optimizes robotic surgery and adaptive treatment regimens, such as AI-driven insulin therapy adjusting dosages in real time. Deep learning advances early disease detection, with Google Health's AI achieving over 90% accuracy in diagnosing diabetic retinopathy. Natural Language Processing (NLP) streamlines clinical documentation and diagnostics by analyzing unstructured patient records, improving efficiency in healthcare workflows. These AI-driven advancements demonstrate the growing role of machine learning in transforming medical decision-making and patient outcomes.

Supervised Learning

Supervised learning is a type of machine learning where the algorithm is trained on a labeled dataset, which means that the data has predefined categories or classes. The algorithm learns the relationship between input features and the corresponding labels and then can predict the label of new, unseen data. In healthcare, supervised learning can be used for tasks such as diagnosis, prediction of patient outcomes, and personalized treatment recommendations.

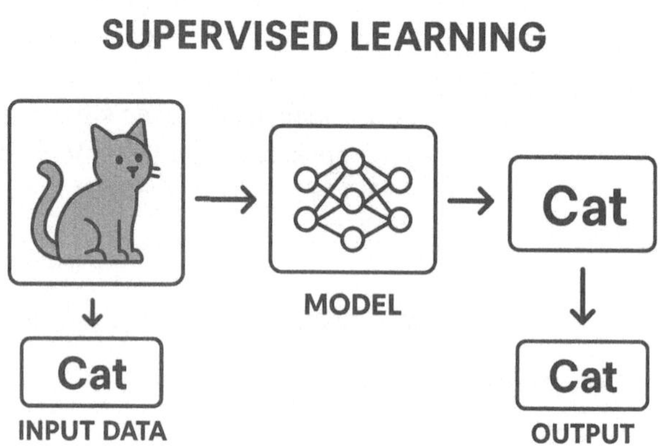

***Figure 2.1**: Supervised Learning*

Supervised learning is a powerful machine learning technique where algorithms learn from labeled datasets to make predictions about new, unseen data. In healthcare, this approach has significant applications in diagnosis, patient outcome prediction, and personalized treatment recommendations. The following are the high-level examples of supervised learning across various industries, showcasing its transformative impact:

- **Healthcare**
  - **Disease Diagnosis**: AI models trained on labeled medical images (X-rays, MRIs, CT scans) can detect diseases such as lung cancer, brain tumors, and diabetic retinopathy with high accuracy. For example, Google's DeepMind AI has been used to diagnose breast cancer more accurately than human radiologists.

  - **Patient Outcome Prediction**: AI algorithms analyze Electronic Health Records (EHRs) to predict patient readmissions, sepsis risks, and heart attack likelihood, enabling early intervention and preventive care.
  - **Personalized Treatment Plans**: Machine learning helps oncologists customize chemotherapy treatments based on patient genetics and response patterns, improving treatment effectiveness.
- **Finance**
  - **Fraud Detection**: AI models analyze labeled financial transaction data to detect suspicious activity, preventing credit card fraud and cybercrime.
  - **Credit Scoring**: Banks use supervised learning to assess loan eligibility based on a customer's financial history, spending behavior, and repayment patterns.
- **Retail and E-Commerce**
  - **Product Recommendation Systems**: AI models predict customer preferences based on purchase history, providing personalized shopping experiences (for example, Amazon, Netflix).
  - **Customer Sentiment Analysis**: AI analyzes customer reviews and social media posts to classify sentiment as positive, neutral, or negative, helping brands improve products and services.
- **Security and Cybersecurity**
  - **Spam Filtering**: Email services such as Gmail use supervised learning to classify emails as spam or non-spam, reducing phishing attacks.
  - **Anomaly Detection in Cybersecurity**: AI monitors network traffic to detect unusual login attempts or potential security breaches, helping prevent cyber threats.
- **Transportation and Autonomous Systems**
  - **Autonomous Vehicle Navigation**: Self-driving cars use AI to classify objects (for example, pedestrians, stop signs, other vehicles) and make real-time driving decisions.
  - **Traffic Prediction**: AI analyzes real-time road data to forecast traffic congestion and suggest optimal driving routes.
- **Natural Language Processing (NLP) and Communication**
  - **Speech Recognition**: AI models, such as Siri and Google Assistant, transcribe speech into text for voice commands and virtual assistants.
  - **Language Translation**: Platforms such as Google Translate use supervised learning to convert text from one language to another with improved contextual accuracy.

Supervised learning is transforming industries by enabling more accurate predictions, automation, and data-driven decision-making, making it a critical tool in advancing healthcare, finance, security, and beyond.

Unsupervised Learning

Unsupervised learning is a type of machine learning where the algorithm is trained on an unlabeled dataset, which means that the data does not have predefined categories or classes. The algorithm learns the underlying structure and patterns in the data, allowing for the discovery of new insights or hidden relationships. In healthcare, unsupervised learning can be used for tasks such as clustering patients based on similar clinical features or identifying subtypes of diseases.

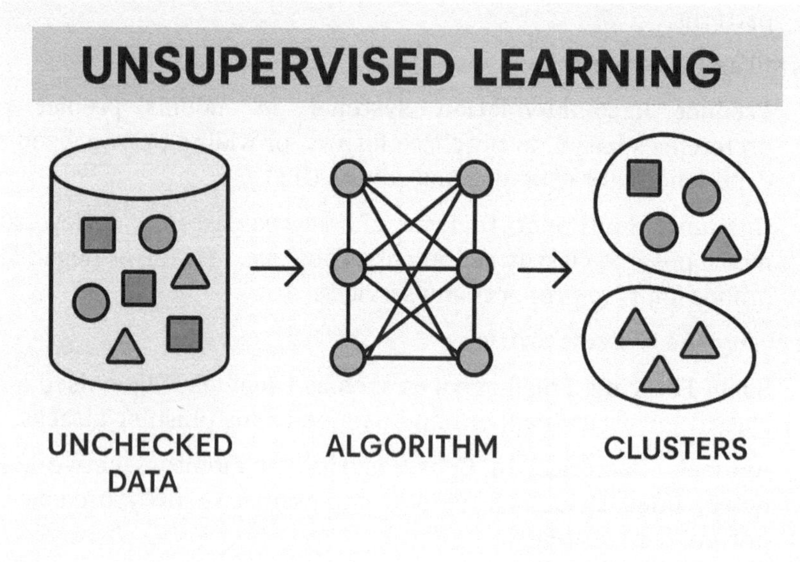

Figure 2.2: *Unsupervised Learning*

- **Healthcare**
    - **Clustering Patients for Personalized Medicine**: AI groups patients with similar genetic markers or medical histories, enabling precision medicine and targeted therapies. For example, AI models have discovered new cancer subtypes by clustering tumor genetic profiles, improving treatment strategies.
    - **Disease Subtyping and Progression Analysis**: AI can cluster patients based on symptom progression, identifying new forms of diseases that may require specialized treatment. For example, Machine learning identified five subtypes of diabetes, leading to better treatment planning beyond Type 1 and Type 2 classifications.

  - **Anomaly Detection in Medical Imaging**: AI detects abnormal patterns in X-rays, MRIs, and CT scans, flagging potential signs of diseases such as early-stage tumors that may not be easily noticed by radiologists.
  - **Genomic Data Analysis and Drug Discovery**: AI models uncover gene expression patterns that help in identifying new drug targets for rare diseases.
- **Retail and Marketing**
  - **Customer Segmentation**: AI clusters customers based on shopping behavior, demographics, or preferences to improve marketing campaigns and product recommendations. For example, Amazon and Netflix use clustering techniques to personalize shopping recommendations and content suggestions.
  - **Market Basket Analysis**: AI identifies purchase patterns to recommend products frequently bought together. For example, Supermarkets use association rule mining to optimize product placements (for example, people buying bread are likely to buy butter).
- **Natural Language Processing (NLP) and AI Creativity**
  - **Topic Modeling in Research Papers and Medical Literature**: AI organizes large amounts of unstructured text into meaningful themes, helping researchers find relevant publications quickly.
  - **AI-Generated Art and Music**: Generative models such as Generative Adversarial Networks (GANs) create realistic medical images, AI-generated music, and deepfake videos.
  - **Neural Network Autoencoders for Image Compression**: AI compresses and reconstructs high-resolution medical images for faster data transmission and storage efficiency.
- **Space Exploration and Climate Science**
  - **Astronomical Data Clustering**: AI classifies galaxies, stars, and exoplanets based on observed features, aiding in astronomical discoveries.
  - **Climate Pattern Recognition**: AI detects shifts in weather and climate patterns, predicting extreme weather events such as hurricanes and droughts.

Semi-Supervised Learning

Semi-supervised learning is a type of machine learning that combines both labeled and unlabeled data. This approach can be useful in healthcare when labeled data is scarce or expensive to obtain. The algorithm can learn from the labeled data and then use that knowledge to make predictions on the unlabeled data.

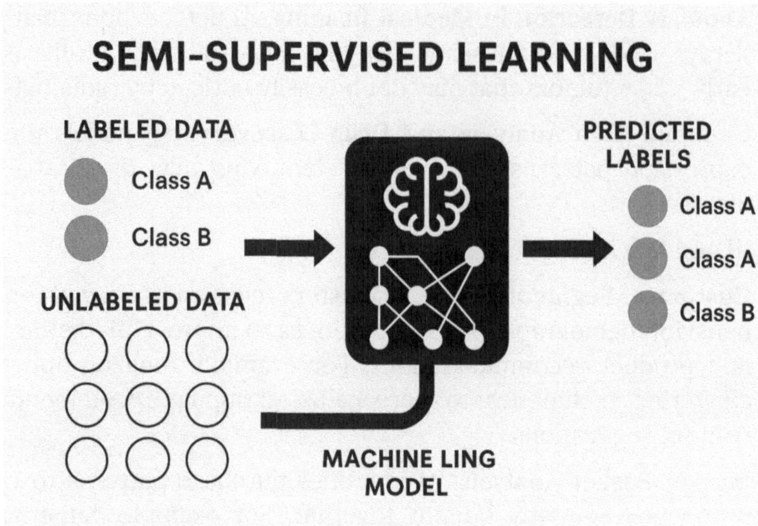

Figure 2.3: *Semi-supervised Learning*

Semi-supervised learning is a type of machine learning in which an algorithm learns from both labeled and unlabeled data. The following are some examples of semi-supervised learning:

- **Speech Recognition**: A small portion of the speech data may be labeled, while the majority of it is unlabeled. The algorithm can use the labeled data to train a model and then use the unlabeled data to improve the model's accuracy.
- **Text Classification**: In this case, the algorithm may have a small number of labeled documents, while the majority of documents are unlabeled. The algorithm can use the labeled data to train a model and then use the unlabeled data to refine the model's classification abilities.
- **Image Classification**: A small set of labeled images may be used to train a model, while the majority of images are unlabeled. The model can use the labeled data to learn the relationship between the features and the labels and then use the unlabeled data to fine-tune the model's classification accuracy.
- **Fraud Detection**: In this case, there may be a small number of labeled fraudulent transactions, while the majority of transactions are unlabeled. The algorithm can use the labeled data to train a model and then use the unlabeled data to detect new fraudulent transactions.
- **Active Learning**: In active learning, the algorithm selects which data points to label based on its uncertainty about the classification of the data. This can help to improve the accuracy of the model while minimizing the amount of labeled data needed.
- **Video Classification**: A small set of labeled video clips may be used to train a model, while the majority of video clips are unlabeled. The model can use the

labeled data to learn the relationship between the features and the labels and then use the unlabeled data to fine-tune the model's classification accuracy.

Challenges in Obtaining Labeled Data in Healthcare and the Role of Semi-Supervised Learning

Challenges in Labeling Healthcare Data

The success of AI-driven healthcare solutions relies heavily on high-quality labeled data, but obtaining such data poses several challenges:

- **High Cost and Time-Intensive Process**
  - Labeling medical images, patient records, or genomic data requires expert radiologists, pathologists, or clinicians, making the process costly and time-consuming.

    Example: Annotating a single CT scan or MRI can take several hours for a radiologist, significantly slowing down AI model training.
- **Scarcity of Expert-Labeled Datasets**
  - Unlike other domains, healthcare data cannot be labeled by general annotators; it requires domain experts.

    Example: In oncology, accurately labeling tumor boundaries in pathology slides requires an experienced pathologist, making large-scale labeled datasets difficult to obtain.
- **Data Privacy and Compliance Regulations**
  - Patient confidentiality laws (HIPAA, GDPR) restrict access to detailed patient data, limiting the availability of labeled datasets for AI model training.

    Example: AI-driven predictive analytics models for cardiovascular disease must comply with strict data protection laws, limiting data-sharing capabilities.
- **Limited Data for Rare Diseases**
  - For rare diseases, only a small number of patient cases exist, making it difficult to collect sufficient labeled data.

    Example: Amyotrophic Lateral Sclerosis (ALS) and orphan diseases have very few diagnosed cases globally, hindering AI model development.

How Semi-Supervised Learning Addresses These Issues

Semi-Supervised Learning (SSL) bridges the gap between supervised and unsupervised learning by using a small amount of labeled data along with a large pool of unlabeled data to train AI models. This approach is particularly useful in healthcare, where labeling data is expensive and time-consuming.

- **AI-Powered Medical Imaging Interpretation**
    - **Case Study**: Google Health's AI for Diabetic Retinopathy
        - Google Health developed an AI model to detect diabetic retinopathy in retinal scans using semi-supervised learning.
        - Since manually labeling thousands of retinal images was impractical, they used a small set of labeled images and a large set of unlabeled images, allowing the model to learn more efficiently.
        - The AI achieved over 90% accuracy, matching expert ophthalmologists in diagnosing the disease.
- **Early Cancer Detection with Pathology AI**
    - **Case Study**: PathAI's Digital Pathology Model
        - PathAI developed a deep learning model for cancer diagnosis by leveraging semi-supervised learning to analyze digital pathology slides.
        - Using a small subset of pathologist-labeled images, the model trained on millions of unlabeled biopsy samples, improving detection accuracy and reducing pathologists' workload.
        - The AI is now assisting hospitals in detecting breast cancer and prostate cancer with improved accuracy.
- **Predictive Modeling for Disease Progression**
    - **Case Study**: AI in Sepsis Detection (Johns Hopkins Hospital)
        - AI models predicting sepsis in ICU patients used semi-supervised learning to combine a small labeled dataset of diagnosed sepsis cases with vast EHR data from thousands of patients.
        - This approach allowed the AI to detect early sepsis warning signs, improving ICU patient survival rates by enabling earlier intervention.
- **Drug Discovery for Rare Diseases**
    - **Case Study**: Healx's AI for Rare Diseases
        - Healx, a biotech company, uses semi-supervised learning to identify potential treatments for rare diseases by combining labeled pharmaceutical data with vast unlabeled genomic data.
        - The AI identified drug repurposing opportunities faster than traditional methods, accelerating new drug discovery for orphan diseases.

- **COVID-19 Detection and Response**
    - **Case Study**: AI-Based Chest X-ray Analysis
        - During the COVID-19 pandemic, AI models for detecting pneumonia in chest X-rays were trained using semi-supervised learning, as only a limited number of COVID-positive cases were labeled initially.
        - By leveraging a large dataset of unlabeled X-rays, AI models were able to differentiate COVID-19 pneumonia from other lung infections, improving triage efficiency in hospitals.

Reinforcement Learning

Reinforcement learning is a type of machine learning where the algorithm learns from trial and error. The algorithm receives feedback in the form of rewards or penalties based on its actions and uses that feedback to improve its decision-making over time. In healthcare, reinforcement learning can be used for tasks such as optimizing treatment plans or identifying the best strategies for disease prevention.

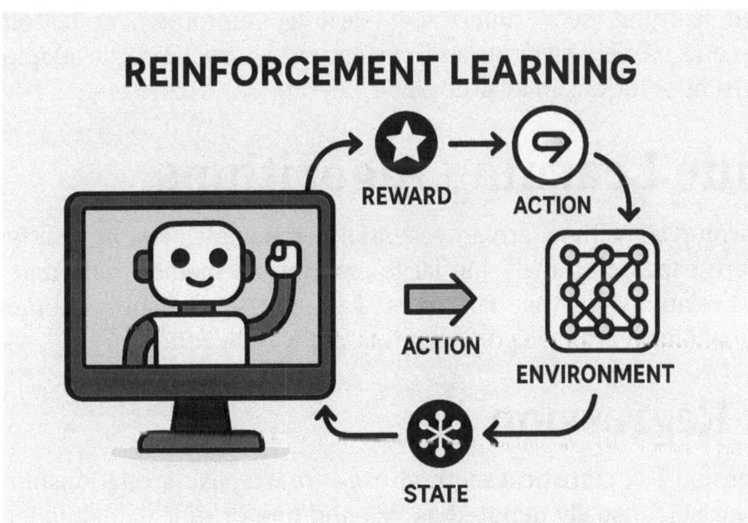

Figure 2.4: *Reinforcement Learning*

Reinforcement learning is a type of machine learning in which an agent learns to make decisions by interacting with an environment and receiving rewards or punishments for its actions. The following are some examples of reinforcement learning:

- **Game Playing**: An agent can learn to play games such as chess, Go, or video games by receiving a reward for winning and a penalty for losing.
- **Robotics**: Robots can learn to perform tasks such as grasping, walking, or driving by receiving a reward for successful completion and a penalty for failure.

- **Advertising**: An agent can learn to optimize advertising strategies by receiving a reward for clicks or conversions and a penalty for low engagement.
- **Finance**: An agent can learn to optimize investment strategies by receiving a reward for profit and a penalty for loss.
- **Traffic Management**: An agent can learn to optimize traffic flows by receiving a reward for reducing congestion and a penalty for causing accidents.
- **Dialogue Systems**: An agent can learn to carry on a conversation by receiving a reward for successfully answering a user's question or completing a task.
- **Robotics**: An agent can learn to explore unknown environments, avoid obstacles, and search for rewards.
- **Manufacturing**: An agent can learn to optimize production processes by receiving a reward for increased efficiency and a penalty for waste.

Machine learning is a powerful tool that can be applied to a wide range of healthcare tasks, from diagnosis and treatment to patient outcomes and disease prevention. Understanding the basic concepts of machine learning, including supervised and unsupervised learning, semi-supervised learning, reinforcement learning, feature engineering, and model selection and evaluation, is crucial to developing effective machine learning solutions in healthcare.

Machine Learning Algorithms

Machine learning algorithms are an essential component of AI in healthcare. These algorithms are capable of analyzing large amounts of medical data and identifying patterns and relationships that can be used to improve patient outcomes. Here are some basic machine learning algorithms that apply to healthcare.

Linear Regression

Linear regression is a statistical method used to establish a relationship between a dependent variable (usually denoted as "y") and one or more independent variables (usually denoted as "x"). The method assumes a linear relationship between the variables and seeks to find the best-fit line that can predict the dependent variable based on the independent variable(s).

Here is an example to help illustrate the concept of linear regression:

Suppose you are an analyst at a real estate company, and you want to predict the selling price of a house based on its size (in square feet). You have a dataset that includes the size of 100 houses and their corresponding selling prices.

You can use linear regression to create a model that predicts the selling price based on the size of the house. In this case, the size of the house is the independent variable, and the selling price is the dependent variable.

To begin, you can plot the data points on a scatter plot, with the size of the house on the x-axis and the selling price on the y-axis. The scatter plot will help you visualize any possible relationship between the variables.

Once you have plotted the data, you can use a mathematical formula to find the best-fit line that predicts the selling price based on the size of the house. This line is often referred to as the "*regression line*" *or the* "*line of best fit.*"

The equation of the regression line can be represented as:

$$y = mx + b$$

Where y is the predicted value of the dependent variable (selling price), x is the value of the independent variable (house size), m is the slope of the line, and b is the y-intercept.

To find the values of m and b that best fit the data, you can use a method called "*least squares regression.*" This involves finding the line that minimizes the sum of the squared differences between the predicted values and the actual values.

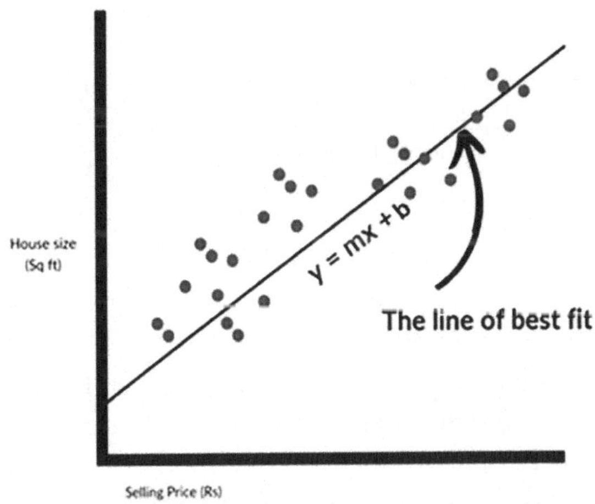

Figure 2.5: *Scatter Plot Showing the Relationship between the Selling Price and the Size of the House*

Once you have the equation for the regression line, you can use it to predict the selling price of a house based on its size. For example, if you want to predict the selling price of a house that is 2000 square feet, you can plug that value into the equation and solve for y:

```
y = mx + b
y = 200 * 50 + 100000
y = 1,010,000
```

According to this model, the predicted selling price of a 2000-square-foot house is $1,010,000.

Of course, this is just a simplified example, and in practice, there may be many other factors that affect the selling price of a house. Nonetheless, linear regression can be a useful tool for analyzing relationships between variables and making predictions based on those relationships.

Here is a Python code example for Linear regression using the scikit-learn library:

```
import numpy as np
from sklearn.linear_model import LinearRegression

# Creating some random data for demonstration
X = np.array([[1], [2], [3], [4], [5]])
y = np.array([2, 4, 5, 4, 5])

# Creating a linear regression model
model = LinearRegression()

# Training the model on the data
model.fit(X, y)

# Printing the slope and intercept of the regression line
print('Slope:', model.coef_[0])
print('Intercept:', model.intercept_)

# Predicting on new data
X_new = np.array([[6], [7], [8]])
y_new = model.predict(X_new)
print('Predicted values:', y_new)
```

In this example, we create a simple dataset of 5 points, with X being the independent variable and y being the dependent variable. We then create a linear regression model, fit it on the data, and print out the slope and intercept of the regression line. Finally, we use the model to predict the values of y for new data points.

Logistic Regression

Logistic regression is a type of regression analysis that is used to model the relationship between a binary dependent variable and one or more independent variables. The dependent variable can only take on two possible values, usually represented as 0 or 1, and the goal of logistic regression is to predict the probability that the dependent variable takes on a value of 1, given the values of the independent variables.

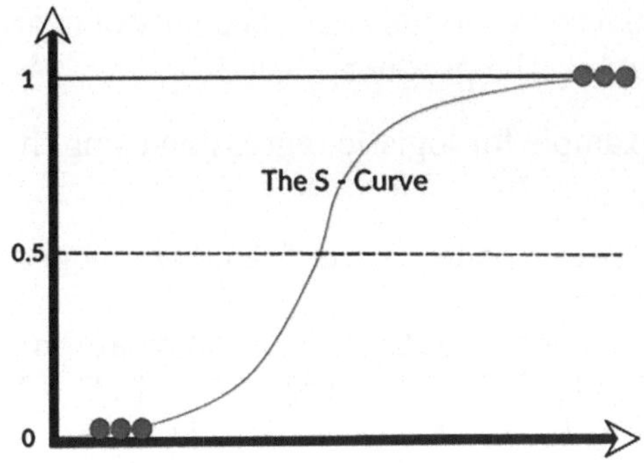

Figure 2.6: *Logistic Regression S - Curve Which Differentiates between 0 and 1*

For example, suppose we want to predict whether or not a customer will buy a product based on their age and income. We can use logistic regression to model the probability that the customer will buy the product as a function of their age and income.

To fit a logistic regression model, we first need to choose a set of independent variables and estimate the parameters of the model.

The logistic regression model is specified as:

```
log(p / (1-p)) = β0 + β1X1 + β2X2 + ... + βk*Xk
```

Where p is the probability of the dependent variable taking on a value of 1, X1, X2, ..., Xk are the independent variables, and β0, β1, β2, ..., βk are the regression coefficients.

The left-hand side of the equation is the log-odds ratio, also known as the logit function, which is used to transform the probability into a linear function of the independent variables.

Once we have estimated the parameters of the model, we can use it to predict the probability of the dependent variable taking on a value of 1, given the values of the independent variables.

For example, suppose we have estimated the following logistic regression model:

```
log(p / (1-p)) = -2 + 0.5Age + 0.01Income
```

This model suggests that the log-odds of buying the product increase by 0.5 for each additional year of age, and by 0.01 for each additional dollar of income.

To predict the probability that a 35-year-old customer with an income of $50,000 will buy the product, we can substitute the values of the independent variables into the model:

```
log(p / (1-p)) = -2 + 0.535 + 0.0150000
log(p / (1-p)) = -2 + 17.5 + 500
log(p / (1-p)) = 515.5
```

The log-odds ratio of 515.5 corresponds to a probability of nearly 1, indicating that this customer is very likely to buy the product.

Here is a Python code example for logistic regression using the scikit-learn library:

```
import numpy as np
from sklearn.linear_model import LogisticRegression

# Creating some random data for demonstration
X = np.array([[1], [2], [3], [4], [5], [6], [7], [8]])
y = np.array([0, 0, 0, 0, 1, 1, 1, 1])

# Creating a logistic regression model
model = LogisticRegression()

# Training the model on the data
model.fit(X, y)

# Printing the slope and intercept of the regression line
print('Slope:', model.coef_[0][0])
print('Intercept:', model.intercept_[0])

# Predicting on new data
X_new = np.array([[9], [10], [11]])
y_new = model.predict(X_new)
print('Predicted values:', y_new)
```

Logistic regression is a powerful tool for predicting binary outcomes and has a wide range of applications, including in fields such as finance, marketing, and healthcare. However, as with any statistical model, it is important to carefully evaluate the assumptions of the model and validate its predictions using independent data.

Decision Trees

A decision tree is a type of supervised learning algorithm that is used to predict the value of a target variable by learning decision rules from data. It is a popular machine learning technique used for both classification and regression problems.

Here is an example of a decision tree used for classification:

Suppose we want to classify whether or not a person is likely to buy a new car based on their age, income, and gender. We can build a decision tree that looks like this:

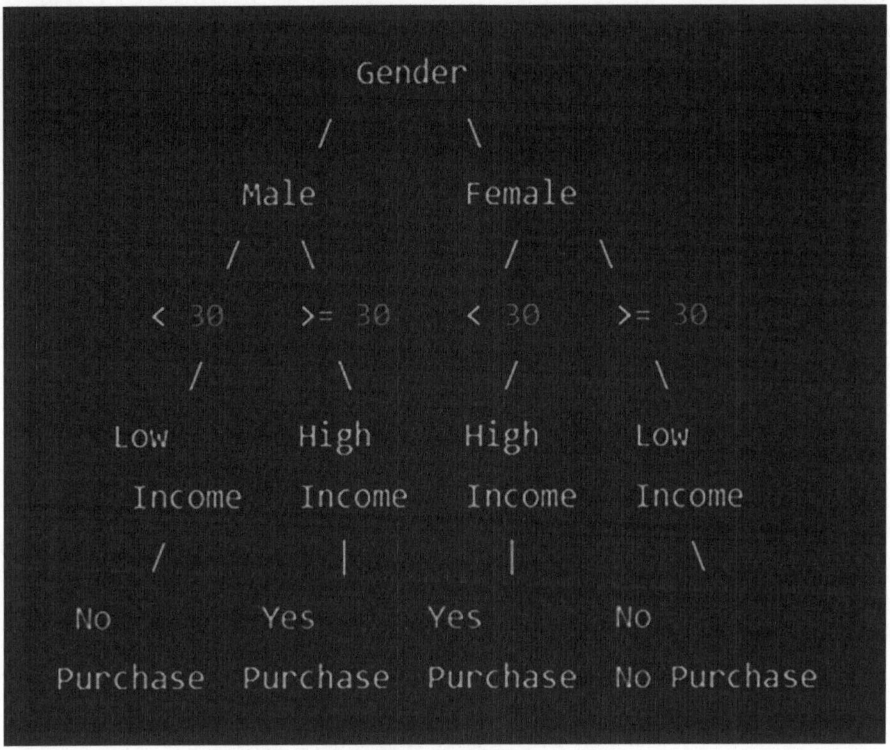

Figure 2.7: *Decision Tree*

The decision tree shown in *Figure* 2.7 has several levels, with each level representing a decision based on one of the input variables. The root node represents the first decision, which is based on gender. The tree then splits into two branches based on the gender of the person, and each branch represents a decision based on age.

Finally, the tree splits again based on income, and the final node indicates whether or not the person is likely to make a purchase.

To use this decision tree to classify a new person, we would start at the root node and follow the appropriate branch based on their gender. We would then follow the branch based on their age, and finally, we would follow the branch based on their income to reach the final decision node.

For example, suppose we have a new person who is a 25-year-old male with a low income. We would start at the root node and follow the left branch since the person is male. We would then follow the left branch again since the person is under 30. Finally, we would follow the left branch again, since the person has a low income. This leads us to the final decision node, which indicates that the person is unlikely to make a purchase.

Decision trees can also be used for regression problems.

Here is an example:

Suppose we want to predict the price of a house based on its size, number of bedrooms, and neighborhood. We can build a decision tree that looks like this:

```
                 Neighborhood
                /            \
           Urban            Suburban
          /     \            /     \
      < 4BR    >= 4BR    < 4BR    >= 4BR
        /          \        /          \
    Large       Small    Large       Small
     House      House    House       House
     /            |        |             \
 $400K         $200K     $300K          $150K
```

Figure 2.8: *Decision Tree with three levels*

The decision tree shown in *Figure* 2.8 has three levels, with each level representing a decision based on one of the input variables. The root node represents the first decision, which is based on neighborhood. The tree then splits into two branches based on the size of the house, and finally, the tree splits again based on the number of bedrooms. The final nodes indicate the predicted price of the house.

To use this decision tree to predict the price of a new house, we would start at the root node and follow the appropriate branch based on the neighborhood. We would then follow the branch based on the size of the house, and finally, we would follow the branch based on the number of bedrooms to reach the final prediction node.

For example, suppose we have a new house that is located in a suburban area, has three bedrooms, and is small in size. We would start at the root node and follow the right branch since the house is located in a suburban area.

Random Forests

Random Forest is an ensemble learning algorithm that is used for both classification and regression tasks. It is a type of decision tree algorithm that creates multiple decision trees and combines their predictions to produce a more accurate and robust model.

Here is an example of the Random Forest used for classification:

Suppose we have a dataset of patients with diabetes, and we want to predict whether or not a patient will be readmitted to the hospital within 30 days of their discharge. We have several features such as age, gender, BMI, blood pressure, and several lab test results. We can use Random Forest to create a model that can predict whether or not a patient will be readmitted to the hospital within 30 days.

In Random Forest, we create multiple decision trees on random subsets of the data and features. Each decision tree is built using a different subset of the data and features, and the final prediction is made by combining the predictions of all the decision trees. This helps to reduce overfitting and improve the accuracy of the model.

For example, let us say we have a dataset with 1000 patients, and we randomly select 500 patients to train each decision tree. We also randomly select a subset of features, let us say 5 out of 10 features, to use for each decision tree. We create 100 decision trees in this way, and the final prediction for each patient is made by combining the predictions of all 100 decision trees.

Here is a detailed example code in Python that demonstrates how to implement the Random Forest algorithm using the scikit-learn library:

```
# Import necessary libraries
from sklearn.ensemble import RandomForestClassifier
from sklearn.datasets import load_iris
from sklearn.model_selection import train_test_split

# Load the iris dataset iris = load_iris()

# Split the dataset into training and testing sets
X_train, X_test, y_train, y_test = train_test_split(iris.data,
iris.target, test_size=0.3)

# Create a Random Forest classifier with 100 trees
rfc = RandomForestClassifier(n_estimators=100)

# Fit the model on the training data
rfc.fit(X_train, y_train)

# Predict the classes of the testing data
y_pred = rfc.predict(X_test)

# Evaluate the model
print("Accuracy:", rfc.score(X_test, y_test))
```

Now, let us walk through the code and explain each step in detail:

1. **Import Necessary Libraries**: We start by importing the necessary libraries for the Random Forest algorithm. We import '`RandomForestClassifier`' from '`sklearn.ensemble`', '`load_iris`' from '`sklearn.datasets`', and '`train_test_split`' from '`sklearn.model_selection`'. These libraries will be used to create, load, and evaluate the model.

2. **Load the Dataset**: We then load the iris dataset using the '`load_iris`' function from '`sklearn.datasets`'. This dataset contains information about three types of iris flowers, with 4 features for each flower.

3. **Split the Dataset into Training and Testing Sets**: We split the dataset into training and testing sets using the '`train_test_split`' function from '`sklearn.model_selection`'. We set the `test_size` parameter to 0.3, which means that 30% of the data will be used for testing and 70% for training.

4. **Create a Random Forest Classifier with 100 Trees**: We create a Random Forest classifier using the '`RandomForestClassifier`' class from '`sklearn.ensemble`'. We set the `n_estimators` parameter to 100, which means that 100 decision trees will be generated and used to create the Random Forest.

5. **Fit the Model on the Training Data**: We fit the Random Forest model on the training data using the fit method of the '`RandomForestClassifier`' class.

6. **Predict the Classes of the Testing Data**: We use the predict method of the '`RandomForestClassifier`' class to predict the classes of the testing data.

7. **Evaluate the Model**: Finally, we evaluate the accuracy of the model using the score method of the '`RandomForestClassifier`' class. This method returns the mean accuracy on the given test data and labels. In this example, we print the accuracy of the model.

In summary, the Random Forest algorithm creates multiple decision trees, each trained on a random subset of the features and samples, and combines their predictions to create a more robust and accurate model. The scikit-learn library provides a simple and easy-to-use implementation of the Random Forest algorithm.

Support Vector Machines

Support Vector Machines (SVM) is a supervised machine learning algorithm used for classification and regression analysis. In classification tasks, SVM seeks to find the hyperplane that best separates the data into different classes. The hyperplane is chosen to maximize the margin between the two classes, which is the distance between the hyperplane and the nearest data points from each class.

Here is a detailed example code in Python that demonstrates how to implement SVM:

```
from sklearn import datasets
from sklearn.model_selection import train_test_split
from sklearn.svm import SVC
from sklearn.metrics import accuracy_score

# Load the iris dataset
iris = datasets.load_iris()
X = iris.data
y = iris.target

# Split the dataset into training and testing sets
X_train, X_test, y_train, y_test = train_test_split(X, y, test_
size=0.3)

# Create an SVM classifier object
classifier = SVC(kernel='linear')

# Train the classifier on the training set
classifier.fit(X_train, y_train)

# Predict the labels of the test set
y_pred = classifier.predict(X_test)

# Calculate the accuracy of the classifier
accuracy = accuracy_score(y_test, y_pred)

print("Accuracy:", accuracy)
```

In this example, we are using the Iris dataset, which contains information about the sepal length, sepal width, petal length, and petal width of three different species of iris flowers. We split the dataset into training and testing sets, and then create an SVM classifier object with a linear kernel.

We then train the classifier on the training set and use it to predict the labels of the test set. Finally, we calculate the accuracy of the classifier by comparing the predicted labels to the actual labels of the test set.

SVM can be used for both binary and multi-class classification problems, as well as for regression problems. It is widely used in various fields, such as image classification, text classification, and bioinformatics. SVM has the advantage of being able to handle high-dimensional data and can achieve high accuracy on a wide range of datasets. However, it can be computationally intensive and requires careful tuning of hyperparameters.

K-Nearest Neighbors

K-Nearest Neighbor (KNN) is a machine learning algorithm used for classification and regression tasks. KNN is a non-parametric algorithm, which means it does not make any assumptions about the distribution of the data. Instead, it uses the distance between data points to classify or predict new data points.

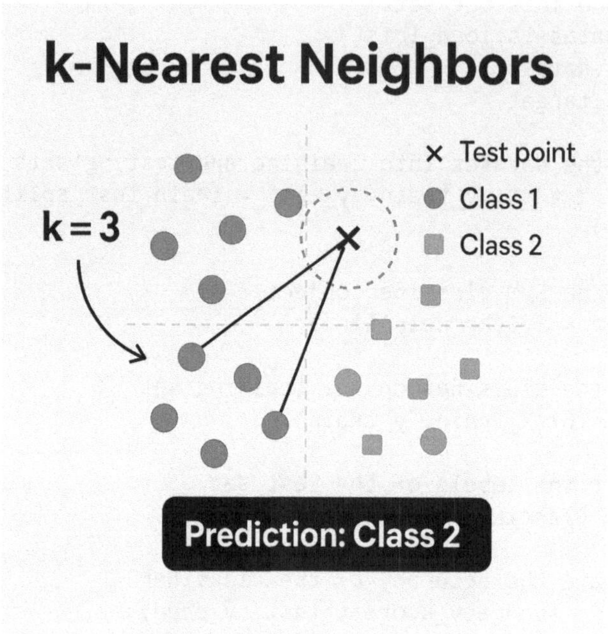

Figure 2.9: *K-Nearest Neighbors*

Here is an example to help illustrate the concept of KNN:

Suppose you are an analyst at a healthcare company, and you want to predict whether a patient has a particular disease based on their symptoms. You have a dataset that includes the symptoms and disease status of 100 patients.

You can use KNN to create a model that predicts the disease status based on the symptoms. In this case, the symptoms are the independent variables, and the disease status is the dependent variable.

To begin, you can plot the data points on a scatter plot, with the symptoms on the x-axis and y-axis. The scatter plot will help you visualize any possible relationship between the variables.

Once you have plotted the data, you can use KNN to find the K nearest neighbors to a new data point based on their distance in the feature space. In the simplest case, the distance can be the Euclidean distance between the two points.

For example, suppose a new patient comes in with the following symptoms:

- Fever: 102°F
- Headache: Yes
- Nausea: No
- Fatigue: Yes

To predict the disease status of this patient, you can calculate the distance between this patient's symptoms and the symptoms of the existing patients in the dataset. You can then select the K nearest neighbors and take a majority vote to predict the disease status of the new patient.

For instance, if K=5, the algorithm will find the 5 closest patients to the new patient and classify the new patient based on the majority disease status of those 5 patients. If 3 out of 5 of the closest patients have the disease, the KNN algorithm will predict that the new patient also has the disease.

Of course, this is just a simplified example, and in practice, there may be many other factors that affect the disease status of a patient. Nonetheless, KNN can be a useful tool for analyzing relationships between variables and making predictions based on those relationships.

Here is a detailed example code in Python that demonstrates how to implement K-Neighbors:

```
from sklearn import datasets
from sklearn.model_selection import train_test_split
from sklearn.neighbors import KNeighborsClassifier
from sklearn.metrics import accuracy_score

# Load the iris dataset
iris = datasets.load_iris()
X = iris.data
y = iris.target

# Split the dataset into training and testing sets
X_train, X_test, y_train, y_test = train_test_split(X, y,
test_size=0.3)

# Create a KNN classifier object
classifier = KNeighborsClassifier(n_neighbors=5)

# Train the classifier on the training set
classifier.fit(X_train, y_train)

# Predict the labels of the test set
y_pred = classifier.predict(X_test)
```

```
# Calculate the accuracy of the classifier
accuracy = accuracy_score(y_test, y_pred)

print("Accuracy:", accuracy)
```

In this example, we are using the Iris dataset again. We split the dataset into training and testing sets and then created a KNN classifier object with a k value of 5. We then train the classifier on the training set and use it to predict the labels of the test set. Finally, we calculate the accuracy of the classifier by comparing the predicted labels to the actual labels of the test set.

KNN is a non-parametric algorithm that can be used for both classification and regression tasks. It is easy to understand and implement and can work well on a wide range of datasets. However, it can be computationally expensive and may not work well with high-dimensional data. Additionally, the choice of k can have a significant impact on the performance of the algorithm.

Clustering

Clustering is a machine learning technique used to group similar data points based on their characteristics or features. Clustering is an unsupervised learning method, which means it does not require labeled data to train the model. Instead, clustering algorithms try to identify patterns in the data and group similar data points together into clusters.

Clustering is a type of unsupervised learning algorithm that is used to group similar data points based on their features or characteristics. There are various clustering algorithms available, each with its strengths and weaknesses. Here are some examples of clustering algorithms with code:

K-Means Clustering

K-Means clustering is one of the most popular clustering algorithms. It works by partitioning the data points into k clusters based on the minimum distance to the cluster centroids. Here is an example code of K-Means clustering using Scikit-learn in Python:

```
from sklearn.cluster import KMeans
import numpy as np

# Create a random dataset
X = np.random.rand(100, 2)

# Create a KMeans clustering object
kmeans = KMeans(n_clusters=3)
```

```
# Fit the KMeans object to the dataset
kmeans.fit(X)

# Get the cluster labels for each data point
labels = kmeans.labels_

# Get the cluster centroids
centroids = kmeans.cluster_centers_
```

In this example, we create a random dataset with 100 data points and 2 features. We then create a KMeans clustering object with 3 clusters and fit it to the dataset. We can then get the cluster labels for each data point and the cluster centroids.

Hierarchical Clustering

Hierarchical clustering is a clustering algorithm that builds a hierarchy of clusters by either merging smaller clusters or dividing larger clusters. There are two types of hierarchical clustering: agglomerative and divisive. Here is an cxample code of agglomerative hierarchical clustering using Scikit-learn in Python:

```
from sklearn.cluster import AgglomerativeClustering
import numpy as np

# Create a random dataset
X = np.random.rand(100, 2)

# Create an AgglomerativeClustering object
agg_clustering = AgglomerativeClustering(n_clusters=3)

# Fit the AgglomerativeClustering object to the dataset
agg_clustering.fit(X)

# Get the cluster labels for each data point
labels = agg_clustering.labels_
```

In this example, we create a random dataset with 100 data points and 2 features. We then create an **AgglomerativeClustering** object with 3 clusters and fit it to the dataset. We can then get the cluster labels for each data point.

DBSCAN Clustering

Density-Based Spatial Clustering of Applications with Noise (DBSCAN) clustering is a density-based clustering algorithm that groups data points that are close to each other in high-density regions and considers points in low-density regions as noise. Here is an example code of DBSCAN clustering using Scikit-learn in Python:

```
from sklearn.cluster import DBSCAN
import numpy as np

# Create a random dataset
X = np.random.rand(100, 2)

# Create a DBSCAN clustering object
dbscan = DBSCAN(eps=0.3, min_samples=5)

# Fit the DBSCAN object to the dataset
dbscan.fit(X)

# Get the cluster labels for each data point
labels = dbscan.labels_
```

In this example, we create a random dataset with 100 data points and 2 features. We then create a DBSCAN clustering object with an epsilon value of 0.3 and a minimum number of samples of 5. We fit the DBSCAN object to the dataset and get the cluster labels for each data point.

Clustering algorithms can be used in a variety of applications, such as customer segmentation, image segmentation, and anomaly detection. It is important to choose the right clustering algorithm and parameters based on the problem at hand and the nature of the data.

Deep learning algorithms have shown promising results in healthcare and are being used in various applications such as medical image analysis, clinical decision support systems, drug discovery, and personalized medicine. Here are some examples of deep learning algorithms used in healthcare:

Autoencoders

Autoencoders are a type of neural network used for unsupervised learning tasks, such as data compression and feature extraction. The basic idea behind autoencoders is to compress the input data into a lower-dimensional representation and then reconstruct the original data from the compressed representation.

An autoencoder consists of two main parts: an encoder and a decoder. The encoder takes the input data and maps it to a lower-dimensional representation. The decoder takes this representation and maps it back to the original data space. The encoder and decoder are trained together to minimize the difference between the input data and the reconstructed data.

Here is an example of how an autoencoder can be used for image compression:

1. We start with an input image, such as a 28×28 pixel image of a handwritten digit.

2. The autoencoder's encoder network takes this input image and compresses it into a lower-dimensional representation, such as a 10-dimensional vector.
3. The decoder network takes this 10-dimensional vector and maps it back to the original 28x28 pixel image.
4. During training, the autoencoder is trained to minimize the difference between the input image and the reconstructed image.
5. Once the autoencoder is trained, we can use the encoder to compress new images into a lower-dimensional representation and the decoder to reconstruct the compressed image back to its original size.

Autoencoders can also be used for feature extraction, where the encoder is used to extract important features from the input data, and the decoder is discarded. These extracted features can then be used for downstream tasks such as classification or clustering.

Autoencoders have many applications in various fields, including computer vision, natural language processing, and recommendation systems.

Here is a detailed example code in Python that demonstrates how to implement the Autoencoders:

```
from keras.layers import Input, Dense
from keras.models import Model

# Define the input shape
input_shape = (784,)

# Define the size of the encoded representation
encoding_dim = 32

# Define the input layer
input_layer = Input(shape=input_shape)

# Define the encoder layers
encoded = Dense(encoding_dim, activation='relu')(input_layer)

# Define the decoder layers
decoded = Dense(input_shape[0], activation='sigmoid')(encoded)

# Define the autoencoder model
autoencoder = Model(input_layer, decoded)

# Define the encoder model
encoder = Model(input_layer, encoded)
```

```
# Define the decoder model
encoded_input = Input(shape=(encoding_dim,))
decoder_layer = autoencoder.layers[-1]
decoder = Model(encoded_input, decoder_layer(encoded_input))

# Compile the autoencoder model
autoencoder.compile(optimizer='adadelta', loss='binary_
crossentropy')

# Train the autoencoder model
from keras.datasets import mnist

(x_train, _), (x_test, _) = mnist.load_data()

# Normalize the input data
x_train = x_train.astype('float32') / 255.
x_test = x_test.astype('float32') / 255.

# Flatten the input data
x_train = x_train.reshape((len(x_train), np.prod(x_train.
shape[1:])))
x_test = x_test.reshape((len(x_test), np.prod(x_test.shape[1:])))

# Train the autoencoder model
autoencoder.fit(x_train, x_train,
                epochs=50,
                batch_size=256,
                shuffle=True,
                validation_data=(x_test, x_test))

# Evaluate the autoencoder model
encoded_imgs = encoder.predict(x_test)
decoded_imgs = decoder.predict(encoded_imgs)
```

In this example, we create a simple autoencoder for the MNIST dataset, which consists of 28x28 grayscale images of handwritten digits. We define the input shape as a flattened 784-dimensional vector and the size of the encoded representation as 32. We define the encoder and decoder layers using dense (fully connected) layers with ReLU and sigmoid activations, respectively. We then define the autoencoder model using the input and output layers, and the encoder and decoder models using the input and bottleneck layers, respectively.

We compile the autoencoder model using the adadelta optimizer and binary cross-entropy loss and train it on the normalized and flattened input data for 50 epochs with a batch size of 256. Finally, we evaluate the autoencoder model by generating compressed and reconstructed images from the test data.

Autoencoders can be used for various tasks such as data compression, image denoising, and feature extraction. The architecture and parameters of the autoencoder can be adjusted based on the requirements of the specific task.

Convolutional Neural Networks (CNNs)

Convolutional Neural Networks (CNNs) are a type of neural network commonly used in computer vision tasks such as image recognition, object detection, and segmentation. CNNs are designed to automatically learn and extract features from images, making them well-suited for tasks that involve visual data.

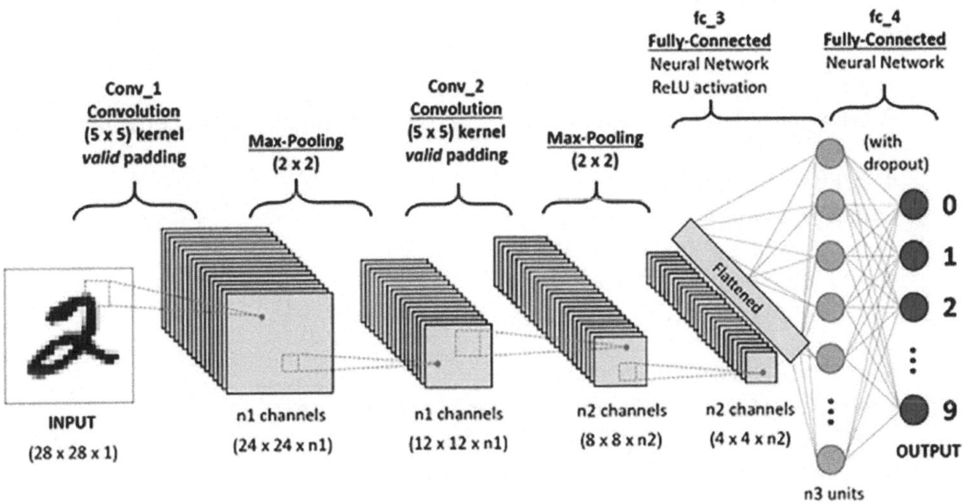

Figure 2.10: *Parts of a CNN Architecture*

The key idea behind CNNs is to use convolutional layers to detect local patterns in the input images, such as edges, textures, and shapes. The output of the convolutional layers is then fed into fully connected layers for classification or regression.

Here is an example of how a CNN can be used for image recognition:

1. We start with an input image, such as a 224×224 pixel image of a cat.
2. CNN's convolutional layers use a set of filters to detect local patterns in the image. Each filter is convolved with the input image to produce a feature map that highlights the presence of that pattern in the image.
3. The output of the convolutional layers is then fed into fully connected layers, which perform classification or regression. In the case of image recognition, the output layer would have a number of nodes corresponding to the number of classes in the dataset (for example, cat, dog, bird).

4. During training, the CNN is trained to minimize the difference between the predicted output and the true label using a loss function such as cross-entropy loss.
5. Once CNN is trained, we can use it to classify new images into different categories.

CNNs have revolutionized the field of computer vision and have achieved state-of-the-art performance on many image recognition tasks. They have also been applied to other domains such as natural language processing and speech recognition with great success.

Here is a detailed example code in Python that demonstrates how to implement CNN Algorithm:

```
from keras.models import Sequential
from keras.layers import Conv2D, MaxPooling2D, Flatten, Dense

# Define the CNN model
model = Sequential()

# Add the convolutional layers
model.add(Conv2D(32, (3, 3), activation='relu', input_shape=(28,
28, 1)))
model.add(MaxPooling2D((2, 2)))
model.add(Conv2D(64, (3, 3), activation='relu'))
model.add(MaxPooling2D((2, 2)))
model.add(Conv2D(64, (3, 3), activation='relu'))

# Add the fully connected layers
model.add(Flatten())
model.add(Dense(64, activation='relu'))
model.add(Dense(10, activation='softmax'))

# Compile the model
model.compile(optimizer='adam', loss='categorical_crossentropy',
metrics=['accuracy'])

# Train the model
from keras.datasets import mnist
from keras.utils import to_categorical

# Load the MNIST dataset
(x_train, y_train), (x_test, y_test) = mnist.load_data()

# Normalize the input data
x_train = x_train.astype('float32') / 255.
```

```
x_test = x_test.astype('float32') / 255.

# Reshape the input data to add a channel dimension
x_train = x_train.reshape((x_train.shape[0], 28, 28, 1))
x_test = x_test.reshape((x_test.shape[0], 28, 28, 1))

# Convert the target labels to categorical
y_train = to_categorical(y_train)
y_test = to_categorical(y_test)

# Train the model
model.fit(x_train, y_train, epochs=5, batch_size=64, validation_
data=(x_test, y_test))
```

In this example, we create a simple CNN for the MNIST dataset, which consists of 28×28 grayscale images of handwritten digits. We define the CNN model using a sequential model and add convolutional layers with ReLU activations and max pooling, followed by fully connected layers with ReLU and SoftMax activations, respectively.

We compile the model using the Adam optimizer and categorical cross-entropy loss and train it on the normalized and reshaped input data for 5 epochs with a batch size of 64. Finally, we evaluate the model on the test data.

CNNs can be used for various tasks such as image classification, object detection, and segmentation. The architecture and parameters of the CNN can be adjusted based on the requirements of the specific task.

Recurrent Neural Networks (RNNs)

Recurrent Neural Networks (RNNs) are a type of neural network commonly used in sequence modeling tasks such as language modeling, speech recognition, and machine translation. Unlike feedforward neural networks, which process inputs independently, RNNs are designed to handle sequential data by maintaining an internal state that captures information about the previous inputs.

The key idea behind RNNs is to use feedback loops to propagate information from previous inputs to the current input. This allows the network to maintain a memory of previous inputs and use that memory to inform its current prediction.

Here is an example of how an RNN can be used for language modeling:

1. We start with a sentence, such as "*The cat sat on the mat.*"
2. The RNN's input layer takes in the first word of the sentence, "*The*," and updates its internal state based on that input.
3. The RNN's output layer generates a probability distribution over all possible words that could come next in the sentence, based on the current internal state.

4. We feed the next word in the sentence, "*cat*," into the RNN, which updates its internal state again based on the current input and previous internal state.
5. The RNN's output layer generates a new probability distribution over all possible words that could come next in the sentence, based on the updated internal state.
6. We continue this process for each subsequent word in the sentence, with the RNN updating its internal state and generating new output probabilities for each input.
7. During training, the RNN is trained to predict the next word in the sequence based on the previous words using a loss function such as cross-entropy loss.

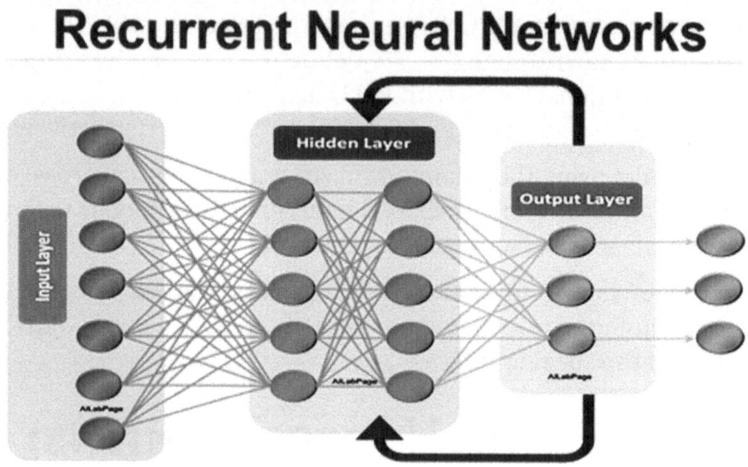

Figure 2.11: *RNN Architecture Showing All the Layers*

RNNs have many applications in various fields, including natural language processing, speech recognition, and time series prediction. However, traditional RNNs have difficulty learning long-term dependencies due to the vanishing gradient problem, which limits their ability to capture information from inputs that occurred many time steps ago. To address this issue, various RNN variants such as Long Short-Term Memory (LSTM) and Gated Recurrent Unit (GRU) have been developed, which use additional gates to control the flow of information and avoid the vanishing gradient problem.

Here is a detailed example code in Python that demonstrates how to implement RNN:

```
from keras.models import Sequential
from keras.layers import SimpleRNN, Dense

# Define the RNN model
model = Sequential()
```

```
# Add the recurrent layer
model.add(SimpleRNN(32, input_shape=(10, 1)))

# Add the output layer
model.add(Dense(1, activation='sigmoid'))

# Compile the model
model.compile(optimizer='adam', loss='binary_crossentropy',
metrics=['accuracy'])

# Train the model
import numpy as np

# Generate some dummy data
x_train = np.random.random((1000, 10, 1))
y_train = np.random.randint(2, size=(1000, 1))

# Train the model
model.fit(x_train, y_train, epochs=10, batch_size=32)
```

In this example, we create a simple RNN for a binary classification task. We define the RNN model using a sequential model and add a SimpleRNN layer with 32 hidden units and an input shape of (10, 1), which means that we will feed the RNN 10 timesteps of 1-dimensional input data.

We then add an output layer with a sigmoid activation and compile the model using the Adam optimizer and binary cross-entropy loss. We generate some dummy data for training the model and fit the model on the input and target data for 10 epochs with a batch size of 32.

RNNs can be used for various tasks such as natural language processing, speech recognition, and time-series prediction. The architecture and parameters of the RNN can be adjusted based on the requirements of the specific task.

Long Short-Term Memory

Long Short-Term Memory (LSTM) is a type of RNN that is designed to handle the vanishing gradient problem that arises in traditional RNNs. LSTMs use a memory cell and several gates to selectively update and forget information over time, allowing them to capture long-term dependencies in sequences.

Here is an example of how an LSTM can be used for sequence prediction:

1. We start with a sequence of inputs, such as a sequence of stock prices over time.
2. The LSTM's input gate determines which information from the current input to store in the memory cell.

3. The LSTM forget gate determines which information from the previous memory cell to forget.
4. The LSTM's output gate determines which information from the memory cell to output to the next layer of the network.
5. We continue this process for each input in the sequence, with the LSTM updating its memory cell and output at each time step.
6. During training, the LSTM is trained to predict the next value in the sequence based on the previous values using a loss function such as mean squared error.

LSTMs have many applications in various fields, including natural language processing, speech recognition, and time series prediction. They are effective at capturing long-term dependencies in sequences and have achieved state-of-the-art performance on many sequence prediction tasks.

Here is a detailed example code in Python that demonstrates how to implement the LSTM:

```
from keras.models import Sequential
from keras.layers import LSTM, Dense

# Define the LSTM model
model = Sequential()

# Add the LSTM layer
model.add(LSTM(32, input_shape=(10, 1)))

# Add the output layer
model.add(Dense(1, activation='sigmoid'))

# Compile the model
model.compile(optimizer='adam', loss='binary_crossentropy',
metrics=['accuracy'])

# Train the model
import numpy as np

# Generate some dummy data
x_train = np.random.random((1000, 10, 1))
y_train = np.random.randint(2, size=(1000, 1))

# Train the model
model.fit(x_train, y_train, epochs=10, batch_size=32)
```

In this example, we create a simple LSTM network for a binary classification task.

We define the LSTM model using a sequential model and add an LSTM layer with 32 hidden units and an input shape of (10, 1), which means that we will feed the LSTM 10 timesteps of 1-dimensional input data.

We then add an output layer with a sigmoid activation and compile the model using the Adam optimizer and binary cross-entropy loss. We generate some dummy data for training the model and fit the model on the input and target data for 10 epochs with a batch size of 32.

LSTM networks can be used for various tasks such as natural language processing, speech recognition, and time-series prediction. The architecture and parameters of the LSTM can be adjusted based on the requirements of the specific task.

Gated Recurrent Units

Gated Recurrent Units (GRUs) are a type of RNN that are similar to LSTMs in that they can handle long-term dependencies in sequences. However, GRUs have a simpler architecture than LSTMs, with fewer gates and a shorter memory cell, which makes them faster and easier to train.

Here is an example of how a GRU can be used for sequence prediction:

1. We start with a sequence of inputs, such as a sequence of weather observations over time.
2. The GRU's reset gate determines which information from the previous hidden state to forget.
3. The GRU's update gate determines which information from the current input to store in the hidden state.
4. The GRU updates its hidden state by interpolating between the previous hidden state and the candidate hidden state, which is calculated based on the current input.
5. We continue this process for each input in the sequence, with the GRU updating its hidden state and output at each time step.
6. During training, the GRU is trained to predict the next value in the sequence based on the previous values using a loss function such as mean squared error.

GRUs have many applications in various fields, including natural language processing, speech recognition, and time series prediction. They are effective at capturing long-term dependencies in sequences and have achieved state-of-the-art performance on many sequence prediction tasks

Here is a detailed example code in Python that demonstrates how to implement GRUs:

```
from keras.models import Sequential
from keras.layers import GRU, Dense

# Define the GRU model
model = Sequential()

# Add the GRU layer
model.add(GRU(32, input_shape=(10, 1)))

# Add the output layer
model.add(Dense(1, activation='sigmoid'))

# Compile the model
model.compile(optimizer='adam', loss='binary_crossentropy',
metrics=['accuracy'])

# Train the model
import numpy as np

# Generate some dummy data
x_train = np.random.random((1000, 10, 1))
y_train = np.random.randint(2, size=(1000, 1))

# Train the model
model.fit(x_train, y_train, epochs=10, batch_size=32)
```

In this example, we create a simple GRU network for a binary classification task. We define the GRU model using a sequential model and add a GRU layer with 32 hidden units and an input shape of (10, 1), which means that we will feed the GRU 10 timesteps of 1-dimensional input data.

We then add an output layer with a sigmoid activation and compile the model using the Adam optimizer and binary cross-entropy loss. We generate some dummy data for training the model and fit the model on the input and target data for 10 epochs with a batch size of 32.

GRU networks can be used for various tasks such as natural language processing, speech recognition, and time-series prediction. The architecture and parameters of the GRU can be adjusted based on the requirements of the specific task.

Generative Adversarial Networks (GANs)

Generative Adversarial Networks (GANs) are a type of deep learning model that consists of two networks: a generator network and a discriminator network. The generator network generates synthetic data that is similar to the real data, while the discriminator network distinguishes between the synthetic and real data. The two networks are trained together in a process called adversarial training, where the generator learns to create more realistic data while the discriminator learns to distinguish better between the synthetic and real data.

Here is an example of how GANs can be used for image generation:

1. The generator network takes in a random noise vector as input and produces a synthetic image as output.
2. The discriminator network takes in an image as input and produces a probability score indicating whether the image is real or synthetic.
3. During training, the generator and discriminator networks are trained in an adversarial manner. The generator tries to generate synthetic images that fool the discriminator into thinking they are real, while the discriminator tries to correctly classify the images as real or synthetic.
4. As the generator gets better at generating more realistic images, the discriminator also gets better at distinguishing between real and synthetic images, and the two networks continue to improve through adversarial training.
5. Once the training is complete, the generator network can be used to generate new synthetic images that are similar to the real images.

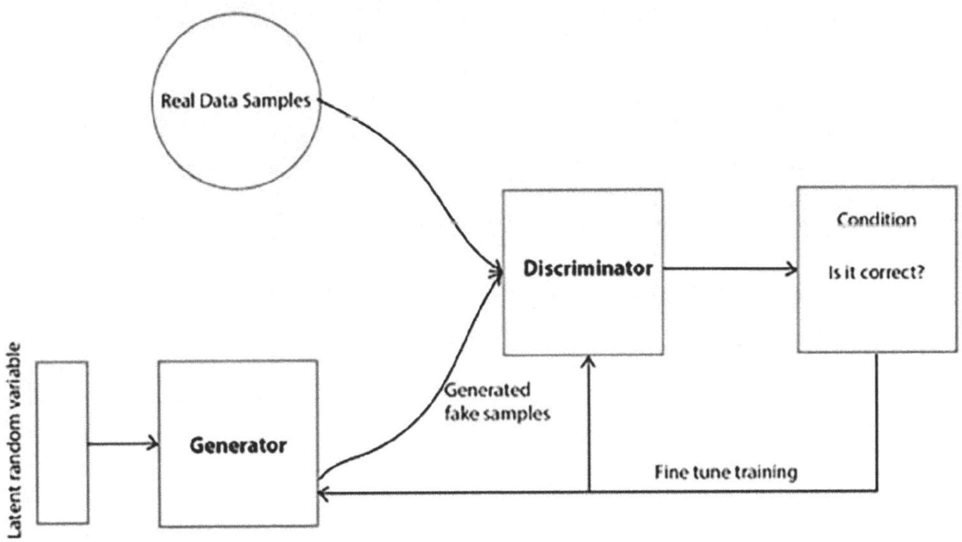

Figure 2.12: *GAN Architecture Showing the Working of a Generator and Discriminator*

GANs have many applications in various fields, including image and video generation, data augmentation, and anomaly detection. They have been used to generate realistic images of faces, animals, and landscapes, among other things.

Here is a detailed example code in Python that demonstrates how to implement GANs:

```
import tensorflow as tf
import numpy as np
import matplotlib.pyplot as plt

# Define the generator network
def make_generator_model():
    model = tf.keras.Sequential()
    model.add(tf.keras.layers.Dense(7*7*256, use_bias=False,
input_shape=(100,)))
    model.add(tf.keras.layers.BatchNormalization())
    model.add(tf.keras.layers.LeakyReLU())

    model.add(tf.keras.layers.Reshape((7, 7, 256)))
    assert model.output_shape == (None, 7, 7, 256) # Note: None
is the batch size

    model.add(tf.keras.layers.Conv2DTranspose(128, (5, 5),
strides=(1, 1), padding='same', use_bias=False))
    assert model.output_shape == (None, 7, 7, 128)
    model.add(tf.keras.layers.BatchNormalization())
    model.add(tf.keras.layers.LeakyReLU())

    model.add(tf.keras.layers.Conv2DTranspose(64, (5, 5),
strides=(2, 2), padding='same', use_bias=False))
    assert model.output_shape == (None, 14, 14, 64)
    model.add(tf.keras.layers.BatchNormalization())
    model.add(tf.keras.layers.LeakyReLU())

    model.add(tf.keras.layers.Conv2DTranspose(1, (5, 5),
strides=(2, 2), padding='same', use_bias=False, activa-
tion='tanh'))
    assert model.output_shape == (None, 28, 28, 1)

    return model

# Define the discriminator network
def make_discriminator_model():
    model = tf.keras.Sequential()
    model.add(tf.keras.layers.Conv2D(64, (5, 5), strides=(2, 2),
padding='same',
```

```
                                        input_shape=[28, 28, 1]))
    model.add(tf.keras.layers.LeakyReLU())
    model.add(tf.keras.layers.Dropout(0.3))

    model.add(tf.keras.layers.Conv2D(128, (5, 5), strides=(2, 2),
padding='same'))
    model.add(tf.keras.layers.LeakyReLU())
    model.add(tf.keras.layers.Dropout(0.3))

    model.add(tf.keras.layers.Flatten())
    model.add(tf.keras.layers.Dense(1))

    return model

# Define the loss functions for the generator and discriminator
networks
cross_entropy = tf.keras.losses.BinaryCrossentropy(from_log-
its=True)

def discriminator_loss(real_output, fake_output):
    real_loss = cross_entropy(tf.ones_like(real_output), real_
output)
    fake_loss = cross_entropy(tf.zeros_like(fake_output), fake_
output)
    total_loss = real_loss + fake_loss
    return total_loss

def generator_loss(fake_output):
    return cross_entropy(tf.ones_like(fake_output), fake_output)

# Define the optimizers for the generator and discriminator
networks
generator_optimizer = tf.keras.optimizers.Adam(1e-4)
discriminator_optimizer = tf.keras.optimizers.Adam(1e-4)

# Define the training loop for the GAN
@tf.function
def train_step(images):
    noise = tf.random.normal([BATCH_SIZE, 100])

    with tf.GradientTape() as gen_tape, tf.GradientTape() as
disc_tape:
        generated_images = generator(noise, training=True)

        real_output = discriminator(images, training=True)
        fake_output = discriminator(generated_images,
training=True)
```

```
        gen_loss = generator_loss(fake_output)
        disc_loss = discriminator_loss(real_output, fake_output)

gradients_of_generator = gen_tape.gradient(gen_loss, generator.
trainable_variables)
    gradients
```

Haar Cascades

Haar cascades are used for object detection tasks in medical imaging, such as detecting tumors or lesions in radiological images.

Optical Coherence Tomography (OCT) Analysis

OCT is a non-invasive imaging technique used to capture high-resolution cross-sectional images of the retina. OCT analysis algorithms are used for detecting and diagnosing eye diseases such as macular degeneration, diabetic retinopathy, and glaucoma.

Deep Reinforcement Learning (DRL)

Deep Reinforcement Learning (DRL) is a type of machine learning technique that involves training an artificial agent to make sequential decisions based on environmental feedback, using a combination of deep neural networks and reinforcement learning algorithms.

In reinforcement learning, an agent learns to take actions in an environment to maximize a reward signal that it receives from the environment. Deep neural networks are used to represent the agent's policy and/or value function, which maps states to actions and/or expected rewards.

DRL has shown remarkable success in a range of applications, including gaming, robotics, and self-driving cars. For example:

- In the game of Go, the AlphaGo and AlphaZero systems, developed by DeepMind, used DRL to defeat some of the best human players in the world.
- DRL has been used to train robots to perform a variety of tasks, such as grasping objects, walking, and playing ping-pong.
- DRL has also been used to develop autonomous vehicles, which can learn to navigate complex environments and make decisions in real time.
- DRL has been used to optimize energy consumption in data centers, reducing energy usage by up to 40%.

- DRL has also been applied to healthcare, such as training agents to diagnose diseases and develop personalized treatment plans for patients.

Overall, DRL has proven to be a powerful technique for training agents to make decisions in complex, dynamic environments, with potential applications across a wide range of fields.

Here is a detailed example code in Python that demonstrates how to implement Q-network:

```
import gym
import numpy as np
import tensorflow as tf

env = gym.make('CartPole-v0')
state_size = 4
action_size = 2

# Define the Q-network
model = tf.keras.Sequential([
    tf.keras.layers.Dense(24, input_dim=state_size, activation='
relu'),
    tf.keras.layers.Dense(24, activation='relu'),
    tf.keras.layers.Dense(action_size, activation='linear')
])
model.compile(loss='mse', optimizer=tf.keras.optimizers.
Adam(lr=0.001))

# Define the hyperparameters
gamma = 0.95
epsilon = 1.0
epsilon_min = 0.01
epsilon_decay = 0.995
batch_size = 64
memory = []

# Define the function for choosing an action
def choose_action(state, epsilon):
    if np.random.rand() <= epsilon:
        return env.action_space.sample()
    else:
        q_values = model.predict(state)
        return np.argmax(q_values[0])

# Define the function for updating the Q-network
def update_model(batch_size, gamma):
    global memory
```

```
        if len(memory) < batch_size:
            return
        batch = np.array(memory)
        states = np.vstack(batch[:, 0])
        actions = np.array(batch[:, 1], dtype=np.int32)
        rewards = np.array(batch[:, 2], dtype=np.float32)
        next_states = np.vstack(batch[:, 3])
        dones = np.array(batch[:, 4], dtype=np.bool)
        q_values = model.predict(states)
        next_q_values = model.predict(next_states)
        max_next_q_values = np.max(next_q_values, axis=1)
        targets = rewards + (1 - dones) * gamma * max_next_q_values
        targets_full = q_values.copy()
        targets_full[np.arange(len(actions)), actions] = targets
        model.fit(states, targets_full, epochs=1, verbose=0)
        if epsilon > epsilon_min:
            epsilon *= epsilon_decay

    # Train the agent
    for i_episode in range(1000):
        state = env.reset()
        state = np.reshape(state, [1, state_size])
        done = False
        total_reward = 0
        while not done:
            action = choose_action(state, epsilon)
            next_state, reward, done, info = env.step(action)
            next_state = np.reshape(next_state, [1, state_size])
            total_reward += reward
            memory.append((state, action, reward, next_state, done))
            state = next_state
            update_model(batch_size, gamma)
        print('Episode {}: Total reward = {}'.format(i_episode + 1,
    total_reward))
```

In this example, the Q-network is implemented using a multi-layer perceptron with two hidden layers. The agent selects an action using an epsilon-greedy policy, where it chooses a random action with probability epsilon and the action with the highest Q-value with probability 1 - epsilon. The Q-network is updated using the Q-learning algorithm, where the target Q-value is calculated as the reward plus the discounted maximum Q-value of the next state. The hyperparameters are tuned to balance exploration.

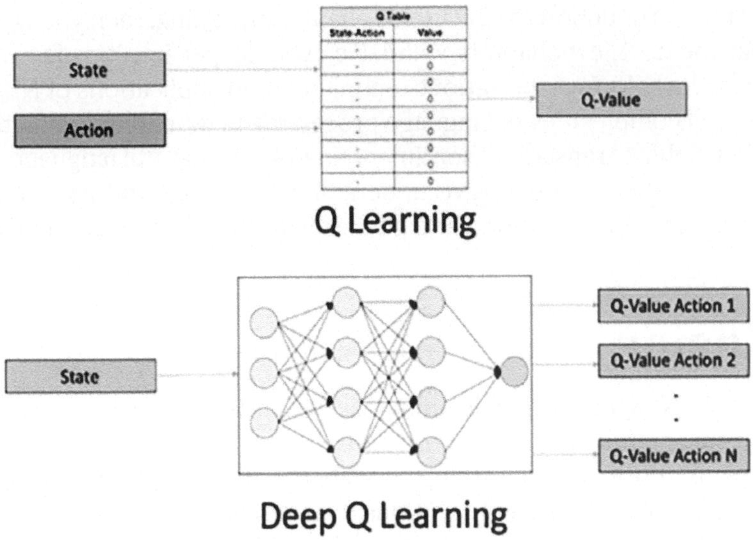

Figure 2.13: *State-Wise Break Up of Q-Learning and Deep-Q Learning Algorithm*

Natural Language Processing (NLP) is a subfield of artificial intelligence that deals with processing and analyzing natural language data. Here are some of the algorithms used for NLP in healthcare:

- **Named Entity Recognition (NER)**: NER is used to identify and classify named entities such as drugs, diseases, symptoms, and procedures in text data.
- **Text Classification**: Text classification algorithms are used to classify medical documents such as diagnosis, treatment, and medication.
- **Sentiment Analysis**: Sentiment analysis algorithms are used to analyze patient feedback, reviews, and social media posts to determine the sentiment toward a particular drug, treatment, or healthcare provider.
- **Topic Modeling**: Topic modeling algorithms are used to identify topics and themes in large amounts of text data. They are used for tasks such as discovering hidden relationships between diseases and symptoms, identifying patterns in electronic health records, and detecting emerging healthcare trends.
- **Word Embeddings**: Word embeddings are used to represent words as vectors in a high-dimensional space. These vectors capture the meaning and context of words and are used for tasks such as document classification, sentiment analysis, and text generation.
- **Machine Translation**: Machine translation algorithms are used to translate medical documents and clinical notes from one language to another.
- **Information Extraction**: Information extraction algorithms are used to extract relevant information from unstructured medical data sources such as medical literature and clinical trial reports.

If you found the introduction to NLP in this chapter intriguing, then you will be excited to know that the next few chapters will delve even deeper into this fascinating field. We will take a closer look at the various techniques and applications of NLP, exploring the nuances and complexities of language processing in more detail. Whether you are interested in machine translation, sentiment analysis, or natural language generation, you will gain a more comprehensive understanding of NLP and its potential in the upcoming chapters. So, stay tuned and get ready to take your NLP knowledge to the next level.

Conclusion

AI and its various algorithms hold immense potential to revolutionize healthcare, offering advancements in medical diagnosis, drug discovery, and personalized treatment plans. With the increasing availability of large-scale medical data and computational power, AI-driven solutions can enhance accuracy, efficiency, and accessibility in healthcare delivery. However, alongside these promising developments, significant challenges remain that must be carefully navigated.

Key concerns include data quality and interoperability issues, as AI models require vast and diverse datasets to ensure reliability and generalizability across different patient populations and healthcare settings. Privacy and security risks are also major hurdles, given the sensitive nature of patient data and the need for compliance with strict regulations such as HIPAA and GDPR. Furthermore, ethical concerns—including algorithmic bias, transparency in decision-making, and the risk of over-reliance on AI systems—raise important questions about trust, accountability, and equitable access to AI-powered healthcare.

Additionally, the regulatory landscape for AI in healthcare is still evolving, with ongoing debates about how to validate AI-driven medical interventions, ensure patient safety, and establish ethical AI governance. Striking a balance between innovation and regulation is crucial to preventing unintended consequences while maximizing AI's benefits.

Despite these challenges, AI continues to drive meaningful progress, with efforts to create more interpretable, secure, and ethically sound AI systems. The success of AI in healthcare will depend not only on technological advancements but also on collaborative efforts between healthcare professionals, AI developers, policymakers, and patients.

In the next chapter, we will explore the application of predictive analytics in healthcare, examining how AI-driven forecasting can enhance patient care, optimize resource utilization, and reduce costs. We will also address the ethical and regulatory challenges that come with implementing predictive models in clinical decision-making, ensuring that AI remains a tool for empowering healthcare professionals rather than replacing them.

Points to Remember

There are three main types of machine learning algorithms: supervised learning, unsupervised learning, and reinforcement learning.

- Supervised learning algorithms require labeled data to learn from and are used for classification and regression problems.
- Unsupervised learning algorithms do not require labeled data and are used for clustering and dimensionality reduction.
- Reinforcement learning algorithms learn from a reward signal and are used for sequential decision-making problems.
- Deep learning algorithms are a type of machine learning algorithm that uses deep neural networks to learn from data.
- Some popular deep learning algorithms include CNNs, RNNs, and GANs.
- It is important to choose the right algorithm for your problem based on the data you have, the type of problem you are trying to solve, and your computational resources.

Further Readings

- "*Hands-On Machine Learning with Scikit-Learn, Keras, and TensorFlow*" by Aurélien Géron: This book provides a practical approach to understanding the most popular machine learning algorithms and techniques. It also includes code examples and exercises to help you build your own machine learning models.
- "*Deep Learning*" by Ian Goodfellow, Yoshua Bengio, and Aaron Courville: This is a comprehensive book that covers deep learning algorithms and techniques. It includes both theoretical and practical aspects of deep learning and provides code examples in Python.
- "*Pattern Recognition and Machine Learning*" by Christopher Bishop: This book covers the basics of machine learning, including linear regression, Bayesian networks, and neural networks. It also provides code examples in MATLAB and includes exercises to help you apply the concepts.

Chapter 3
Predictive Analysis in Healthcare

Introduction

Predictive analytics in healthcare is transforming the way medical professionals diagnose diseases, manage treatments, and optimize healthcare resources. By leveraging data analytics, statistical modeling, and machine learning, predictive analytics enables healthcare providers to anticipate patient health outcomes, disease progression, treatment effectiveness, and resource utilization. These AI-driven models analyze historical and real-time data to identify patterns and trends that support proactive decision-making, early disease detection, and personalized care strategies.

In addition, predictive analysis can aid in healthcare resource management. By analyzing data on patient demographics, historical trends, and disease prevalence, predictive models can help healthcare organizations allocate resources effectively. This includes predicting patient admissions, bed occupancy rates, and demand for specific services or procedures. By optimizing resource allocation, healthcare providers can improve efficiency, reduce costs, and enhance patient satisfaction.

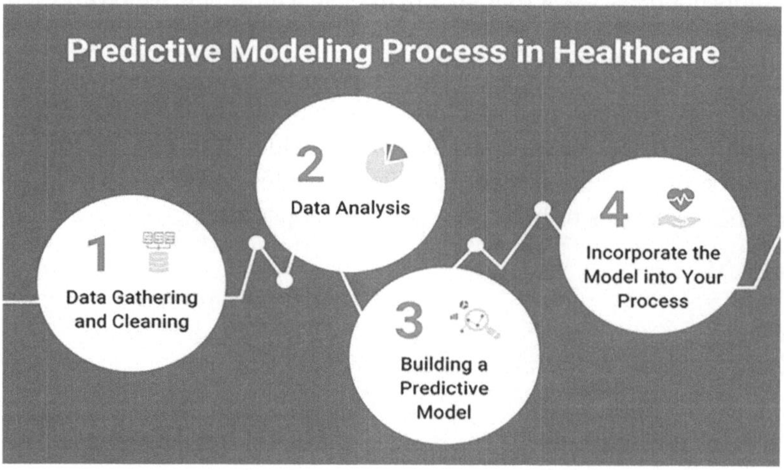

***Figure 3.1**: Predictive Modelling Process in Healthcare*

One of the most impactful applications of predictive analytics is hospital readmission prediction, where AI models assess patient records to identify those at high risk of returning to the hospital. For instance, Penn Medicine implemented a machine learning model to analyze Electronic Health Records (EHRs), vital signs, and medication adherence, enabling timely interventions and significantly reducing hospital readmission rates.

Beyond individual patient care, predictive analytics also aids in healthcare resource management. By forecasting patient admissions, bed occupancy rates, and demand for specialized treatments, hospitals can allocate staff, medical equipment, and critical care units more efficiently. This ensures better patient flow, reduced operational costs, and enhanced hospital efficiency.

On a broader scale, predictive models play a crucial role in public health by analyzing large-scale datasets, including population health records, environmental factors, and social determinants of health. These insights help predict epidemic outbreaks, disease spread patterns, and community health risks, allowing governments and public health agencies to deploy targeted interventions, vaccination campaigns, and resource distribution strategies.

While predictive analytics offers immense potential, it also presents challenges, including data privacy concerns, model biases, and the need for accurate, high-quality data. This chapter will explore real-world case studies, implementation strategies, and ethical considerations surrounding predictive analytics in healthcare, illustrating how advanced analytics and AI-driven insights are shaping the future of patient care, disease prevention, and hospital operations.

Structure

In this chapter, the following topics will be covered:

- Fundamentals of Predictive Analysis
- Data Sources and Preprocessing
- Predictive Analysis in Disease Diagnosis and Early Detection
- Ethical Considerations and Challenges
- Future Scope and Direction of Predictive Analysis in Healthcare

Fundamentals of Predictive Analysis

Predictive analysis is a powerful field that enables businesses and organizations to make informed decisions by using historical data and statistical models to forecast future outcomes. In this chapter, we will explore the fundamentals of predictive analysis, including its definition, process, and key concepts.

Predictive Analysis

Predictive analysis is the practice of extracting information from historical data to identify patterns, relationships, and trends that can be used to make predictions about future events or outcomes. It involves the application of statistical algorithms and machine learning techniques to analyze data and develop predictive models.

The Predictive Analysis Process

The predictive analysis process typically consists of the following steps:

1. **Data Collection**: The first step is to gather relevant data from various sources, such as databases, data warehouses, or external datasets. The quality and completeness of the data play a crucial role in the accuracy of predictions.

2. **Data Preprocessing**: Once the data is collected, it needs to be cleaned and preprocessed to ensure its quality and suitability for analysis. This step involves handling missing values, removing outliers, normalizing variables, and transforming data as required.

3. **Exploratory Data Analysis (EDA)**: EDA involves exploring and visualizing the data to gain insights and understand its characteristics. It helps identify relationships between variables, detect patterns, and determine the most relevant features for prediction.

4. **Feature Selection and Engineering**: In this step, the most informative features are selected from the dataset or new features are created by transforming existing ones. Feature engineering aims to improve the predictive power of the models.

5. **Model Development**: Once the data is prepared, predictive models are developed using statistical techniques or machine learning algorithms. These models are trained on historical data, and their performance is evaluated using appropriate metrics.

6. **Model Evaluation**: The performance of the predictive models is assessed by evaluating their accuracy, precision, recall, or other relevant metrics. The models may be refined or tuned based on the evaluation results.

7. **Model Deployment**: After the model is deemed satisfactory, it is deployed for making predictions on new, unseen data. The deployment can be done in real-time systems or integrated into existing business processes.

8. **Monitoring and Maintenance**: Predictive models need to be monitored and maintained to ensure their ongoing accuracy and relevance. They may require periodic updates or retraining with new data as patterns and relationships evolve over time.

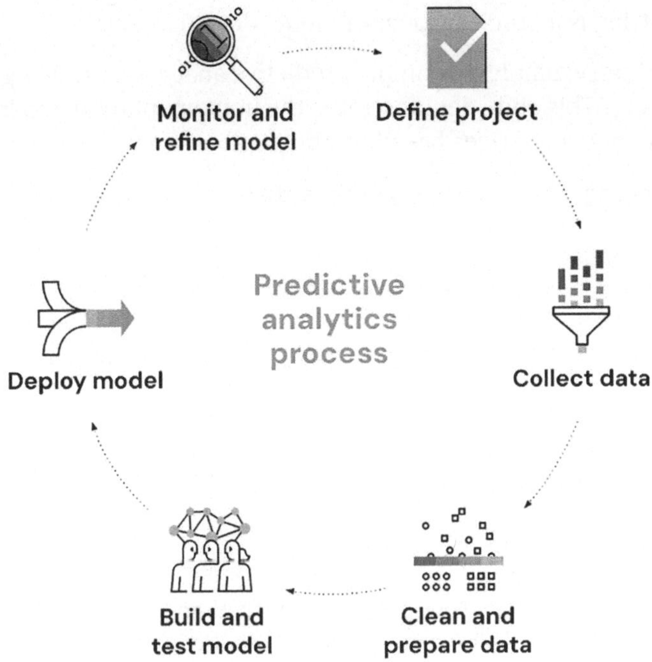

Figure 3.2: *Process of Predictive Analysis*

Key Concepts in Predictive Analysis

To grasp the fundamentals of predictive analysis, it is essential to understand the following key concepts:

- **Training Data and Test Data**: Predictive models are trained using historical data, which is divided into training data and test data. The training data is used to build the models, while the test data is reserved to evaluate their performance on unseen examples.
- **Predictive Models**: Predictive models are algorithms that learn patterns from historical data to make predictions on new data. These models can range from simple linear regression to complex machine learning algorithms such as decision trees, random forests, or neural networks.
- **Variables**: In predictive analysis, variables can be classified as independent variables (input) and dependent variables (output). The independent variables are used to predict the dependent variable, also known as the target variable or the variable being predicted.
- **Overfitting and Underfitting**: Overfitting occurs when a predictive model performs well on training data but fails to generalize to new, unseen data. Underfitting, on the other hand, happens when a model is too simple to

capture the underlying patterns in the data. Balancing between overfitting and underfitting is a crucial aspect of model development.

Certainly! Here is an example of a simple predictive analysis code using Python and the scikit-learn library. This code demonstrates the implementation of a linear regression model to predict housing prices based on the number of rooms in a house.

```
# Importing the necessary libraries

import pandas as pd
from sklearn.model_selection import train_test_split
from sklearn.linear_model import LinearRegression
from sklearn.metrics import mean_squared_error

# Load the dataset

data = pd.read_csv('housing_data.csv')

# Prepare the data

X = data[['RM']] # Input feature: Number of rooms
y = data['Price'] # Target variable: Housing price

# Split the data into training and test sets

X_train, X_test, y_train, y_test = train_test_split(X, y, test_
size=0.2, random_state=42)

# Create a linear regression model = LinearRegression()

# Train the model model.fit(X_train, y_train)

# Make predictions on the test set y_pred = model.predict(X_test)

# Evaluate the model

mse = mean_squared_error(y_test, y_pred)
print("Mean Squared Error:", mse)

# Predict the price of a house with 5 rooms

rooms = [[5]] predicted_price = model.predict(rooms)
print("Predicted price for a house with 5 rooms:", predicted_
price[0])
```

Steps to be followed:

1. In this example, the code assumes that the housing data is stored in a CSV file named '**housing_data.csv**,' where the **'RM'** column represents the number of rooms, and the **'Price'** column represents the housing price.
2. The code begins by importing the necessary libraries, including pandas for data manipulation, scikit-learn for machine learning algorithms, and metrics from scikit-learn for evaluation.
3. Next, the dataset is loaded using **pd.read_csv()**, and the input feature (**'RM'**) and target variable (**'Price'**) are extracted.
4. The data is then split into training and test sets using **train_test_split()**, with 80% of the data used for training and 20% for testing.
5. A linear regression model is created using **LinearRegression()**, and the model is trained on the training data using **fit()**.
6. The trained model is used to make predictions on the test set with **predict()**.
7. The model's performance is evaluated using Mean Squared Error (MSE) by comparing the predicted housing prices (**y_pred**) with the actual prices (**y_test**).
8. Finally, the model is used to predict the price of a house with 5 rooms, and the result is printed.

Note: *This is a simplified example for illustration purposes. In real-world scenarios, data preprocessing, feature engineering, model tuning, and cross-validation should be considered for a more comprehensive and accurate predictive analysis.*

Data Sources and Preprocessing

The integration and preprocessing of diverse healthcare data sources are essential for building accurate and reliable predictive models. Healthcare data originates from Electronic Health Records (EHRs), wearable devices, clinical trials, insurance claims, and public health databases, each presenting unique challenges in standardization, interoperability, and security. Variations in medical terminology, missing values, and incompatible EHR systems can lead to inconsistencies that compromise data accuracy and AI model reliability. Effective data cleaning, standardization (for example, ICD, SNOMED-CT), and feature selection ensure that only the most relevant health indicators are used for predictive analytics. Interoperability frameworks such as FHIR and HL7 enable seamless data exchange, allowing AI models to utilize comprehensive patient histories for improved diagnostics and treatment predictions. Additionally, privacy and security measures such as data anonymization, encryption, and compliance with regulations such as HIPAA and GDPR are crucial to maintaining patient confidentiality while allowing AI-driven insights. Properly preprocessed data enhances AI applications such as sepsis prediction, personalized cancer treatments, and hospital resource optimization, leading to improved patient care, operational efficiency, and advancements in medical research. By addressing these challenges through structured preprocessing techniques, healthcare organizations can fully leverage predictive analytics to drive better clinical and operational outcomes.

Data sources and preprocessing play a critical role in healthcare analytics, ensuring that the data used for analysis is accurate, reliable, and appropriately prepared. Here is an overview of commonly used data sources and preprocessing steps in healthcare:

Data Sources

- **Electronic Health Records (EHR)**: EHR systems store patient health information, including medical history, diagnoses, treatments, laboratory results, and more. EHR data is a valuable source for healthcare analytics as it provides a comprehensive view of patient health.

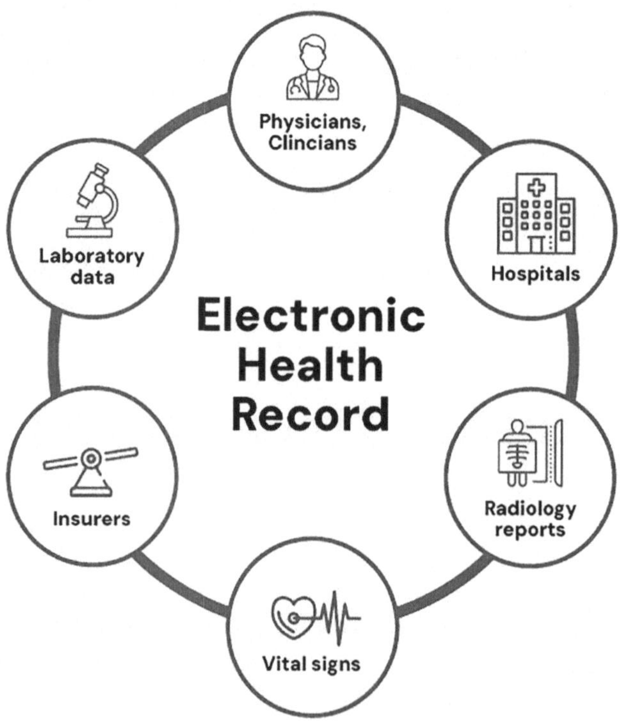

Figure 3.3: *Different Types of Electronic Health Records*

- **Claims and Billing Data**: Claims and billing data contain information related to medical procedures, services, and costs. These datasets are often used for billing and reimbursement purposes, but they can also be leveraged for healthcare analytics to understand utilization patterns, costs, and reimbursement trends.

- **Clinical Trials and Research Studies**: Data from clinical trials and research studies provide valuable insights into treatment outcomes, effectiveness, adverse events, and patient characteristics. These datasets are often used to assess the efficacy and safety of medical interventions.
- **Wearable Devices and Remote Monitoring**: With the increasing popularity of wearable devices and remote monitoring technologies, healthcare data can be collected from devices such as fitness trackers, smartwatches, and remote sensors. These devices capture information about vital signs, activity levels, sleep patterns, and other relevant health metrics.

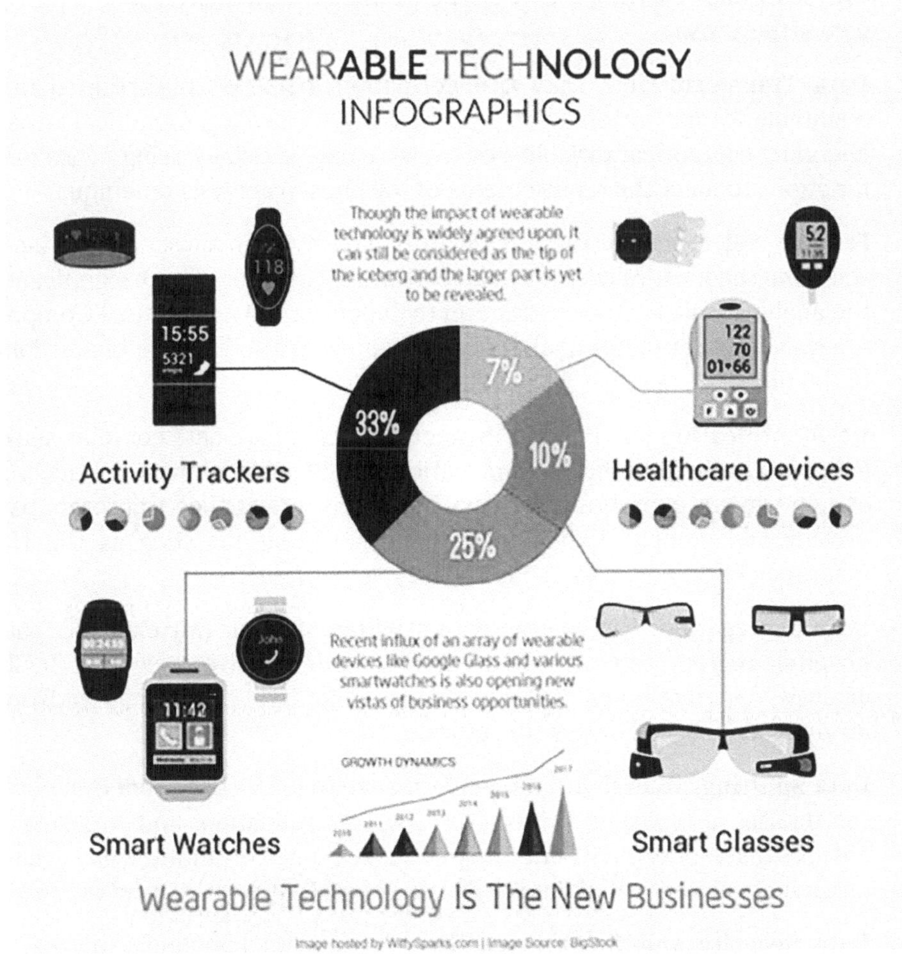

Figure 3.4: *Wearable Market in 2023*

- **Public Health Datasets**: Public health agencies and organizations collect and publish data related to disease surveillance, population health, epidemiology, and health outcomes. Examples include national health surveys, mortality and morbidity data, disease registries, and infectious disease data.

Preprocessing Steps:

1. **Data Cleaning**: Data cleaning involves removing or correcting errors, inconsistencies, and missing values in the dataset. This step ensures the data quality and reliability before analysis. Techniques such as outlier detection, imputation, and data validation are applied to handle missing or erroneous data.

2. **Data Integration**: In healthcare analytics, data often comes from multiple sources. Data integration involves combining and merging data from different sources while resolving inconsistencies in data formats, variable names, and data structures.

3. **Data Transformation**: Data transformation includes converting data into a suitable format for analysis. This may involve scaling numerical variables, encoding categorical variables, or transforming variables using mathematical functions to meet the requirements of the chosen analysis technique.

4. **Feature Selection/Extraction**: Feature selection involves identifying and selecting the most relevant variables (features) that contribute significantly to the analysis task. Feature extraction techniques such as Principal Component Analysis (PCA) or factor analysis can be applied to reduce the dimensionality of the dataset.

5. **De-Identification and Privacy Protection**: Healthcare data contains sensitive and personally identifiable information. De-identification techniques, such as removing or encrypting personal identifiers, are applied to protect patient privacy and comply with data protection regulations such as the Health Insurance Portability and Accountability Act (HIPAA).

6. **Data Aggregation**: Aggregating data at different levels (for example, patient, hospital, region) can provide a more comprehensive view and facilitate analysis. Aggregation can involve summarizing data, calculating statistics, or grouping data based on specific criteria.

7. **Data Splitting**: To evaluate the performance of predictive models accurately, the dataset is typically divided into training, validation, and test sets. This ensures that models are trained on one subset, tuned on another, and evaluated on an independent set of data to assess generalization and avoid overfitting.

8. **Data Security and Governance**: Healthcare data handling requires strict adherence to data security and governance practices to ensure confidentiality, integrity, and availability. This includes access controls, encryption, audit trails, and compliance with relevant regulations.

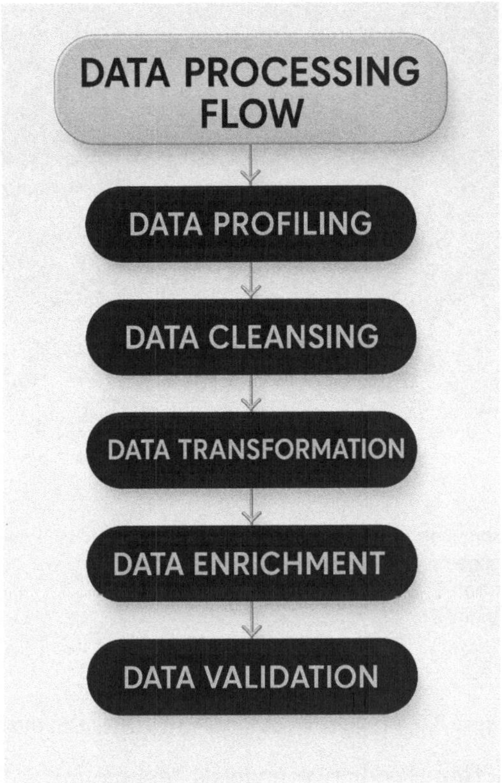

Figure 3.5: *Steps for Data Preprocessing*

Predictive Analysis in Disease Diagnosis and Early Detection

Predictive analysis plays a significant role in disease diagnosis and early detection by leveraging historical data, patient characteristics, and advanced analytics techniques to identify patterns and make predictions. This proactive approach enables healthcare professionals to intervene early, improve treatment outcomes, and potentially save lives. Here is an overview of how predictive analysis is applied in disease diagnosis and early detection:

- **Risk Stratification**: Predictive models are developed to stratify individuals into different risk categories based on their likelihood of developing a particular disease. By analyzing various factors such as demographics, genetic information, lifestyle habits, and medical history, these models can identify individuals who are at a higher risk of developing certain conditions.

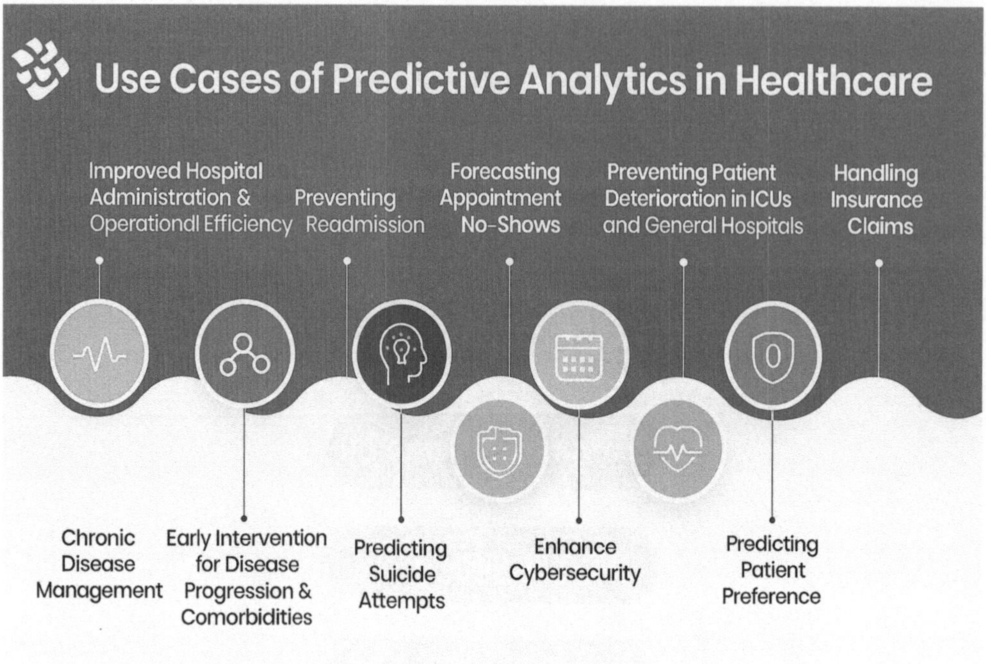

***Figure 3.6:** Predictive Analysis in Disease Diagnosis*

- **Disease Prediction**: Predictive analysis techniques are employed to predict the probability of a person developing a specific disease within a certain timeframe. By considering risk factors, biomarkers, genetic predisposition, and environmental factors, these models help healthcare professionals identify individuals who may benefit from targeted screening, prevention strategies, or early intervention.

  Let us Predict Heart Disease Prediction Using Machine Learning.

  Filename: `heart.csv`

  This dataset is sourced from the online repository of UCI.

  Link: https://archive.ics.uci.edu/ml/datasets/Heart+Disease

  Importing Libraries: The required libraries, such as NumPy, pandas, matplotlib, seaborn, and the necessary scikit-learn modules, are imported to facilitate data manipulation, visualization, and logistic regression modeling

```
import numpy as np
import pandas as pd
import matplotlib.pyplot as plt
import seaborn as sns from sklearn.model_selection
import train_test_split from sklearn.linear_model
```

```
import LogisticRegression from sklearn.metrics import confusion_
matrix

# Importing the required libraries

import seaborn as sns
from sklearn.model_selection import train_test_split
from sklearn.linear_model import LogisticRegression
from sklearn.metrics import confusion_matrix
```

- **Reading the Dataset**: The dataset is loaded into a pandas DataFrame using the **`pd.read_csv()`** function. The **`head(10)`** method displays the first 10 rows of the DataFrame

```
# Read the dataset
dataframe = pd.read_csv("/content/heart.csv")
dataframe.head(10)
```

- **Correlation Heatmap**: A correlation heatmap is generated using **`sns.heatmap()`** and displayed using **`plt.show()`**. This heatmap visualizes the correlation between different features in the dataset.

```
# Plot correlation heatmap
plt.figure(figsize=(15, 10))
sns.heatmap(dataframe.corr(), linewidth=0.01, annot=True,
cmap="winter")
plt.show()
plt.savefig('correlationfigure')

# Plot feature histograms
dataframe.hist(figsize=(12, 12))
plt.savefig('featuresplot')
```

- **Train-Test Split**: The dataset is split into training and testing sets using **`train_test_split()`** from scikit-learn. The independent variables are assigned to X, and the target variable is assigned to y.

```
# Train-Test Split
X = dataframe.drop('target', axis=1)
y = dataframe['target']
X_train, X_test, y_train, y_test = train_test_split(X, y, test_
size=0.25, random_state=40)

# Logistic Regression
lr = LogisticRegression(C=1.0, class_weight='balanced', dual=-
False, fit_intercept=True, intercept_scaling=1, l1_ratio=None,
max_iter=100, multi_class='auto', n_jobs=None, penalty='l2',
random_state=1234, solver='lbfgs', tol=0.0001, verbose=0, warm_
start=False)
```

```
model1 = lr.fit(X_train, y_train)
prediction1 = model1.predict(X_test)
cm = confusion_matrix(y_test, prediction1)
```

- **Plotting the Confusion Matrix**: The confusion matrix is plotted as a heatmap using **`sns.heatmap()`**. Annotations are added, and the plot is customized with linewidths and line colors.

```
# Plotting confusion matrix
sns.heatmap(cm, annot=True, cmap='winter', linewidths=0.3, line-
color='black', annot_kws={"size": 20})
```

- **Calculating Performance Metrics**: The true positives, true negatives, false positives, and false negatives are extracted from the confusion matrix to calculate various performance metrics.

```
# Calculating True Positives, True Negatives, False Positives,
False Negatives
TP = cm[0][0]
TN = cm[1][1]
FN = cm[1][0]
FP = cm[0][1]
```

- **Printing Performance Metrics**: The performance metrics, including testing accuracy, sensitivity, specificity, and precision, are printed to evaluate the logistic regression model's performance.

```
# Printing performance metrics
print('Testing Accuracy for Logistic Regression:', (TP + TN) /
(TP + TN + FN + FP))
print('Testing Sensitivity for Logistic Regression:', (TP / (TP +
FN)))
print('Testing Specificity for Logistic Regression:', (TN / (TN +
FP)))
print('Testing Precision for Logistic Regression:', (TP / (TP +
FP)))
```

Try out more algorithms such as Decision Tree, Random Forest, and Support Vector Machine (SVM) and compare the results for the best algorithm:

- **Diagnostic Support:** Predictive models can assist in disease diagnosis by analyzing patient data, symptoms, and test results to provide additional insights to healthcare professionals. These models can suggest potential diagnoses based on patterns observed in similar patient cases or provide probability scores to aid in decision-making.
- **Early Warning Systems:** Predictive analytics is used to develop early warning systems for diseases with acute or rapidly progressing symptoms. By continuously monitoring vital signs, laboratory values, and other relevant

data, these systems can identify deviations from normal patterns and alert healthcare providers to intervene promptly.

- **Image Analysis:** In medical imaging, predictive analysis techniques such as machine learning algorithms can be utilized to analyze images and aid in disease detection. For example, these models can be trained to detect patterns and anomalies in X-rays, mammograms, or MRI scans, assisting radiologists in early diagnosis and detection of conditions such as tumors or abnormalities.

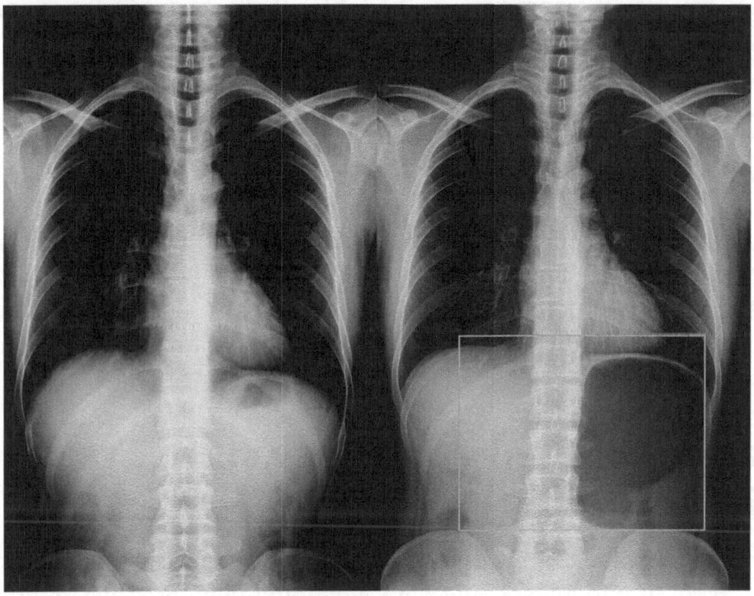

Figure 3.7: *AI in Chest X-ray for Pleural Effusion Detection*

- **Genetic Risk Assessment:** Predictive analysis techniques combined with genetic information can assess an individual's risk of developing inherited diseases. By analyzing genetic variants and their associations with diseases, these models provide personalized risk assessments, empowering individuals to make informed decisions about their healthcare and engage in preventive measures.
- **Prognosis and Treatment Response Prediction:** Predictive models can be used to predict the prognosis and treatment response of individuals diagnosed with specific diseases. By considering clinical data, biomarkers, and treatment history, these models assist in tailoring treatment plans and providing personalized care to improve outcomes.

By leveraging predictive analysis in disease diagnosis and early detection, healthcare professionals can identify high-risk individuals, make timely interventions, optimize treatment strategies, and ultimately improve patient outcomes. These predictive models, coupled with advancements in technology and data availability, have the potential to transform healthcare and promote proactive and preventive care practices.

Predictive Analysis in Treatment Optimization

Predictive analysis, in conjunction with advanced data analytics and machine learning techniques, has the potential to revolutionize treatment optimization in healthcare. By leveraging large datasets, patient characteristics, treatment outcomes, and clinical guidelines, predictive analysis can provide valuable insights into tailoring treatment plans, predicting treatment response, and optimizing therapeutic interventions. This chapter explores the applications, benefits, challenges, and future prospects of predictive analysis in treatment optimization.

Understanding Predictive Analysis in Treatment Optimization

Predictive analysis in treatment optimization involves the use of historical treatment data, patient profiles, and clinical parameters to develop models that predict treatment outcomes and guide decision-making processes. It aims to identify the most effective treatment options for individual patients, optimize treatment plans, and enhance patient outcomes.

Applications of Predictive Analysis in Treatment Optimization

- **Personalized Treatment Selection**: Predictive analysis models can analyze a vast array of patient-specific data, including demographics, medical history, genetic information, and biomarkers, to predict the most suitable treatment options for an individual. By considering multiple variables and their interactions, these models can assist healthcare providers in selecting the treatment that is most likely to be effective for a particular patient, improving treatment response rates.
- **Treatment Response Prediction**: Predictive analysis can help predict how an individual patient will respond to a specific treatment. By analyzing historical treatment data and patient characteristics, these models can estimate the likelihood of treatment success, potential adverse effects, and the optimal dosage or duration of treatment. This information can guide treatment decisions, reduce trial and error, and improve patient outcomes.

Benefits and Advantages

- **Personalized Treatment Plans**: Predictive analysis enables the development of personalized treatment plans tailored to individual patient's characteristics and needs. By considering a wide range of patient-specific variables, including genetics, lifestyle factors, comorbidities, and treatment history, these models can provide treatment recommendations that maximize effectiveness while minimizing risks and side effects.

- **Improved Treatment Outcomes:** By predicting treatment responses and guiding treatment selection, predictive analysis can lead to improved treatment outcomes. Healthcare providers can make more informed decisions, choose the most appropriate therapies, and adjust treatment plans based on individual patient characteristics. This personalized approach can optimize treatment efficacy, reduce adverse effects, and enhance patient satisfaction.

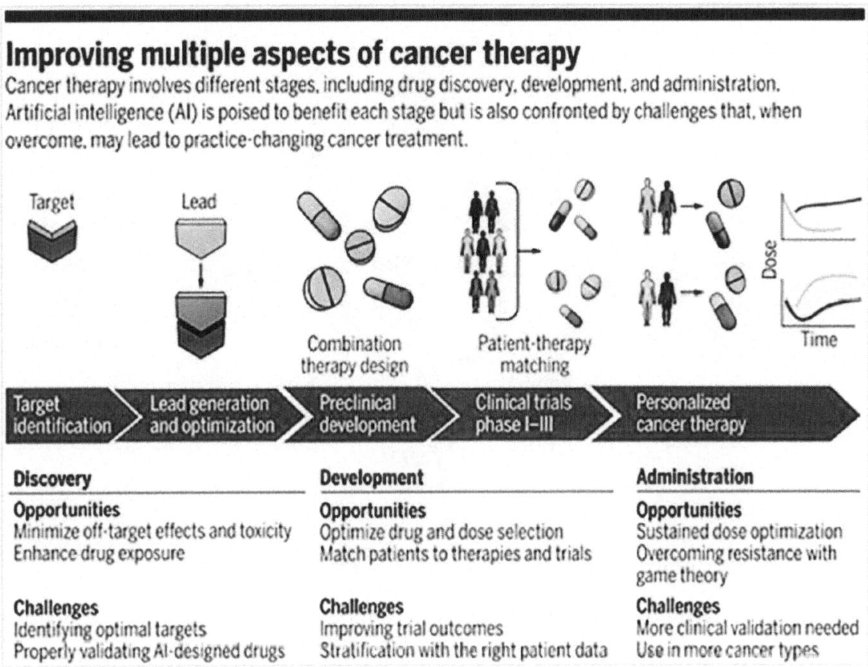

Figure 3.8: *Predictive Analysis Use in Cancer Therapy*

- **Cost Optimization**: Predictive analysis can also help optimize healthcare costs by identifying the most cost-effective treatment options. By considering treatment effectiveness, potential risks, and associated costs, these models can assist in decision-making processes and resource allocation. This can result in better allocation of healthcare resources, reduced healthcare expenses, and improved cost-effectiveness in treatment strategies.

Challenges and Considerations

- **Data Availability and Quality**: The predictive analysis relies on comprehensive and high-quality data to develop accurate models. However, healthcare data is often fragmented, dispersed across various systems, and subject to data privacy and security concerns. Integrating diverse data sources, ensuring data quality, and addressing data governance issues are crucial challenges that need to be overcome to effectively leverage predictive analysis in treatment optimization.

- **Ethical and Legal Considerations:** The use of predictive analysis in treatment optimization raises ethical and legal considerations. Patient privacy, data security, informed consent, and fairness in algorithmic decision-making are important factors that need to be addressed. Transparent and interpretable models, along with robust governance frameworks, are necessary to maintain trust and ensure the responsible use of predictive analysis in treatment optimization.

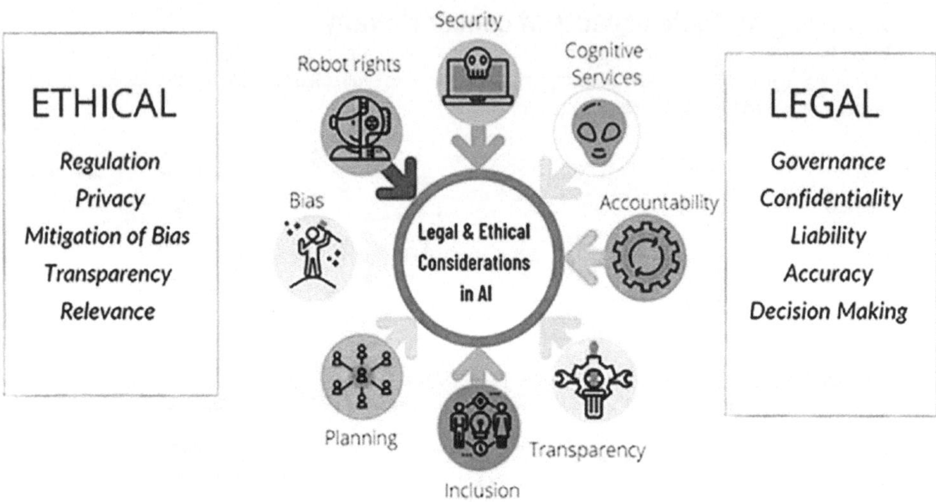

Figure 3.9: *Ethical Challenges in Predictive Analysis*

- **Future Prospects:** The future of predictive analysis in treatment optimization holds significant promise. Advancements in data collection methods, wearable devices, electronic health records, and real-time patient monitoring will generate more extensive and diverse datasets. This, combined with evolving machine learning algorithms and artificial intelligence techniques, will enhance the accuracy and applicability of predictive models in treatment optimization.

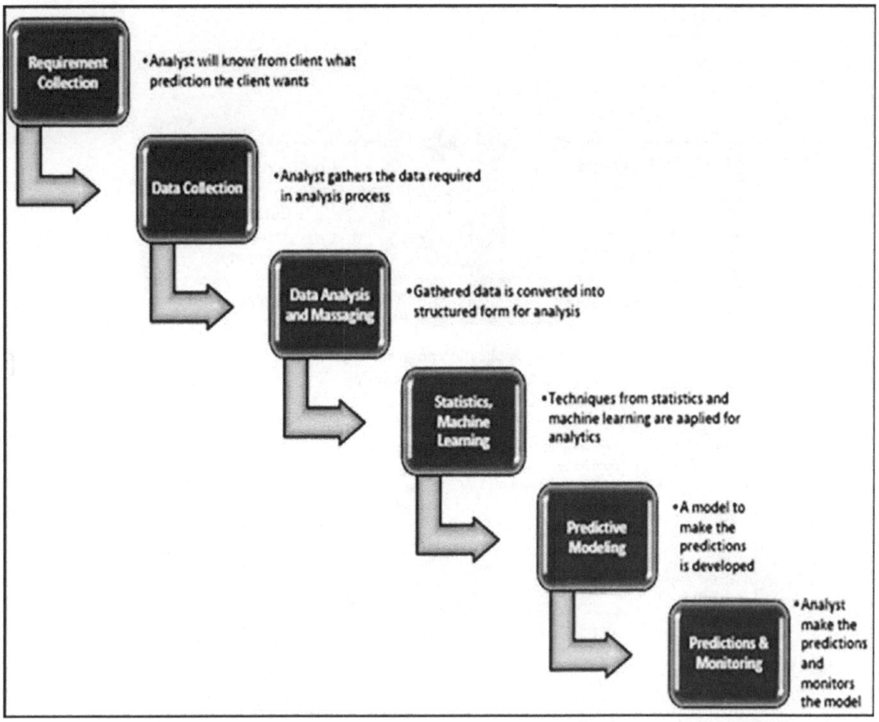

Figure 3.10: *Process of Predictive Analysis*

Predictive analysis offers immense potential in optimizing treatment decisions and improving patient outcomes. By leveraging data-driven insights, healthcare providers can personalize treatment plans, predict treatment response, and optimize therapeutic interventions. However, overcoming data challenges, addressing ethical considerations, and ensuring transparency and accountability are crucial for the responsible and effective implementation of predictive analysis in treatment optimization. With continued advancements in technology and data analytics, predictive analysis will undoubtedly play a vital role in shaping the future of healthcare.

Predictive Analysis for Healthcare Resource Management

Predictive analysis plays a crucial role in healthcare resource management by utilizing historical data and statistical models to make predictions about future healthcare resource needs. Here are some areas where predictive analysis can be applied in healthcare resource management:

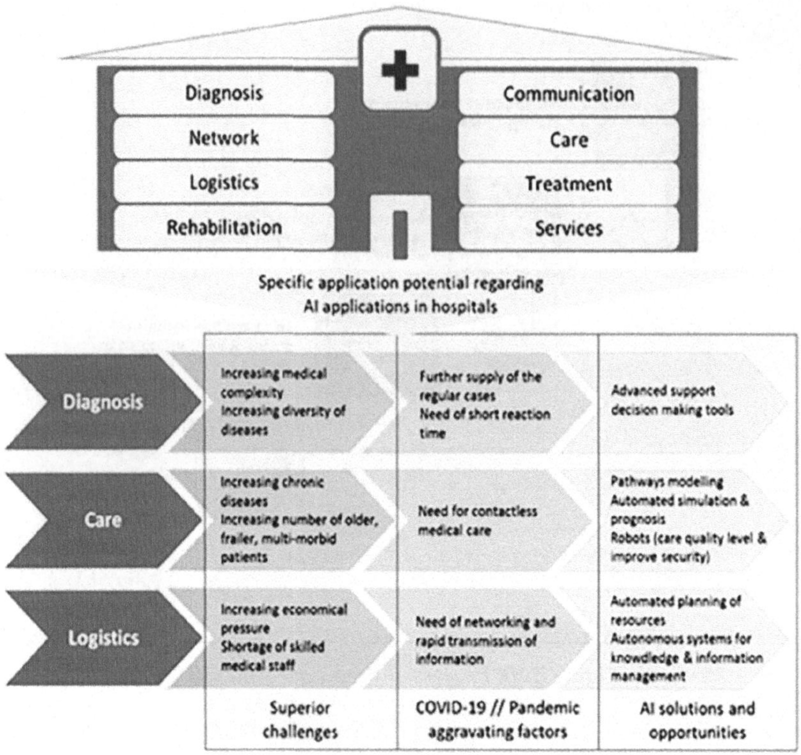

Figure 3.11: *AI Applications in Hospitals*

- **Demand Forecasting**: Predictive analysis can be used to forecast patient volumes, bed occupancy rates, and the demand for specific healthcare services. By analyzing historical data, such as patient admissions, seasonal patterns, and demographic factors, healthcare organizations can anticipate future resource requirements and plan accordingly. This helps optimize resource allocation, avoid shortages or overcapacity, and improve overall operational efficiency.
- **Staffing Optimization**: Predictive analysis can assist in predicting staffing needs based on patient demand and expected workload. By considering factors such as patient volumes, acuity levels, and historical data on staff-to-patient ratios, healthcare organizations can determine the optimal number of healthcare professionals required in each department or shift. This ensures that staffing levels are aligned with patient needs, improving patient care and reducing costs associated with overstaffing or understaffing.
- **Inventory Management**: Predictive analysis can be employed to optimize inventory management of medical supplies, medications, and equipment. By analyzing usage patterns, expiration dates, and demand fluctuations, healthcare organizations can predict when and how much inventory should

be replenished. This helps prevent stockouts, minimize waste, and reduce the financial burden associated with excessive inventory or emergency orders.

- **Patient Readmission Risk**: Predictive analysis can be used to identify patients at high risk of readmission. By analyzing patient characteristics, medical history, and clinical data, predictive models can assess the likelihood of a patient being readmitted within a certain timeframe. Healthcare organizations can then proactively intervene by providing appropriate follow-up care, home monitoring, or additional support to reduce readmission rates and optimize resource allocation.
- **Equipment Maintenance and Failure Prediction**: Predictive analysis can help predict equipment failures and maintenance needs. By monitoring real-time data from medical devices, such as vital signs monitors or imaging equipment, and applying predictive algorithms, healthcare organizations can anticipate equipment failures before they occur. This enables proactive maintenance scheduling, reduces downtime, and ensures the availability of functional equipment when needed.

Overall, predictive analysis in healthcare resource management allows organizations to make informed decisions, optimize resource allocation, improve patient outcomes, and reduce costs. By leveraging historical data and advanced analytics techniques, healthcare organizations can anticipate future needs, identify potential bottlenecks, and take proactive measures to ensure efficient and effective resource utilization.

Predictive Analysis in Public Health

Predictive analysis in public health involves using data and statistical models to forecast and anticipate health-related events, patterns, and outcomes. Here are some key applications of predictive analysis in public health:

- **Disease Outbreak Prediction**: Predictive analysis can help identify patterns and indicators that precede disease outbreaks. By analyzing various data sources, such as epidemiological data, environmental factors, social media trends, and healthcare utilization patterns, predictive models can provide early warnings of potential disease outbreaks. This allows public health officials to take proactive measures, such as targeted interventions, resource allocation, and public awareness campaigns, to prevent the spread of diseases.

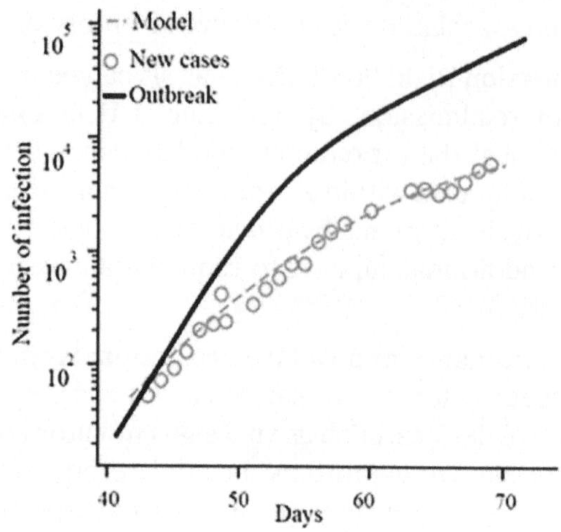

Figure 3.12: *COVID-19 Outbreak Prediction*

- **Epidemic Modeling**: Predictive analysis is used to create mathematical models that simulate the spread of infectious diseases within populations. These models consider factors such as disease transmission dynamics, population demographics, mobility patterns, and intervention strategies. By running simulations based on different scenarios, public health authorities can assess the potential impact of interventions, evaluate the effectiveness of control measures, and inform decision-making to mitigate the impact of epidemics.

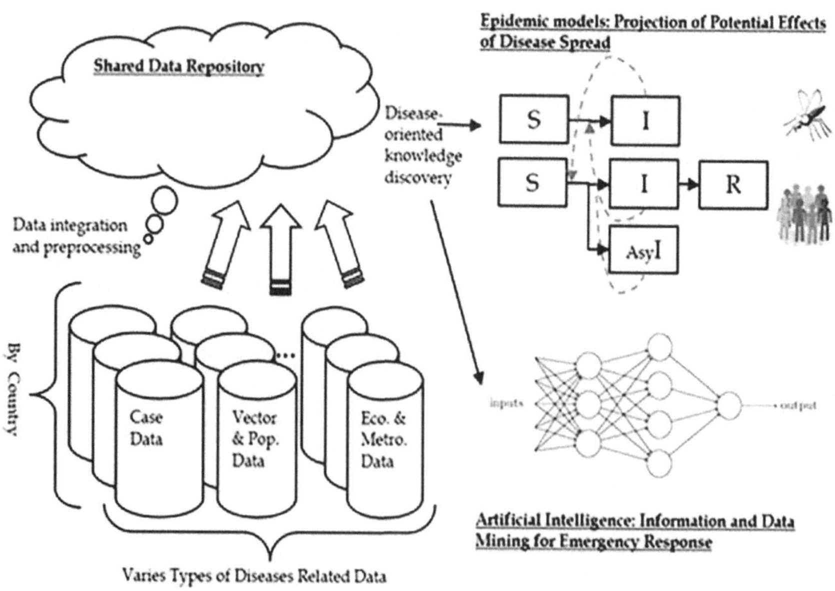

Figure 3.13: *Data Architecture for Emergency Response*

- **Public Health Resource Allocation**: Predictive analysis helps optimize the allocation of public health resources, such as vaccines, medications, and healthcare personnel. By analyzing data on population demographics, disease prevalence, and healthcare utilization, predictive models can estimate the demand for specific resources in different regions or communities. This information allows public health agencies to distribute resources strategically, prioritize high-risk populations, and ensure equitable access to healthcare services.
- **Risk Assessment and Early Intervention**: Predictive analysis can be used to assess individuals' risk of developing certain health conditions or experiencing adverse health outcomes. By analyzing demographic data, medical records, genetic information, lifestyle factors, and environmental factors, predictive models can identify individuals at higher risk. This enables targeted interventions, such as preventive screenings, health education programs, or personalized interventions, to mitigate risks and improve health outcomes.
- **Health Service Planning**: Predictive analysis supports the planning and provision of healthcare services. By analyzing population demographics, health needs, healthcare utilization patterns, and capacity data, predictive models can estimate future healthcare service demands. This information helps public health agencies and healthcare providers allocate resources effectively, plan for infrastructure development, and ensure adequate service capacity to meet the population's healthcare needs.
- **Public Health Surveillance**: Predictive analysis enhances public health surveillance systems by identifying patterns and trends in health-related data. By analyzing data from various sources, such as electronic health records, syndromic surveillance systems, social media, and environmental sensors, predictive models can detect early signals of disease outbreaks, monitor the spread of infectious diseases, and identify emerging health threats. This enables timely response and targeted interventions to mitigate risks and protect public health.

Predictive analysis in public health empowers decision-makers with valuable insights and actionable information to prevent and control diseases, optimize resource allocation, and improve overall population health. By leveraging data-driven approaches, public health agencies can proactively address health challenges, enhance preparedness, and make informed decisions to protect and promote the well-being of communities.

Ethical Considerations and Challenges

Predictive analysis in healthcare brings forth several ethical considerations and challenges that need to be carefully addressed. Here are some key ethical considerations and challenges associated with predictive analysis in healthcare:

- **Privacy and Data Security**: Predictive analysis relies heavily on collecting and analyzing large volumes of personal health data. Ensuring the privacy and security of this sensitive information is crucial. Healthcare organizations must implement robust data protection measures, adhere to relevant privacy regulations (such as HIPAA in the United States), and obtain informed consent from individuals whose data is being used. Anonymization and de-identification techniques should be applied to minimize the risk of re-identification.
- **Fairness and Bias**: Predictive models can inadvertently perpetuate or amplify existing biases in healthcare. If the training data used to develop predictive models is biased, such as the underrepresentation of certain demographic groups, the models may produce biased predictions and exacerbate healthcare disparities. It is essential to regularly assess and mitigate biases in data, algorithms, and decision-making processes to ensure fairness and equity in healthcare outcomes.
- **Informed Consent and Transparency**: Individuals whose data is being used for predictive analysis should be informed about the purposes, potential benefits, and risks involved. Transparent communication is necessary to ensure individuals understand how their data will be used and have the opportunity to provide informed consent. Healthcare organizations should also be transparent about the limitations and uncertainties associated with predictive models, setting realistic expectations for their performance.
- **Accountability and Explainability**: Predictive models can be complex, making it challenging to understand and explain the factors influencing their predictions. Healthcare providers and organizations must be able to explain the rationale behind the predictions generated by these models. Ensuring transparency and accountability in the decision-making process is crucial, especially when it comes to high-stakes decisions that may significantly impact patient care.
- **Continual Validation and Updating**: Predictive models require continuous monitoring, validation, and updating to maintain their accuracy and effectiveness. As new data becomes available and healthcare practices evolve, models must be re-evaluated and updated accordingly. Failure to validate and update models may lead to outdated or inaccurate predictions, potentially compromising patient care and safety.

- **Impact on the Patient-Provider Relationship**: The use of predictive analysis can influence the patient-provider relationship. Providers must carefully navigate the introduction of predictive models into clinical practice to ensure they enhance, rather than undermine, the trust and communication between patients and healthcare professionals. Patients should be informed about the role of predictive analysis and how it complements clinical judgment, ensuring they remain active participants in their healthcare decisions.
- **Unintended Consequences and Overreliance**: Predictive analysis is a powerful tool, but it is not infallible. Relying solely on predictive models without considering clinical expertise and context may lead to errors or inappropriate interventions. Healthcare professionals should maintain a balanced approach, utilizing predictive insights to inform decision-making while considering individual patient circumstances and preferences.

Addressing these ethical considerations and challenges requires interdisciplinary collaboration among healthcare professionals, data scientists, ethicists, policymakers, and patients. Ethical frameworks, guidelines, and regulatory frameworks should be developed and regularly updated to ensure the responsible and ethical use of predictive analysis in healthcare, promoting patient autonomy, equity, and the overall well-being of individuals and communities.

Predictive analysis in healthcare faces several challenges and limitations that impact its effectiveness and implementation. Here are some key challenges and limitations to consider:

- **Data Quality and Availability**: The accuracy and reliability of predictive models heavily depend on the quality and availability of data. Healthcare data can be incomplete, inconsistent, or contain errors, which can introduce biases and affect the performance of predictive models. Additionally, data may be fragmented across different systems and not easily accessible for analysis. Improving data quality, standardization, and interoperability is essential to enhance the reliability and utility of predictive analysis in healthcare.
- **Data Representativeness and Bias**: Biases present in the data used to train predictive models can result in biased predictions and exacerbate healthcare disparities. Data may be skewed towards specific populations, leading to underrepresentation or misrepresentation of certain demographic groups. This can result in inequitable healthcare outcomes. Addressing biases in data collection and ensuring diverse and representative datasets are used for training is crucial to mitigate these issues.
- **Interpretability and Explainability**: Many predictive models, such as deep learning algorithms, are often considered black boxes, making it challenging to understand and interpret the factors influencing their predictions. Lack of interpretability can hinder trust and acceptance among healthcare professionals, patients, and regulatory bodies. Ensuring models are explainable

and providing clear justifications for their predictions is important to gain stakeholders' confidence and facilitate decision-making.

- **Generalizability and External Validity**: Predictive models developed and validated using specific datasets or patient populations may not generalize well to different populations or healthcare settings. Models need to be evaluated and validated across diverse populations to ensure their effectiveness and generalizability. It is important to consider the context and population characteristics when applying predictive analysis to different healthcare scenarios.
- **Overfitting and Model Complexity**: Overfitting occurs when a predictive model performs well on the training data but fails to generalize to new data. Overly complex models with excessive parameters can be prone to overfitting, leading to inaccurate predictions. Striking a balance between model complexity and generalization is crucial to avoid overfitting and ensure models are robust and reliable.
- **Ethical and Legal Considerations**: Predictive analysis in healthcare raises ethical and legal concerns, including privacy, consent, fairness, and accountability. As mentioned earlier, protecting patient privacy, ensuring informed consent, addressing biases, and being transparent about the limitations and uncertainties of predictive models are essential to maintain ethical standards and comply with legal requirements.
- **Integration into Clinical Workflows**: Integrating predictive analysis seamlessly into clinical workflows can be challenging. Clinicians may have limited time and resources to engage with complex predictive models. It is crucial to design user-friendly interfaces and decision support tools that present actionable insights in a timely manner and align with clinicians' workflow to facilitate their adoption and utilization.

Addressing these challenges and limitations requires collaborative efforts from healthcare providers, data scientists, policymakers, and regulatory bodies. Improving data quality, promoting transparency and interpretability of models, addressing biases, and fostering interdisciplinary collaborations are vital steps toward harnessing the potential of predictive analysis in healthcare while ensuring patient safety, fairness, and ethical standards.

Future Scope and Direction of Predictive Analysis in Healthcare

The future scope and direction of predictive analysis in healthcare are promising and poised to bring significant advancements to the field. Here are some key areas where predictive analysis is expected to make a substantial impact:

- **Personalized Medicine**: Predictive analysis can contribute to the advancement of personalized medicine by utilizing patient-specific data, such as genetic information, medical history, lifestyle factors, and environmental data, to predict disease risks, treatment responses, and prognosis. This can enable tailored interventions and treatment plans that maximize patient outcomes and minimize adverse effects.
- **Preventive Healthcare and Early Intervention**: Predictive analysis can help identify individuals at high risk of developing certain diseases or experiencing adverse health outcomes. By analyzing various data sources, including electronic health records, wearable devices, and social determinants of health, predictive models can provide insights into early warning signs and facilitate proactive interventions, preventive measures, and lifestyle modifications to mitigate risks and promote better health.
- **Real-Time Monitoring and Decision Support**: Advances in data analytics and machine learning techniques can enable real-time monitoring of patient data, such as vital signs, lab results, and patient-reported outcomes. Predictive analysis can identify abnormal patterns or predict deteriorating health conditions, providing timely alerts to healthcare providers. This facilitates early intervention, reduces hospital readmissions, and improves patient outcomes.
- **Integration with Digital Health Technologies**: Predictive analysis can be integrated with emerging digital health technologies, such as remote patient monitoring, telehealth, and wearable devices. These technologies generate vast amounts of real-time data, which can be leveraged by predictive models to provide actionable insights and support remote diagnosis, personalized recommendations, and virtual care delivery.
- **Health System Optimization and Resource Management**: Predictive analysis can contribute to optimizing healthcare resource allocation, improving operational efficiency, and reducing costs. By forecasting patient volumes, demand for services, and resource needs, healthcare organizations can allocate resources effectively, streamline workflows, and reduce wait times. Predictive models can also assist in optimizing staffing levels, inventory management, and healthcare facility planning to ensure efficient service delivery.
- **Population Health Management and Public Health Planning**: Predictive analysis can support population health management initiatives and public health planning. By analyzing population-level data, such as epidemiological data, social determinants of health, and environmental factors, predictive models can identify health trends, assess disease burdens, and anticipate healthcare needs at a community or regional level. This facilitates targeted interventions, resource allocation, and policy development to improve population health outcomes.

- **Integration of Multi-Modal Data**: The future of predictive analysis lies in the integration of diverse data sources, including genomics, proteomics, electronic health records, social determinants of health, and patient-generated data. Integrating and analyzing these multi-modal data sets can provide a more comprehensive understanding of health conditions, disease mechanisms, and treatment responses, leading to more accurate predictions and personalized healthcare approaches.

To realize the full potential of predictive analysis in healthcare, ongoing research and development efforts are necessary. Collaboration among healthcare providers, data scientists, policymakers, and technology developers is crucial to addressing the challenges related to data quality, privacy, interpretability, and ethical considerations. Additionally, robust regulatory frameworks and standards for data sharing, interoperability, and model validation are essential to ensure the responsible and effective implementation of predictive analysis in healthcare.

Conclusion

This chapter on predictive analytics in healthcare highlights the remarkable potential of data-driven insights in transforming patient care, optimizing resource allocation, and improving healthcare operations. By systematically analyzing vast amounts of patient data, predictive analytics empowers healthcare providers to anticipate adverse events, enhance clinical decision-making, and implement targeted preventive measures. The applications explored–including early disease detection, treatment optimization, readmission prediction, and medication adherence improvements–demonstrate the ability of predictive models to drive better health outcomes and cost efficiencies across healthcare systems.

However, while predictive analytics offers immense benefits, its real-world implementation faces several ongoing challenges. Data integration and interoperability remain major obstacles, as healthcare data is often fragmented across multiple systems, formats, and institutions, making seamless data exchange difficult. Additionally, ethical concerns around patient privacy, algorithmic bias, and transparency in AI-driven predictions must be addressed to build trust in predictive models. Another critical challenge is the need for rigorous validation and clinical trials to ensure that predictive models are accurate, reliable, and generalizable across diverse patient populations. Without robust model validation and regulatory oversight, the risk of misleading predictions could undermine patient safety.

To fully harness the potential of predictive analytics, healthcare organizations must prioritize data standardization, invest in privacy-preserving technologies, and foster collaboration between healthcare professionals, data scientists, and policymakers. As AI-driven analytics continues to evolve, ensuring responsible deployment, ethical governance, and continuous model refinement will be key to bridging the gap between innovation and real-world impact.

In the next chapter, we will explore how the convergence of Artificial Intelligence (AI) and telemedicine is driving a transformative shift in healthcare delivery, with Remote Patient Monitoring (RPM) emerging as a powerful tool for improving patient care and expanding access to healthcare services.

Questions

- What is predictive analysis in healthcare?
- True or False: Predictive analysis uses historical data and statistical algorithms to forecast future outcomes in healthcare.
- What are some common applications of predictive analysis in healthcare?
- Name one statistical algorithm commonly used in predictive analysis for healthcare.
- What is the difference between predictive analysis and diagnostic analysis in healthcare?
- True or False: Predictive analysis can help identify patients at risk of developing certain medical conditions or complications.
- How does predictive analysis contribute to personalized medicine in healthcare?
- What are the main challenges or limitations of predictive analysis in healthcare?
- Describe the process of building a predictive model in healthcare.
- Give an example of how predictive analysis can be used to improve healthcare outcomes.

Chapter 4
Artificial Intelligence in Telemedicine Remote Patient Monitoring

Introduction

In recent years, the rapid evolution of healthcare technologies has positioned Artificial Intelligence (AI) as a transformative force in medicine, particularly in the realm of telemedicine and **Remote Patient Monitoring (RPM)**. AI-powered RPM solutions are revolutionizing chronic disease management, enabling continuous monitoring of diabetes, hypertension, and cardiovascular conditions, ensuring early intervention and personalized treatment adjustments. In mental health, AI-integrated wearables and mobile apps analyze speech patterns, sleep cycles, and physiological markers to detect early signs of anxiety and depression, facilitating timely interventions.

Beyond chronic disease and mental health care, AI-enhanced RPM is also transforming postoperative recovery, elderly care, and Intensive Care Unit (ICU) monitoring, reducing hospital readmissions and improving patient safety. By leveraging real-time data from smart sensors, wearable devices, and AI-driven analytics, RPM enhances clinical decision-making, enables proactive interventions, and fosters a more patient-centric approach to care. This chapter explores real-world applications, technological advancements, and the challenges of AI-powered RPM, shedding light on how this innovation is reshaping the doctor-patient relationship and the future of healthcare delivery.

Structure

In this chapter, we will cover the following topics:

- The Evolving Face of Telemedicine
- Predictive Analytics for Early Intervention
- Personalized Treatment Plans
- Natural Language Processing (NLP) for Virtual Consultations
- Future Trends and Innovations

The Evolving Face of Telemedicine

The evolving face of telemedicine reflects a dynamic and transformative shift in healthcare delivery, driven by advancements in technology, changing patient preferences, and the ongoing need for accessible and efficient healthcare services. Here are key aspects that characterize the evolving landscape of telemedicine:

Technological Advancements

- **Integration of AI and Machine Learning**: Telemedicine is increasingly incorporating AI and machine learning algorithms to enhance diagnostic capabilities, analyze patient data, and provide personalized treatment recommendations.
- **Wearables and Remote Monitoring Devices**: The integration of wearables and remote monitoring devices allows for continuous tracking of patient health metrics, enabling real-time data collection and personalized interventions.
- **Telehealth Platforms and Apps**: The development of user-friendly telehealth platforms and mobile applications facilitates seamless virtual consultations, enabling patients to connect with healthcare providers from the comfort of their homes.

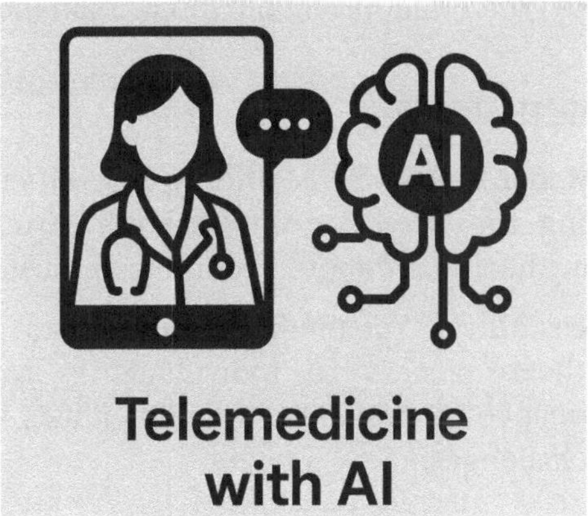

***Figure 4.1**: AI in Telemedicine*

Expanding Scope of Services

- **Beyond Primary Care**: Telemedicine has expanded beyond primary care to include specialized services such as mental health consultations, dermatology assessments, chronic disease management, and post-surgical follow-ups.
- **Remote Surgical Procedures**: Advancements in telemedicine technology, including robotics and haptic feedback systems, are paving the way for remote surgical procedures performed by surgeons from different locations.
- **Remote Patient Monitoring (RPM)**: RPM has become an integral part of telemedicine, allowing for continuous monitoring of patients with chronic conditions, early detection of health issues, and proactive interventions.

Patient-Centric Care

- **Personalized Treatment Plans**: Telemedicine is moving towards more personalized treatment plans, integrating patient data, preferences, and feedback to tailor interventions based on individual needs.
- **Patient Education and Engagement**: Telehealth platforms are incorporating features to educate and engage patients in their healthcare journey, promoting active participation in managing their health.
- **Virtual Support Groups**: The evolving face of telemedicine includes virtual support groups and communities, fostering connections among patients with similar conditions, and providing emotional support.

Regulatory Changes and Acceptance

- **Regulatory Support**: Many countries are adapting and updating regulations to support the widespread adoption of telemedicine. Regulatory changes aim to ensure quality care, patient safety, and the ethical use of technology.
- **Increased Acceptance**: Patients and healthcare providers are increasingly accepting and embracing telemedicine as a viable and convenient healthcare option, leading to greater adoption and integration into traditional healthcare systems.

Economic and Accessible Healthcare

- **Cost-Efficient Model**: Telemedicine offers a cost-efficient model of healthcare delivery, reducing the need for physical infrastructure and streamlining processes, making healthcare more economically sustainable.
- **Improved Accessibility**: Telemedicine addresses geographical barriers, providing healthcare access to individuals in remote or underserved areas. It also enhances accessibility for individuals with mobility issues or transportation challenges.

Data Security and Privacy

- **Emphasis on Security Measures**: As telemedicine usage grows, there is an increased emphasis on implementing robust data security measures. Adherence to privacy regulations and secure transmission of patient data are critical considerations.
- **Technological Safeguards**: The evolving face of telemedicine involves the integration of secure communication channels, encryption protocols, and technologies such as blockchain to safeguard patient information.

Global Response to Healthcare Challenges

- **Pandemic Response**: The COVID-19 pandemic accelerated the adoption of telemedicine globally as healthcare systems adapted to the need for remote care and social distancing measures.
- **Public Health Preparedness**: Telemedicine is increasingly recognized as a tool for public health preparedness, enabling healthcare systems to respond more effectively to public health emergencies and ensuring continuity of care.

Research and Continuous Innovation

- **Ongoing Research**: Continuous research and innovation in telemedicine focus on addressing challenges, improving technologies, and exploring new applications. Research efforts aim to enhance the effectiveness and scalability of telehealth solutions.

The evolving face of telemedicine is marked by a shift towards a more integrated, patient-centric, and technologically advanced healthcare model. As telemedicine continues to evolve, it is expected to play a central role in shaping the future of healthcare delivery, offering solutions to challenges and improving access to quality care for diverse populations.

AI-Powered Diagnostic Tools

AI can significantly enhance diagnostic capabilities in telemedicine by leveraging advanced algorithms, machine learning, and data analytics. Here are several ways AI contributes to improving diagnostics in the context of telemedicine:

Medical Imaging Analysis

- **Image Recognition**: AI algorithms can analyze medical images, such as X-rays, MRIs, and CT scans, with high accuracy. This can help in detecting abnormalities, tumors, or other conditions without the need for an in-person visit.
- **Radiology Assistance**: AI can assist radiologists by quickly highlighting potential areas of concern, reducing the time required for image interpretation, and improving overall diagnostic efficiency.

Remote Monitoring and Data Analysis

- **Continuous Monitoring**: AI algorithms can analyze continuous streams of patient data from wearable devices and remote monitoring equipment. This enables the early detection of anomalies or changes in health status that may indicate a potential medical issue.
- **Predictive Analytics**: By processing historical patient data, AI can predict the likelihood of certain health events, allowing for proactive interventions and personalized care plans.

***Figure 4.2**: Remote Monitoring*

Clinical Decision Support Systems

- **Assisting Healthcare Professionals**: AI-powered clinical decision support systems can provide real-time insights to healthcare professionals during virtual consultations. This includes relevant medical literature, treatment guidelines, and potential diagnostic options.
- **Risk Assessment**: AI algorithms can assess patient risk factors and suggest appropriate diagnostic tests or procedures, helping clinicians make more informed decisions.

Natural Language Processing (NLP) for Virtual Consultations

- **Interpreting Patient Narratives**: NLP allows AI systems to understand and interpret natural language, enabling them to analyze patient descriptions of symptoms during virtual consultations. This aids in gathering crucial information for diagnostic purposes.
- **Chatbots for Triage**: AI-driven chatbots can assist in initial patient triage by asking relevant questions about symptoms, medical history, and lifestyle factors. This information can then be used to prioritize and guide the diagnostic process.

Integration of Genomic and Clinical Data

- **Genomic Analysis**: AI can integrate genomic data with clinical information to identify genetic markers associated with specific conditions. This can contribute to more accurate diagnoses and personalized treatment plans.
- **Pattern Recognition**: AI algorithms can identify complex patterns in large datasets, allowing for the identification of subtle correlations between genetic variations and disease susceptibility.

Remote Laboratory Testing and Analysis

- **Automated Lab Results Interpretation**: AI can assist in interpreting laboratory test results, ensuring accurate and timely assessments without the need for a physical presence in a healthcare facility.
- **Efficient Data Processing**: AI helps manage and process large volumes of lab data, improving the speed and accuracy of diagnostic reporting.

Reducing Diagnostic Errors

- **Flagging Unusual Patterns**: AI algorithms can flag unusual patterns or inconsistencies in patient data, reducing the likelihood of diagnostic errors caused by oversights or cognitive biases.
- **Continuous Learning**: AI systems can continuously learn from new data and updates, refining their diagnostic capabilities over time and adapting to evolving medical knowledge.

By combining these capabilities, AI in telemedicine not only extends the reach of healthcare but also enhances the accuracy and efficiency of diagnostics, leading to improved patient outcomes.

AI Algorithms for Image Recognition

AI algorithms for image recognition play a crucial role in the analysis of medical images, such as X-rays, MRIs, and CT scans. These algorithms leverage deep learning techniques to automatically identify patterns, anomalies, or specific features in images, assisting healthcare professionals in diagnosis and treatment planning. Here are some common AI algorithms used in medical image recognition:

Convolutional Neural Networks (CNNs)

- **Application**: CNNs are widely used in medical image analysis due to their ability to automatically learn hierarchical features from images.
- **Use Case**: They can identify structures, abnormalities, or regions of interest in medical images by processing local patterns and gradually combining them to recognize more complex patterns.

Transfer Learning

- **Application**: Transfer learning involves using pre-trained models on large datasets for general image recognition tasks and fine-tuning them for medical image analysis.
- **Use Case**: Models pre-trained on non-medical datasets, such as ImageNet, can be adapted to medical images with smaller datasets, reducing the need for extensive labeled medical data.

U-Net Architecture

- **Application**: U-Net is commonly used for segmentation tasks, where the goal is to outline and identify specific structures or abnormalities within an image.
- **Use Case**: It is frequently employed in segmenting organs or tumors in medical images, providing a detailed analysis of the structures present.

Recurrent Neural Networks (RNNs)

- **Application**: RNNs are useful for analyzing sequential medical data, such as time-series images or 3D scans.
- **Use Case**: They can be applied to analyze changes in medical images over time or to process 3D medical scans for a more comprehensive understanding of volumetric data.

Generative Adversarial Networks (GANs)

- **Application**: GANs are used for generating synthetic medical images, enhancing datasets, and augmenting training data.
- **Use Case**: They can help in scenarios where acquiring a diverse set of real medical images is challenging, allowing for more robust model training.

Attention Mechanisms

- **Application**: Attention mechanisms focus on specific regions of interest within an image, aiding in more accurate and interpretable image analysis.
- **Use Case**: They can highlight critical areas in medical images, guiding clinicians to regions that require closer examination or providing explanations for model predictions.

Capsule Networks (CapsNets)

- **Application**: Capsule networks aim to address some limitations of traditional CNNs in recognizing spatial hierarchies and deformations.
- **Use Case**: They can be beneficial in scenarios where precise spatial relationships between features in medical images are crucial for accurate diagnosis.

Ensemble Learning

- **Application**: Ensemble methods combine predictions from multiple models to enhance overall accuracy and robustness.
- **Use Case**: They are employed to mitigate uncertainties and improve generalization, especially in cases where medical image datasets may be limited or exhibit class imbalances.

It is important to note that the success of these algorithms relies on the availability of high-quality labeled datasets, collaboration with medical professionals for annotation and validation, and adherence to regulatory standards in healthcare AI applications. Ongoing research in this field continues to explore innovative approaches to improve the accuracy and interpretability of AI algorithms in medical image recognition.

AI Assists in Early Detection

The potential for AI to assist in the early detection of diseases through continuous monitoring of patient data is a promising and transformative aspect of healthcare. Continuous monitoring allows for the real-time analysis of various health parameters, enabling early detection of anomalies or changes in a patient's health status. Here are key aspects of how AI can contribute to early disease detection through continuous monitoring:

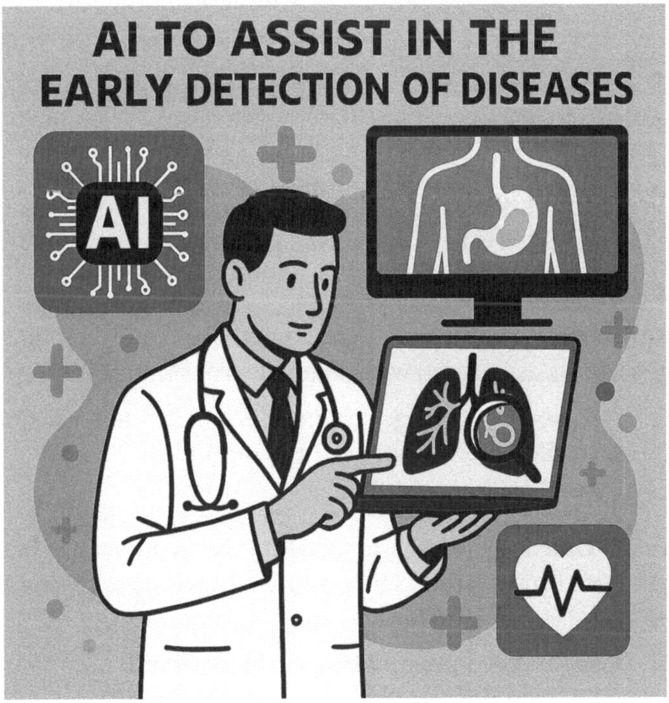

Figure 4.3: *AI in Early Disease Detection*

Continuous Data Collection

- **Wearable Devices and Sensors**: AI can utilize data from wearable devices, such as smartwatches or fitness trackers, and medical sensors to continuously collect information such as heart rate, blood pressure, activity levels, and more.
- **Internet of Things (IoT)**: Integration with IoT devices enables the monitoring of various physiological parameters and environmental factors in real time.

Machine Learning Algorithms

- **Pattern Recognition**: AI algorithms can analyze patterns in continuous data streams to identify deviations from normal health parameters.
- **Predictive Analytics**: By processing historical and real-time data, machine learning models can predict the likelihood of developing certain conditions, allowing for proactive interventions.

Early Warning Systems

- **Alerts and Notifications**: AI can be programmed to generate alerts or notifications for healthcare providers and patients when it detects abnormalities or potential health risks.
- **Customized Thresholds**: Personalized thresholds for each patient can be established, ensuring that alerts are contextually relevant to the individual's baseline health.

Cardiovascular Health Monitoring

- **Arrhythmia Detection**: AI algorithms can continuously monitor electrocardiogram (ECG) data to detect irregular heart rhythms or arrhythmias.
- **Blood Pressure Monitoring**: Continuous blood pressure monitoring through wearable devices provides valuable insights into cardiovascular health.

Respiratory Health Monitoring

- **Sleep Apnea Detection**: AI can analyze data from sleep monitoring devices to identify patterns associated with sleep disorders such as sleep apnea.
- **Respiratory Rate Monitoring**: Continuous monitoring of respiratory rate can aid in the early detection of respiratory conditions.

Blood Glucose Monitoring

- **Continuous Glucose Monitoring (CGM)**: AI can analyze CGM data to detect trends and patterns related to blood glucose levels, benefiting individuals with diabetes.
- **Insulin Dosage Recommendations**: AI-powered systems can provide personalized insulin dosage recommendations based on continuous glucose data.

Cancer Biomarker Monitoring

- **Tumor Marker Analysis**: For cancer patients, continuous monitoring of specific biomarkers through blood tests can help in the early detection of cancer recurrence.
- **Radiological Imaging Analysis**: AI algorithms can assist in analyzing continuous imaging data, such as MRI or CT scans, for signs of tumor growth or metastasis.

Chronic Disease Management

- **Symptom Tracking**: AI-powered apps can continuously monitor and analyze symptoms reported by patients, helping in the management of chronic conditions such as arthritis, asthma, or autoimmune diseases.
- **Medication Adherence**: AI can support medication adherence by reminding patients to take their medications and monitoring compliance.

The integration of AI in continuous patient monitoring not only facilitates early disease detection but also empowers patients to take a more active role in their healthcare. It can lead to timely interventions, improved outcomes, and a shift towards preventive and personalized healthcare. However, ethical considerations, data privacy, and regulatory compliance are critical aspects that need to be addressed in the development and implementation of such systems.

Predictive Analytics for Early Intervention

AI plays a crucial role in analyzing patient data collected through Remote Patient Monitoring (RPM) to predict health deterioration and identify potential issues. The continuous monitoring of vital signs and other health parameters enables AI algorithms to detect subtle changes and patterns that may precede a health decline. Here is how AI contributes to predicting health deterioration through RPM:

Continuous Data Monitoring

- **Vital Signs Monitoring**: RPM collects continuous data on vital signs such as heart rate, blood pressure, respiratory rate, and body temperature. AI algorithms analyze these parameters in real time to identify deviations from baseline values.

Machine Learning for Pattern Recognition

- **Baseline Establishment**: AI models establish a baseline for each individual based on historical data and continuous monitoring. This baseline represents the typical range of vital signs and other relevant parameters for that specific patient.

- **Pattern Recognition**: Machine learning algorithms recognize patterns and trends within the continuous data streams. This includes identifying irregularities, sudden changes, or subtle deviations that may indicate potential health issues.

Predictive Analytics

- **Risk Stratification**: AI models use predictive analytics to stratify patients into different risk categories based on their continuous monitoring data. This helps healthcare providers prioritize interventions for those at higher risk of health deterioration.
- **Early Warning Systems**: AI can generate alerts or notifications for healthcare professionals when it detects patterns indicative of potential health issues. Early warnings allow for timely interventions to prevent or mitigate deterioration.

Integration of Multiple Data Sources

- **Multimodal Data Analysis**: AI can integrate data from various sources, including wearable devices, medical sensors, Electronic Health Records (EHRs), and patient-reported outcomes. Analyzing a diverse set of data provides a comprehensive view of the patient's health status.
- **Contextual Information**: Incorporating contextual information, such as lifestyle factors, environmental data, and social determinants of health, enhances the accuracy of predictions.

Clinical Decision Support Systems (CDSS)

- **Real-time Recommendations**: AI-powered CDSS can provide real-time recommendations to healthcare providers based on the analysis of continuous patient data. This assists clinicians in making informed decisions regarding patient care and intervention strategies.
- **Customized Care Plans**: AI can contribute to the development of personalized care plans by considering individual patient characteristics and response patterns.

Early Intervention and Preventive Measures

- **Proactive Care**: Predicting health deterioration enables healthcare providers to take proactive measures, such as adjusting medication dosages, recommending lifestyle changes, or scheduling additional diagnostic tests.
- **Preventive Strategies**: AI can support the implementation of preventive strategies, reducing the likelihood of hospitalizations and complications by addressing issues before they become critical.

Patient Engagement and Education

- **Patient Feedback Integration**: AI can incorporate patient-reported data and feedback into the analysis, fostering patient engagement and shared decision-making.

- **Health Education**: AI-driven applications can provide patients with personalized health education and self-care recommendations based on their continuous monitoring data.

Early intervention in healthcare plays a crucial role in preventing complications and reducing hospital readmissions. Timely identification and proactive management of health issues contribute to improved patient outcomes, enhanced quality of care, and more efficient healthcare utilization. Here are key reasons highlighting the importance of early intervention:

- **Preventing Disease Progression:** Early intervention can halt or slow down the progression of diseases. By addressing health issues at an early stage, healthcare providers can implement strategies to manage and control the condition before it becomes more severe.
- **Minimizing Complications:** Many health conditions, if left untreated, can lead to complications. Early detection and intervention help prevent the development of complications, reducing the overall burden on the patient and the healthcare system.
- **Improving Patient Outcomes:** Timely medical intervention often results in better patient outcomes. It can lead to faster recovery, reduced morbidity, and an overall improvement in the patient's health and well-being.
- **Reducing Healthcare Costs:** Early intervention can be more cost-effective than treating advanced or complicated conditions. Preventing complications and reducing the need for extensive medical interventions can result in significant cost savings for both patients and healthcare systems.
- **Enhancing Quality of Life:** Addressing health issues early allows individuals to maintain a higher quality of life. It can prevent the deterioration of physical and mental health, enabling patients to continue their daily activities with minimal disruption.
- **Patient Satisfaction:** Early intervention demonstrates a commitment to patient care and can enhance patient satisfaction. Patients appreciate receiving timely attention and appropriate care, which contributes to a positive healthcare experience.
- **Reducing Hospital Readmissions:** Early intervention can prevent the exacerbation of health conditions, reducing the likelihood of hospital readmissions. This is particularly important for chronic conditions where effective management and preventive measures can minimize the need for repeated hospitalizations.
- **Optimizing Resource Utilization:** By addressing health issues early, healthcare

resources can be utilized more efficiently. This includes outpatient services, diagnostic tests, and preventive measures that are often more accessible and less resource-intensive than inpatient care.

- **Supporting Population Health Management:** Early intervention aligns with population health management strategies, focusing on proactive care to improve the health of entire populations. Identifying and addressing health risks early contributes to the overall health and well-being of communities.
- **Promoting Preventive Care:** Early intervention often involves preventive measures, including vaccinations, screenings, and lifestyle interventions. These strategies are key to reducing the incidence of diseases and promoting a culture of health and wellness.
- **Compliance with Value-Based Care Models:** Value-based care models emphasize achieving positive health outcomes and reducing unnecessary healthcare costs. Early intervention aligns with the principles of value-based care by prioritizing preventive measures and proactive management.

In summary, early intervention is a cornerstone of effective healthcare delivery, emphasizing the importance of proactive measures to address health issues before they escalate. It not only benefits individual patients but also contributes to the overall efficiency and sustainability of healthcare systems. Healthcare professionals, policymakers, and patients all play crucial roles in promoting early intervention as a fundamental component of modern healthcare practices.

Personalized Treatment Plans

AI has the potential to revolutionize healthcare by creating personalized treatment plans based on individual patient data. Here are several ways in which AI can contribute to the development of personalized treatment plans:

Data Integration and Analysis

- **Electronic Health Records (EHRs)**: AI can analyze a patient's complete medical history, including diagnoses, medications, lab results, and treatment outcomes stored in EHRs. This comprehensive view helps identify patterns and correlations.

Genomic Data Interpretation

- **Genomic Analysis**: AI can analyze genomic data to identify genetic variations associated with specific diseases or treatment responses. This information helps tailor treatment plans based on an individual's genetic profile.

Clinical Decision Support Systems (CDSS)

- **Real-Time Guidance**: AI-driven CDSS can provide real-time guidance to healthcare professionals by analyzing patient data and recommending evidence-based treatment options. This assists clinicians in making informed decisions.

Predictive Analytics

- **Risk Stratification**: AI models can predict the risk of disease progression or complications based on patient data. This enables the identification of high-risk individuals who may benefit from more aggressive interventions or closer monitoring.

Continuous Monitoring and Feedback

- **Remote Patient Monitoring (RPM)**: AI can analyze continuous patient data from wearables and sensors, providing insights into the effectiveness of ongoing treatments. Adjustments to treatment plans can be made in response to real-time data.

Personalized Medication Plans

- **Pharmacogenomics**: AI can analyze genetic data to predict how individuals may respond to specific medications. This information helps in tailoring drug prescriptions to maximize efficacy and minimize adverse reactions.

Treatment Response Prediction

- **Machine Learning Models**: AI models can analyze historical data to predict how a patient is likely to respond to a particular treatment. This supports the selection of treatments with higher chances of success.

Behavioral and Lifestyle Recommendations

- **Patient-Reported Data**: AI can incorporate patient-reported data on lifestyle factors, preferences, and behaviors. This information is valuable for creating treatment plans that align with the patient's lifestyle and are more likely to be adhered to.

Dynamic Personalization

- **Adaptive Algorithms**: AI algorithms can adapt treatment plans over time based on changing patient conditions, responses to interventions, and new data inputs. This dynamic personalization ensures ongoing relevance and effectiveness.

Collaborative Decision-Making

- **Shared Decision-Making Tools**: AI-powered tools can facilitate collaborative decision-making between healthcare providers and patients. Patients are informed about various treatment options, potential outcomes, and associated risks, enabling them to actively participate in the decision-making process.

Ethical Considerations

- **Bias Mitigation**: AI systems should be designed to mitigate biases and ensure fair treatment recommendations across diverse patient populations.
- **Transparency and Explainability**: Transparent AI models that provide explanations for their recommendations foster trust among healthcare professionals and patients.

The integration of patient history, genetics, and lifestyle factors represents a comprehensive approach to personalized medicine. By combining these diverse sources of information, healthcare providers can tailor medical interventions to individual patients, optimizing treatment outcomes and promoting overall well-being. Here is how the integration of patient history, genetics, and lifestyle factors can contribute to personalized medical interventions:

Patient History

- **Medical History**: The patient's medical history, including past illnesses, surgeries, allergies, and chronic conditions, provides essential context for understanding the patient's health journey.
- **Medication History**: Knowing a patient's response to previous medications helps in selecting the most effective and well-tolerated treatment options.
- **Family History**: Information about familial health conditions and genetic predispositions can guide risk assessments and preventive measures.

Genetic Information

- **Genomic Data**: Genetic testing can reveal specific variations in a patient's DNA that may influence their susceptibility to certain diseases, response to medications, and risk of developing particular conditions.
- **Pharmacogenomics**: Understanding how an individual metabolizes drugs based on genetic factors allows for the customization of medication regimens, minimizing adverse reactions and optimizing efficacy.
- **Genetic Counseling**: Providing patients with genetic information requires proper counseling to help them understand the implications and make informed decisions about their healthcare.

Lifestyle Factors

- **Dietary Habits**: Understanding a patient's dietary preferences, restrictions, and nutritional status is crucial for designing personalized nutrition plans.
- **Physical Activity**: Lifestyle data, including levels of physical activity, exercise routines, and sedentary behavior, informs interventions aimed at promoting a healthy and active lifestyle.

- **Social and Environmental Factors:** Considering factors such as socioeconomic status, living conditions, and social support networks helps in addressing social determinants of health that may impact treatment adherence and outcomes.

Integration of Data

- **Electronic Health Records (EHRs):** The integration of patient history, genetic information, and lifestyle data into EHRs facilitates a holistic view of the patient's health. This integrated data can be accessible to healthcare providers for informed decision-making.
- **Interoperability**: Ensuring interoperability between different health systems and data sources allows for a seamless exchange of information, fostering a more comprehensive understanding of the patient.

Risk Assessment and Prevention

- **Disease Risk Stratification**: Combining genetic and lifestyle data enables the identification of individuals at higher risk for certain diseases, allowing for targeted preventive measures and early interventions
- **Behavioral Interventions**: Personalized lifestyle recommendations can be tailored based on genetic and historical data, promoting behavior change and reducing risk factors for chronic conditions

Treatment Customization

- **Precision Medicine**: Tailoring medical interventions based on genetic information allows for the selection of treatments that are more likely to be effective and with fewer adverse effects.
- **Individualized Medication Plans**: Genetic and historical data can guide the selection of medications and dosages that align with an individual's unique pharmacogenomic profile.

Patient Engagement

- **Shared Decision-Making**: Involving patients in the decision-making process by considering their preferences, values, and lifestyle choices fosters a collaborative approach to healthcare.
- **Health Education**: Providing patients with personalized information about the interplay between genetics, lifestyle, and health empowers them to make informed decisions about their well-being.

Continuous Monitoring and Adjustment

- **Remote Patient Monitoring (RPM)**: Leveraging technology for continuous monitoring of health parameters allows for real-time adjustments to treatment plans based on changes in patient conditions or responses to interventions.

The successful integration of patient history, genetics, and lifestyle factors into personalized medical interventions requires a multidisciplinary approach involving healthcare providers, genetic counselors, data scientists, and patients. Ethical considerations, data privacy, and ongoing patient education are crucial components of this approach, ensuring that personalized medicine is both effective and patient-centered. As technology continues to advance, the potential for refining and expanding personalized interventions based on integrated patient data becomes even more promising.

Natural Language Processing (NLP) for Virtual Consultations

Natural Language Processing (NLP) plays a significant role in enhancing virtual consultations in telemedicine, making communication between healthcare providers and patients more effective. Here are several ways in which NLP is utilized in telemedicine for more efficient and meaningful virtual consultations:

Improved Documentation

- **Automated Note-Taking**: NLP algorithms can transcribe and extract information from spoken conversations during virtual consultations, generating structured and accurate clinical notes. This reduces the administrative burden on healthcare providers and ensures comprehensive documentation.

Speech Recognition for Dictation

- **Voice-to-Text Conversion**: NLP-powered speech recognition systems convert spoken language into text, allowing healthcare providers to dictate notes, prescriptions, and other documentation during virtual consultations. This speeds up the documentation process and enhances provider productivity.

Semantic Understanding

- **Contextual Understanding**: NLP algorithms can analyze and understand the context of patient conversations, enabling more nuanced and context-aware interactions during virtual consultations. This helps in accurately interpreting patient concerns and queries.

Clinical Decision Support

- **Access to Medical Knowledge**: NLP can integrate with medical databases and literature to provide real-time clinical decision support. This ensures that healthcare providers have access to the latest information and evidence-based guidelines during virtual consultations.

Patient History and Record Retrieval

- **Querying Electronic Health Records (EHRs)**: NLP facilitates the extraction of relevant information from EHRs, enabling healthcare providers to quickly retrieve and review patient histories during virtual consultations. This enhances continuity of care and supports more informed decision-making.

Automated Coding and Billing

- **Coding Assistance**: NLP algorithms can assist in coding and billing processes by analyzing clinical documentation during virtual consultations. This ensures accurate coding and billing practices, reducing errors and streamlining administrative tasks.

Virtual Assistants and Chatbots

- **Conversational Agents**: NLP-driven virtual assistants and chatbots can engage with patients in natural language, answering queries, providing information, and guiding patients through pre-consultation assessments. This enhances patient engagement and satisfaction.

Symptom Analysis and Triage

- **Symptom Recognition**: NLP algorithms can analyze patient-reported symptoms during virtual consultations to aid in the recognition of potential health issues. This supports more accurate triage and appropriate referrals.

Language Translation Services

- **Multilingual Support**: NLP can facilitate language translation services during virtual consultations, breaking down language barriers and ensuring effective communication between healthcare providers and patients who speak different languages.

Sentiment Analysis

- **Emotional Understanding**: NLP can perform sentiment analysis on patient interactions, helping healthcare providers gauge the emotional state of patients during virtual consultations. This allows for more empathetic and patient-centered care.

Appointment Scheduling and Follow-Up

- **Automated Appointment Management**: NLP-powered systems can assist in scheduling follow-up appointments, sending reminders, and managing post-consultation care plans, improving continuity of care.

Data Security and Privacy Compliance

- **Text De-Identification**: NLP techniques can be applied to de-identify and anonymize patient data in text form, ensuring compliance with privacy regulations and protecting patient confidentiality during virtual consultations.

AI-powered chatbots or virtual assistants play a valuable role in helping patients understand their conditions, medications, and treatment plans. These tools provide a user-friendly interface for patients to access information, ask questions, and receive guidance. Here is how AI-powered chatbots contribute to patient education and support:

Accessible Information

- **24/7 Availability**: AI-powered chatbots are available around the clock, providing patients with instant access to information whenever they need it, reducing the reliance on office hours.

Patient Education

- **Information Dissemination**: Chatbots can deliver personalized educational content about medical conditions, treatment options, and lifestyle modifications, helping patients understand their health better.

Medication Understanding

- **Medication Information**: Chatbots can provide detailed information about medications, including dosage instructions, potential side effects, and interactions. This supports medication adherence and helps alleviate concerns or confusion.

Treatment Plan Explanation

- **Step-by-Step Guidance**: Chatbots can break down complex treatment plans into simple, step-by-step explanations. This helps patients understand the rationale behind each aspect of their treatment.

Answering Patient Queries

- **Question and Answer Interaction**: Patients can ask questions about their conditions, medications, or treatment plans, and chatbots can provide clear and concise answers, fostering a better understanding.

Language Understanding

- **Natural Language Processing (NLP)**: Chatbots equipped with NLP capabilities can understand and respond to patients' queries in natural language, creating a more conversational and user-friendly interaction.

Tailored Advice

- **Personalized Recommendations**: AI-powered chatbots can offer personalized advice based on the patient's health data, preferences, and treatment history, enhancing the relevance of the information provided.

Health Monitoring and Reminders

- **Tracking Progress**: Chatbots can help patients monitor their health by providing reminders for medication adherence, lifestyle changes, and follow-up appointments. This supports continuous engagement in their care plan.

Interactive Decision Support

- **Informed Decision-Making**: Chatbots can assist patients in making informed decisions about their healthcare by providing information about various treatment options, potential risks, and benefits.

Behavioral Support

- **Motivational Encouragement**: Chatbots can offer motivational messages and encouragement to promote positive health behaviors, such as adhering to treatment plans, exercising, or adopting a healthier lifestyle.

Link to Additional Resources

- **External Information**: Chatbots can guide patients to reliable external resources for further reading or additional information, empowering patients to take an active role in their health education.

Integration with Wearables

- **Health Data Integration**: Chatbots can integrate with wearable devices to provide real-time insights into patients' health metrics. This helps patients visualize the impact of their actions on their health.

Emergency Response Assistance

- **Emergency Information**: In critical situations, chatbots can guide patients on immediate actions to take, provide emergency contact information, or connect them to emergency services.

Continuous Learning and Improvement

- **Feedback Analysis**: Chatbots can analyze user interactions and feedback to continuously improve responses and user experience, ensuring ongoing enhancement in patient education capabilities.

Implementing AI-powered chatbots in healthcare requires careful consideration of patient privacy, data security, and regulatory compliance. Additionally, ensuring that chatbots complement, rather than replace, human interactions is essential for maintaining a patient-centered approach to care. When designed and implemented effectively, AI-powered chatbots contribute significantly to patient education, engagement, and empowerment in understanding their health conditions and treatment plans.

Security and Privacy Considerations

Maintaining patient privacy and data security is of utmost importance in telemedicine and Remote Patient Monitoring (RPM). As these technologies involve the exchange of sensitive health information, protecting patient confidentiality is crucial for building trust, ensuring compliance with regulations, and safeguarding individuals' rights. Here are key reasons highlighting the importance of maintaining patient privacy and data security in telemedicine and RPM:

- **Trust and Patient Confidence:** Ensuring robust privacy and security measures builds trust between patients and healthcare providers. Patients are more likely to engage in telemedicine or RPM when they are confident that their sensitive health information is handled securely.
- **Legal and Regulatory Compliance:** Healthcare data is subject to strict regulations such as the Health Insurance Portability and Accountability Act (HIPAA) in the United States or the General Data Protection Regulation (GDPR) in the European Union. Adherence to these regulations is mandatory to avoid legal consequences and fines.
- **Confidentiality and Ethical Considerations:** Upholding patient privacy is an ethical obligation in healthcare. Patients have a right to expect that their health information will be treated with the utmost confidentiality, and healthcare providers must adhere to ethical standards in handling this information.
- **Preventing Unauthorized Access:** Telemedicine and RPM platforms must implement strong access controls to prevent unauthorized users from accessing patient data. Secure authentication methods, encryption, and role-based access control help ensure that only authorized individuals have access to sensitive information.
- **Data Encryption:** Transmitting patient data securely is essential. Encryption protocols, such as Secure Sockets Layer (SSL) or Transport Layer Security (TLS), should be employed to protect data during transmission, reducing the risk of interception by unauthorized parties.
- **Data Integrity:** Ensuring the integrity of patient data is crucial to prevent tampering or unauthorized alterations. Employing mechanisms to verify data integrity safeguards against malicious activities or inadvertent errors that could compromise the accuracy of health information.
- **Secure Storage:** Patient health data should be securely stored with robust encryption and access controls. Secure storage practices protect patient information from unauthorized access, data breaches, or cyberattacks.
- **Informed Consent and Patient Awareness:** Patients should be fully informed about how their data will be collected, used, and protected. Obtaining informed

consent ensures that patients are aware of privacy and security practices, promoting transparency in the healthcare provider-patient relationship.

- **Mitigating Cybersecurity Risks:** Telemedicine and RPM systems are potential targets for cyberattacks. Regular security assessments, vulnerability testing, and the implementation of cybersecurity best practices help mitigate the risk of data breaches and unauthorized access.
- **Data De-Identification and Anonymization:** De-identifying or anonymizing patient data when possible minimizes the risk of identification and protects patient privacy. Techniques such as removing personally identifiable information contribute to enhanced privacy.
- **Secure Communication Channels:** Secure communication channels, including end-to-end encryption for video consultations and secure messaging systems, protect patient information from interception during virtual interactions.
- **Patient Control Over Data:** Empowering patients with control over their data is essential. Patients should have the ability to access, manage, and, if necessary, revoke their consent for the use of their health information.
- **Training and Awareness:** Healthcare providers and staff involved in telemedicine and RPM should receive ongoing training on privacy and security practices. Raising awareness about the importance of protecting patient data helps create a culture of compliance and diligence.
- **Data Breach Response Plan:** Having a well-defined data breach response plan is essential. In the event of a security incident, prompt detection, containment, notification, and resolution procedures help minimize the impact on patient privacy.

AI can contribute to secure data transmission and storage by implementing advanced technologies and techniques that enhance the confidentiality, integrity, and availability of sensitive information. Here are ways in which AI can play a role in securing the transmission and storage of data:

Encryption Algorithms

- **Advanced Encryption**: AI can be used to implement and optimize advanced encryption algorithms for securing data during transmission and storage. This includes symmetric and asymmetric encryption techniques to protect data at rest and in transit.

Secure Key Management

- **AI-Enhanced Key Management**: AI algorithms can improve key management practices, ensuring secure generation, storage, and distribution of cryptographic keys used for encryption and decryption processes.

Dynamic Threat Detection

- **Anomaly Detection**: AI-driven anomaly detection systems can continuously monitor data transmission and storage environments, identifying unusual patterns or activities that may indicate security threats. This proactive approach helps in early threat detection.

Behavioral Analytics

- **User Behavior Monitoring**: AI-based behavioral analytics can analyze user interactions with data storage and transmission systems, identifying deviations from normal behavior that may indicate unauthorized access or malicious activities.

Intrusion Detection and Prevention

- **AI-Powered IDS/IPS**: Intrusion Detection Systems (IDS) and Intrusion Prevention Systems (IPS) enhanced by AI can effectively identify and block potential security threats, including unauthorized access attempts or data breaches.

Data Masking and Tokenization

- **Sensitive Data Protection**: AI can automate the process of data masking and tokenization, replacing sensitive information with pseudonyms or tokens. This ensures that even if unauthorized access occurs, the exposed data is not meaningful.

Secure Protocols for Communication

- **AI-Optimized Secure Protocols**: AI can contribute to the optimization and improvement of secure communication protocols (for example, TLS/SSL) to protect data during transmission over networks.

Predictive Analytics for Security Threats

- **Predictive Modeling**: AI models can predict potential security threats by analyzing historical data and identifying patterns associated with previous incidents. This enables organizations to take proactive measures to mitigate risks.

Data Loss Prevention (DLP)

- **Automated DLP Solutions**: AI-driven DLP solutions can monitor and control data movement within an organization, preventing unauthorized data transfers and ensuring compliance with security policies.

Secure Cloud Storage

- **AI-Powered Cloud Security**: AI contributes to enhancing the security of cloud storage by continuously monitoring for unauthorized access, implementing encryption, and providing automated responses to security incidents.

Blockchain for Data Integrity

- **Blockchain Technology**: AI and blockchain can be combined to ensure the integrity of stored data. Blockchain's decentralized and tamper-evident nature can be leveraged to maintain an immutable record of data transactions.

Adaptive Access Controls

- **Dynamic Access Controls**: AI can facilitate the implementation of adaptive access controls that adjust permissions based on real-time analysis of user behavior and security conditions, reducing the risk of unauthorized access.

Secure Firmware and Hardware

- **Hardware-Level Security**: AI can be utilized to enhance security at the hardware level, ensuring that devices and storage systems have secure firmware and protection against physical attacks.

Zero-Trust Architecture

- **AI-Enabled Zero Trust**: AI contributes to the implementation of a Zero Trust security model by continuously verifying the identity and security posture of users and devices, irrespective of their location within the network.

Incident Response Automation

- **Automated Incident Response**: AI can automate incident response processes, enabling quick and effective responses to security incidents, such as data breaches or unauthorized access attempts.

By leveraging AI in these ways, organizations can significantly enhance the security of data during transmission and storage, reducing the risk of data breaches, ensuring compliance with privacy regulations, and maintaining the trust of users and stakeholders. However, it is essential to note that the implementation of AI-powered security measures should be part of a comprehensive cybersecurity strategy that includes policies, training, and ongoing risk assessments.

Challenges and Ethical Considerations

While AI in telemedicine holds great promise, there are several challenges and limitations that need to be addressed to ensure its effective and ethical use. Some of the key challenges include:

Algorithmic Bias

- **Potential for Bias**: AI algorithms are trained on historical data, and if that data contains biases, the algorithms may perpetuate and even exacerbate those biases. This could result in disparities in healthcare delivery, diagnosis, and treatment recommendations.

Data Quality and Representativeness

- **Limited Diversity in Training Data**: The quality and representativeness of training data used to develop AI models are crucial. If the data is not diverse or representative of various demographics, it can lead to biased predictions and inaccurate generalizations.

Validation and Generalization

- **Robust Validation**: Ensuring that AI models generalize well to different populations and healthcare settings is challenging. Validation in diverse environments and populations is essential to confirm the reliability and efficacy of telemedicine AI applications.

Interoperability and Integration

- **System Integration Challenges**: Integrating AI systems with existing telemedicine platforms, Electronic Health Records (EHRs), and other healthcare IT systems can be complex. Ensuring interoperability is essential for the seamless and effective use of AI in telemedicine.

Ethical Considerations

- **Informed Consent**: Patients need to be informed about the use of AI in telemedicine, its limitations, and potential risks. Obtaining informed consent becomes crucial, especially when AI algorithms influence medical decisions.

Security and Privacy Concerns

- **Data Security**: Telemedicine involves the transmission and storage of sensitive health information. Ensuring robust cybersecurity measures to protect patient data from unauthorized access or cyberattacks is critical.

Regulatory Compliance

- **Adherence to Regulations**: Telemedicine AI applications must comply with healthcare regulations and standards, such as HIPAA in the United States or GDPR in the European Union, to safeguard patient privacy and ensure legal compliance.

User Acceptance and Trust

- **Provider and Patient Trust**: Building trust among healthcare providers and patients in the accuracy and reliability of AI-driven telemedicine applications is crucial for widespread adoption. User acceptance and confidence in the technology play a pivotal role.

Explainability and Transparency

- **Opaque Algorithms**: Many AI models, especially deep learning models, are considered "*black boxes*" with limited explainability. Ensuring transparency and explainability in AI-driven decisions is challenging but necessary for gaining trust and acceptance.

Integration of Human Expertise

- **Human-AI Collaboration**: AI should complement, not replace human expertise in healthcare. The challenge lies in finding the right balance between automated decision-making and the involvement of healthcare professionals to ensure patient safety and quality care.

Continuous Monitoring and Updating

- **Adaptability to Changing Conditions**: The healthcare landscape evolves, and new medical knowledge emerges. AI models need to be continuously monitored, updated, and adapted to reflect the latest evidence-based practices and medical guidelines.

Resource Constraints

- **Infrastructure and Resource Challenges**: Implementation of AI in telemedicine may face resource constraints, especially in less-developed regions or healthcare systems with limited technological infrastructure.

Liability and Accountability

- **Responsibility for Outcomes**: Determining liability in cases where AI contributes to medical decisions or errors poses legal and ethical challenges. Establishing clear accountability and responsibility is critical.

Addressing these challenges requires collaborative efforts from healthcare professionals, technology developers, policymakers, and regulatory bodies. Rigorous testing, validation, and ongoing monitoring of AI applications, coupled with transparent and ethical practices, are essential to unlock the full potential of AI in telemedicine while mitigating associated risks and limitations.

Ethical considerations are paramount in the development, deployment, and use of AI in healthcare. As AI technologies become integral to healthcare delivery, it is essential to uphold ethical principles to ensure patient trust, privacy, and the responsible application of these technologies. Here are key ethical considerations in the context of AI in healthcare:

Informed Consent

- **Patient Autonomy**: Informed consent is a fundamental ethical principle that respects patients' autonomy. When AI technologies are involved in healthcare, patients should be adequately informed about how AI will be used, its potential implications, and any risks or benefits associated with its use.

Transparency and Explainability

- **Understanding AI Decisions**: Transparency is crucial in AI-driven healthcare to help patients and healthcare professionals understand how AI algorithms make decisions. Explainability ensures that AI systems provide clear and understandable reasons for their recommendations or predictions, promoting trust and accountability.

Equity and Fairness

- **Mitigating Bias**: AI algorithms should be developed and tested to minimize biases and ensure equitable outcomes across diverse patient populations. Ethical AI design considers fairness to avoid perpetuating existing healthcare disparities or introducing new ones.

Privacy Protection

- **Data Security**: Protecting patient privacy is a foundational ethical principle. Robust measures must be in place to secure patient data, especially given the sensitive nature of healthcare information. Patients should have confidence that their health data is handled securely and confidentially.

Data Ownership and Consent for Sharing

- **Patient Control**: Patients should have control over their health data and be informed about how it will be used. Clear consent mechanisms should be in place for data sharing, ensuring that patients are aware of how their information will be utilized for AI development, research, or other purposes.

End-User Training and Competence

- **Healthcare Professional Training**: Healthcare professionals utilizing AI technologies must be adequately trained to understand the capabilities and limitations of AI systems. Ensuring the competence of end-users contributes to ethical and responsible AI use in healthcare.

Accountability and Liability

- **Clear Responsibility**: Establishing clear accountability for AI-related decisions, outcomes, and errors is essential. This includes defining responsibilities for healthcare providers, AI developers, and other stakeholders. Clarity in liability helps address ethical and legal considerations.

Patient-Centeredness

- **Human-Centric Approach**: AI should be designed and implemented with a patient-centered focus, ensuring that technology complements human expertise and supports the patient-doctor relationship. Patient preferences and values should be prioritized in decision-making.

Ongoing Monitoring and Evaluation

- **Continuous Improvement**: Ethical AI use involves ongoing monitoring and evaluation of AI algorithms to ensure their effectiveness, accuracy, and adherence to ethical standards. Regular assessments are necessary to address any emerging issues or biases.

Avoiding Unintended Consequences

- **Risk Mitigation**: AI developers and healthcare providers should proactively identify and mitigate potential unintended consequences of AI use, such as overreliance on technology, erosion of human skills, or the exacerbation of healthcare disparities.

Stakeholder Collaboration

- **Multidisciplinary Approach**: Collaboration between healthcare professionals, AI developers, policymakers, ethicists, and patients is crucial. A multidisciplinary approach ensures that diverse perspectives are considered in the ethical development and deployment of AI in healthcare.

Respect for Cultural and Ethical Values

- **Cultural Sensitivity**: AI applications should be culturally sensitive and respect diverse ethical values and norms. Consideration of cultural contexts is vital to avoid imposing biased or inappropriate practices on different populations.

Regulatory Compliance

- **Adherence to Standards**: Developers and healthcare organizations must adhere to relevant regulatory standards and guidelines governing the use of AI in healthcare. Compliance helps ensure that ethical principles are integrated into legal frameworks.

Patient Education and Empowerment

- **Promoting Understanding**: Patient education is essential to empower individuals with an understanding of AI technologies, their role in healthcare, and their rights. Informed patients are better equipped to make decisions and advocate for their own well-being.

By incorporating these ethical considerations into the development and implementation of AI in healthcare, stakeholders can work towards ensuring the responsible and equitable use of technology, aligning with the overarching goal of improving patient outcomes and healthcare delivery.

Future Trends and Innovations

AI in telemedicine continues to be a rapidly evolving field, with ongoing research and emerging trends contributing to its advancement. Here are some notable trends and areas of ongoing research in AI for telemedicine:

Remote Patient Monitoring (RPM) Advancements

- **Wearable Technology Integration**: Ongoing research focuses on enhancing RPM through the integration of advanced wearable devices. This includes sensors for continuous monitoring of vital signs, activity levels, and other health metrics.

AI-Powered Diagnostic Imaging

- **Advanced Image Analysis**: Research in diagnostic imaging aims to improve the accuracy and efficiency of AI algorithms for analyzing medical images, including X-rays, MRIs, and CT scans. Deep learning models are being developed for more precise and rapid image interpretation.

Natural Language Processing (NLP) for Virtual Consultations

- **Conversational AI**: Ongoing research explores the use of NLP and conversational AI to enhance virtual consultations. Natural language understanding capabilities are being improved to facilitate more natural and effective communication between patients and healthcare providers.

Telepsychiatry and Mental Health Support

- **AI-Based Mental Health Screening**: Researchers are working on AI applications for telepsychiatry, including virtual mental health assessments and screening tools. These tools aim to assist in the early detection and monitoring of mental health conditions.

Predictive Analytics for Disease Prevention

- **Risk Stratification Models**: Ongoing research focuses on developing predictive analytics models that can stratify patient populations based on their risk of developing certain diseases. This enables targeted interventions and preventive measures.

Human Augmentation Technologies

- **Augmented Reality (AR) and Virtual Reality (VR)**: Emerging trends explore the use of AR and VR technologies in telemedicine to enhance the visualization of medical information, surgical planning, and medical training.

Blockchain for Data Security

- **Secure Health Data Exchange**: Research is ongoing to leverage blockchain technology to enhance the security and integrity of health data exchange in telemedicine. Blockchain can provide a decentralized and tamper-resistant platform for storing and sharing patient records.

Explainable AI (XAI)

- **Interpretable AI Models**: As the demand for transparency in AI decision-making grows, ongoing research focuses on developing explainable AI models in telemedicine. This is particularly crucial for gaining the trust of healthcare providers and patients.

Federated Learning in Healthcare

- **Privacy-Preserving AI**: Research explores the use of federated learning to train AI models across decentralized healthcare networks while keeping patient data localized. This approach helps address privacy concerns and regulatory requirements.

AI for Medication Adherence

- **Personalized Medication Plans**: Ongoing research investigates AI applications to improve medication adherence through personalized treatment plans. AI algorithms can consider individual patient factors to tailor medication regimens and reminders.

Robotic Telepresence in Healthcare

- **Teleoperated Robots**: Thc usc of teleoperated robots equipped with AI capabilities is an emerging trend. These robots can assist in tasks such as remote diagnostics, patient monitoring, and even performing simple medical procedures under remote guidance.

Edge Computing for Real-Time Processing

- **On-Device AI**: Edge computing is gaining attention for the real-time processing of healthcare data. AI algorithms are being optimized for on-device processing, reducing latency and enhancing the efficiency of telemedicine applications.

Continuous Monitoring of Chronic Conditions

- **AI-Driven Early Warning Systems**: Ongoing research focuses on developing AI-driven early warning systems for continuous monitoring of chronic conditions. These systems aim to detect subtle changes in health metrics and provide timely alerts.

Collaboration Platforms for Healthcare Teams

- **Integrated Communication Systems**: Research explores the development of AI-enhanced collaboration platforms for healthcare teams. These platforms aim to streamline communication, data sharing, and decision-making among different healthcare professionals involved in telemedicine.

Ethical and Regulatory Guidelines

- **Guidelines for Ethical AI Use**: Researchers are actively working on establishing ethical and regulatory frameworks specific to AI in telemedicine. These guidelines aim to ensure responsible and equitable deployment of AI technologies in healthcare.

These trends and ongoing research efforts underscore the dynamic nature of AI in telemedicine, with a focus on improving patient outcomes, increasing accessibility, and addressing emerging healthcare challenges. As technology continues to advance, these developments are likely to shape the future landscape of AI-powered telemedicine applications.

The future of AI in healthcare promises to bring about several transformative developments, including the integration of wearables, advancements in mental health monitoring, and innovations in remote surgical procedures. Here is an exploration of these potential future developments.

Integration of Wearables

- **Advanced Health Monitoring**: Wearable devices, such as smartwatches, fitness trackers, and biosensors, will play a crucial role in continuous health monitoring. These devices can track a wide range of vital signs, including heart rate, blood pressure, and glucose levels, providing real-time data for personalized health insights.
- **Early Detection and Prevention**: Wearables integrated with AI algorithms can enable early detection of health issues and personalized preventive measures. For example, AI can analyze patterns in data to identify subtle changes that may indicate the onset of a medical condition, allowing for timely intervention.
- **Chronic Disease Management**: Wearable technology, coupled with AI, will facilitate better management of chronic diseases. Patients with conditions such as diabetes, hypertension, or respiratory disorders can benefit from continuous monitoring and AI-driven insights to optimize their treatment plans.

AI in Mental Health Monitoring

- **Digital Biomarkers for Mental Health**: AI algorithms will analyze data from various sources, including wearables, smartphones, and social media, to identify digital biomarkers indicative of mental health conditions. This can aid in early detection, monitoring, and personalized interventions for mental health disorders.
- **Virtual Mental Health Support**: AI-powered chatbots and virtual assistants will play a role in providing mental health support. These tools can offer resources, coping strategies, and immediate assistance, contributing to the accessibility of mental health services.
- **Emotion Recognition**: AI-driven tools that analyze facial expressions, voice tone, and other behavioral cues will enhance the recognition of emotions. This technology can be integrated into telemedicine platforms to provide more nuanced insights into a patient's mental and emotional well-being.

Advancements in Remote Surgical Procedures

- **Telepresence Robotics**: AI-enhanced telepresence robots will enable remote surgical procedures with a high level of precision. Surgeons will be able to control robotic systems equipped with AI capabilities, facilitating minimally invasive surgeries from a distance.
- **Haptic Feedback Systems**: Future developments may include haptic feedback systems that provide surgeons with a sense of touch and tactile feedback during remote procedures. AI algorithms can enhance the interpretation of feedback, allowing for more dexterous and intricate maneuvers.
- **AI-Assisted Surgical Planning**: AI will play a crucial role in pre-operative planning, analyzing patient data to assist surgeons in determining optimal surgical approaches. This includes predicting potential complications, identifying critical structures, and optimizing the overall surgical strategy.
- **Remote Training and Collaboration**: AI-powered platforms will support remote training for surgical procedures, allowing surgeons to collaborate, share expertise, and engage in virtual training sessions. This can enhance the dissemination of surgical knowledge and skills across geographical boundaries.

Personalized Treatment Plans

- **Integration of Multiomic Data**: Future developments will involve the integration of multiomic data, including genomics, proteomics, and metabolomics, to create comprehensive profiles for personalized medicine. AI algorithms will analyze these complex datasets to tailor treatment plans based on individual genetic and molecular characteristics.
- **Dynamic Treatment Adjustments**: AI-driven models will continuously analyze patient data to make real-time adjustments to treatment plans. This dynamic approach allows for personalized interventions that adapt to changes in a patient's health status, ensuring optimal outcomes.
- **Behavioral Interventions**: AI will be increasingly used to develop personalized behavioral interventions. This includes creating individualized plans for lifestyle modifications, physical activity, and dietary changes, taking into account a patient's preferences, habits, and social determinants of health.

Health Information Exchange and Interoperability

- **Seamless Data Sharing**: Future developments will focus on improving interoperability and health information exchange, allowing different healthcare systems and devices to seamlessly share data. AI will play a role in aggregating and analyzing this diverse information for holistic patient care.
- **Unified Electronic Health Records (EHRs)**: AI-powered EHR systems will provide unified and comprehensive health records, ensuring that healthcare

providers have access to up-to-date and relevant information. This will contribute to more informed decision-making and coordinated care.

- **Patient-Controlled Health Data**: Advances in blockchain technology may empower patients to have more control over their health data. Blockchain can provide a secure and decentralized platform for patients to manage and share their health information, ensuring privacy and data ownership.

As these developments unfold, it is essential to consider ethical, regulatory, and privacy implications to ensure the responsible and equitable deployment of AI in healthcare. The future integration of wearables, AI in mental health monitoring, and advancements in remote surgical procedures hold the potential to significantly improve patient outcomes, increase accessibility to healthcare services, and reshape the landscape of healthcare delivery.

Conclusion

The integration of Artificial Intelligence (AI) in telemedicine represents a transformative paradigm shift in healthcare, fundamentally altering how medical services are delivered, accessed, and personalized. The symbiotic relationship between AI and telemedicine has introduced innovative solutions that address longstanding healthcare challenges, enhance diagnostic capabilities, and improve patient outcomes. As we navigate this evolving landscape, several key insights and future considerations emerge.

AI algorithms have demonstrated remarkable accuracy in analyzing medical images, enabling remote detection of diseases with unprecedented precision. This advancement expedites diagnostic processes and supports early intervention, ultimately leading to timely and effective healthcare. Additionally, Remote Patient Monitoring (RPM) combined with predictive analytics allows for continuous tracking of vital signs and health metrics, enabling healthcare professionals to identify early warning signs, personalize interventions, and prevent complications in chronic disease management and post-operative care.

However, despite these advancements, significant challenges persist. Ethical concerns, algorithmic biases, data privacy issues, and regulatory hurdles require careful attention to ensure that AI-driven telemedicine is responsible, equitable, and patient-centric. Addressing these challenges demands collaboration among healthcare providers, policymakers, and technology developers to establish clear regulations, ethical AI frameworks, and standardized interoperability protocols.

To fully realize the potential of AI-driven telemedicine, healthcare providers, policymakers, and industry leaders must actively invest in:

- **AI Infrastructure and Integration**: Healthcare organizations should adopt AI-driven telemedicine platforms that enhance diagnostic accuracy, enable real-time patient monitoring, and improve virtual care delivery.

- **Regulatory and Ethical Governance**: Policymakers must implement robust data security measures, ethical AI guidelines, and standardized telemedicine regulations to safeguard patient privacy and build public trust.
- **Equitable Access to AI-Enabled Healthcare**: Governments and healthcare organizations should ensure that AI-powered telemedicine services are accessible to rural and underserved populations, bridging the gap in global healthcare disparities.
- **Collaboration between AI Developers and Clinicians**: AI solutions must be co-developed with healthcare professionals to ensure clinical relevance, reliability, and ease of integration into existing workflows.

As we embark on this transformative journey, it is imperative to strike a balance between technological innovation and ethical responsibility, ensuring that AI-driven telemedicine is fair, inclusive, and patient-centered. The future of AI in telemedicine holds immense promise, and with the right investments, regulations, and collaborative efforts, we can create a more accessible, efficient, and personalized healthcare system for all.

In the next chapter, we will delve into the pivotal intersection of AI, Clinical Decision Support (CDS), and Electronic Health Records (EHRs), exploring how AI-powered decision-making tools enhance diagnostic accuracy, optimize treatment plans, and streamline healthcare workflows. As AI seamlessly integrates with EHRs, it propels us toward a future of data-driven insights, improved patient care, and a more efficient healthcare ecosystem. Let us explore how AI is redefining clinical decision-making and healthcare delivery in the next chapter.

Points to Remember

- **Remote Healthcare Delivery**: AI in telemedicine enables remote healthcare delivery, allowing patients to access medical services and consultations from the comfort of their homes.
- **Diagnostic Capabilities**: AI algorithms enhance diagnostic capabilities by analyzing medical images such as X-rays, MRIs, and CT scans, aiding in the identification of abnormalities and conditions.
- **Continuous Monitoring**: Remote Patient Monitoring (RPM) powered by AI facilitates continuous monitoring of patient data through wearables and connected devices, enabling proactive healthcare interventions.
- **Predictive Analytics**: AI-driven predictive analytics contributes to early disease detection and prevention by analyzing real-time patient data to identify potential health issues.

- **Personalized Treatment Plans**: AI integrates patient data, genetics, and lifestyle factors to create personalized treatment plans, tailoring interventions based on individual characteristics.
- **NLP in Virtual Consultations**: Natural Language Processing (NLP) enhances virtual consultations by enabling AI to understand and respond to patient queries in natural language, improving the overall telemedicine experience.
- **AI-Powered Support**: Chatbots and virtual assistants assist patients by providing information on conditions, medications, and treatment plans, contributing to patient education and adherence.
- **Privacy and Security**: Ensuring patient privacy and data security is crucial in telemedicine, requiring robust measures to protect sensitive health information and comply with regulations.
- **Ethical Considerations**: Ethical considerations include addressing algorithmic biases, obtaining informed consent, and ensuring responsible AI use in telemedicine to maintain trust and patient well-being.
- **Future Developments**: The future of AI in telemedicine includes the integration of wearables, advancements in mental health monitoring, innovations in remote surgical procedures, and a continued focus on personalized, patient-centric care.

CHAPTER 5
AI in Clinical Decision Support and Electronic Health Record

Introduction

AI-driven solutions are revolutionizing clinical decision support (CDS) systems and electronic health records (EHRs) by enhancing diagnostic accuracy, optimizing treatment recommendations, and streamlining administrative workflows. In real-world applications, AI-powered CDS tools help identify early signs of sepsis, flagging high-risk patients in ICU settings, while predictive models integrated with EHRs assist oncologists in selecting personalized cancer treatments based on genetic markers. AI-enhanced EHR systems also automate documentation, reduce physician burnout, and improve interoperability, ensuring that healthcare providers can access and analyze patient data more efficiently.

Despite these advancements, data fragmentation, interoperability challenges, and AI model transparency remain significant barriers. Healthcare organizations must address these issues by adopting standardized frameworks, ensuring AI explainability, and implementing robust data privacy measures. As AI continues to evolve, its integration into CDS and EHR systems holds immense potential to enhance patient outcomes, reduce medical errors, and optimize healthcare efficiency–paving the way for a smarter, more proactive healthcare system.

Structure

In this chapter, the following topics will be covered:

- AI in Clinical Decision Support Systems
- AI and Electronic Health Records
- Challenges and Ethical Considerations
- Emerging trends in AI for CDS and EHR

AI in Clinical Decision Support Systems

Artificial intelligence (AI) is revolutionizing the field of healthcare, particularly in the area of Clinical Decision Support Systems (CDSS). By integrating AI algorithms and machine learning models, these systems can analyze large volumes of medical data, including patient records, clinical studies, and real-time health signals, to provide healthcare professionals with evidence-based recommendations and diagnostic insights. This can lead to more accurate diagnoses, personalized treatment plans, and improved patient outcomes. Moreover, AI-driven CDSS can identify potential risks and alert clinicians to early signs of complications, ensuring timely intervention. Despite these advantages, the integration of AI in healthcare also presents challenges, such as ensuring data privacy, managing ethical concerns, and maintaining human oversight in decision-making processes. Nonetheless, the potential of AI to enhance CDSS is vast, promising a future where healthcare is more efficient, effective, and patient-centered.

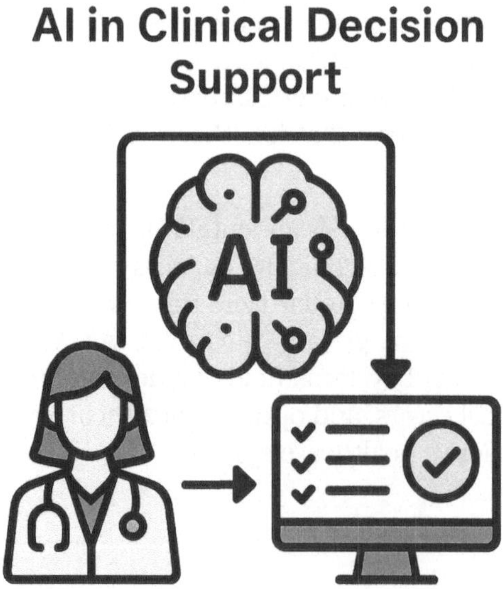

***Figure 5.1**: AI in CDSS*

Foundations of AI in Decision Support Systems

A Decision Support System (DSS) is designed to assist decision-makers in the analysis of data and in the use of data models to solve complex and ill-structured problems. Unlike operational systems that automate repetitive tasks, DSS is aimed at increasing the effectiveness of decision-making by providing relevant information, predictive models, and analytical tools.

Components of DSS

DSS typically consists of three key components:

- **Database Management System (DBMS)**: This component stores and manages the data required for problem-solving. It ensures that data is accessible, reliable, and up-to-date.
- **Model Management System**: This includes the software and computational models that process data and conduct analyses. These models can range from statistical analyses and simulations to complex predictive algorithms.
- **User Interface**: The interface allows users to interact with the DSS, inputting data, setting analysis parameters, and viewing results. An effective interface is critical for ensuring the system is accessible and useful to decision-makers.

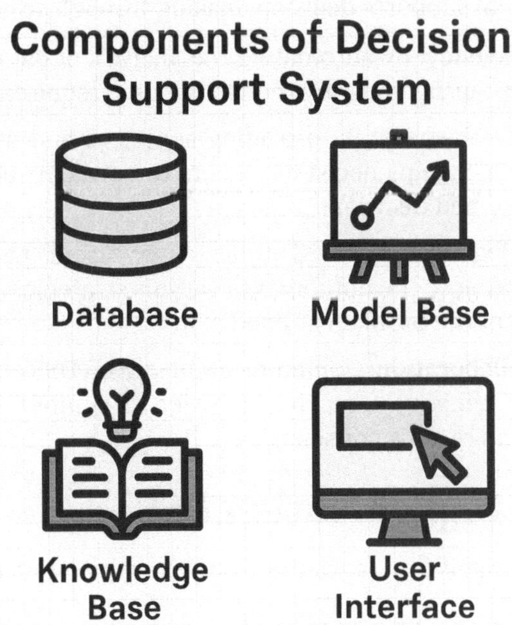

Figure 5.2: *Components of DSS*

Types of DSS

DSS can be categorized based on their primary function or the techniques they employ:

- **Data-driven DSS**: Focus on the management, retrieval, and analysis of large sets of data. Examples include systems that use data warehousing and online analytical processing (OLAP).
- **Model-driven DSS**: Rely on models to perform complex analyses and simulations. These systems are useful for scenarios that require the examination of numerous alternatives under various conditions.
- **Knowledge-driven DSS**: Provide specialized problem-solving expertise and recommendations by utilizing a knowledge base. They often incorporate artificial intelligence to simulate human decision-making processes.
- **Document-driven DSS**: Manage, retrieve, and manipulate unstructured information in various formats and from multiple sources.
- **Communication-driven DSS**: Facilitate collaboration and communication among decision-makers, especially in environments where team decision-making is crucial.

How DSS Supports Decision-Making

Decision Support System supports decision-making through several key functions:

- **Improving Efficiency**: By automating the analysis of data and the generation of reports, DSS can significantly reduce the time required to make decisions.
- **Enhancing Effectiveness**: By providing access to and analysis of a broader range of data, DSS helps decision-makers to consider more alternatives and make more informed decisions.
- **Encouraging Exploration**: DSS tools allow users to simulate different scenarios and explore the outcomes of various strategies, facilitating a deeper understanding of the problem at hand.
- **Supporting Collaboration**: Communication-driven DSS enables teams to work together more effectively, making it easier to compile inputs from various stakeholders and reach a consensus.

Challenges in Implementing DSS

While DSS can offer significant advantages, their implementation is not without challenges:

- **Data Quality and Integration**: Ensuring that the data fed into the DSS is accurate, relevant, and consistently updated is crucial for the reliability of the system.

- **Complexity and Usability**: The complexity of some DSS can be a barrier to effective use, particularly for users without technical expertise. Balancing sophistication with usability is key.
- **Security and Privacy**: Protecting sensitive data within the DSS from unauthorized access and breaches is a major concern, especially for systems handling personal or financial information.

Decision Support Systems represent a critical component in the modern decision-making landscape, offering tools and frameworks to analyze data, predict outcomes, and facilitate informed decisions. As technology advances, the scope and capabilities of DSS are expected to expand, further integrating AI and machine learning to provide even more sophisticated decision support. However, the success of these systems will continue to depend on thoughtful design, effective implementation, and ongoing management to ensure they meet the evolving needs of decision-makers.

The Role of AI in DSS

The integration of Artificial Intelligence (AI) into Decision Support Systems (DSS) has fundamentally transformed the landscape of decision-making tools. AI enhances DSS by introducing capabilities that extend beyond traditional data analysis and manual interpretation, facilitating more efficient, accurate, and sophisticated decision-making processes. This section delves into the role of AI in DSS, highlighting its impact, benefits, and the technologies that enable these advanced systems.

- **Enhancing Data Analysis and Interpretation**: AI significantly augments the data analysis capabilities of DSS. By employing machine learning algorithms and other AI techniques, DSS can analyze complex datasets more effectively than traditional statistical methods. AI algorithms excel at identifying patterns, trends, and correlations within vast amounts of data, many of which may be too subtle or complex for human analysts to detect. This enhanced data analysis capability allows organizations to derive more meaningful insights from their data, leading to better-informed decision-making.
- **Predictive Analytics and Forecasting**: One of the most valuable applications of AI in DSS is predictive analytics. AI models, trained on historical data, can forecast future trends, behaviors, and outcomes with a significant degree of accuracy. These predictive capabilities are crucial for strategic planning, risk management, and optimizing operational efficiencies. In sectors such as finance, healthcare, and retail, AI-driven predictive analytics enable decision-makers to anticipate market movements, patient health outcomes, and consumer behavior, respectively.
- **Automation of Decision Processes**: AI enables the automation of certain decision processes, particularly those involving routine or repetitive tasks. This not only speeds up the decision-making process but also reduces the likelihood

of human error. Automation is especially beneficial in operational decisions, such as inventory management or preventive maintenance scheduling, where AI systems can analyze real-time data to make instant decisions.

- **Enhancing Decision Accuracy**: The precision of AI algorithms contributes to making more accurate decisions. By processing and analyzing data at a granular level, AI-powered DSS can provide recommendations that are specifically tailored to the unique circumstances of a decision scenario. This customization enhances the relevance and effectiveness of decision support, leading to outcomes that are closely aligned with an organization's goals and objectives.

Technologies Powering AI in DSS

- **Machine Learning**: The core technology behind AI's predictive analytics and pattern recognition capabilities, enabling DSS to learn from data and improve over time.
- **Natural Language Processing (NLP)**: Allows DSS to understand and generate human language, facilitating the analysis of text data and enabling users to interact with the system using natural language.
- **Deep Learning**: A subset of machine learning that uses neural networks with many layers, enabling the analysis of complex data structures and the automation of decision processes involving visual data, audio data, and large-scale textual data.
- **Expert Systems**: Mimic the decision-making ability of a human expert, providing specialized guidance and recommendations in specific domains.

The role of AI in DSS represents a paradigm shift in how data is analyzed and decisions are made. By enhancing data analysis, automating decision processes, and improving the accuracy and efficiency of decisions, AI has made DSS more powerful and versatile than ever before. As AI technology continues to evolve, its integration into DSS will further revolutionize decision-making processes across all sectors, making them more data-driven, predictive, and effective in achieving strategic objectives. The future of DSS lies in harnessing the full potential of AI to address increasingly complex decision-making challenges, paving the way for innovative solutions and unprecedented levels of organizational performance.

ML in Powering AI-DSS Technologies

Machine Learning (ML) is a cornerstone of the technological foundation that powers AI-enabled Decision Support Systems (DSS). As a subset of artificial intelligence, ML focuses on developing algorithms that enable computers to learn from and make predictions or decisions based on data. This capability is central to enhancing the functionality, efficiency, and effectiveness of DSS across various applications. Here, we explore the pivotal roles and contributions of machine learning in powering AI-DSS technologies.

- **Enhancing Predictive Analytics**: Machine learning algorithms are at the heart of predictive analytics within AI-DSS. By analyzing historical data, ML models can identify patterns, trends, and relationships that might not be apparent to human analysts. These models are trained to forecast future events, behaviors, and outcomes with a significant degree of accuracy. For example, in finance, ML-powered DSS can predict stock market trends, helping investors make informed decisions. In healthcare, they can forecast disease outbreaks or patient readmissions, enabling proactive care management.
- **Improving Data Processing and Analysis**: ML algorithms excel in processing and analyzing vast amounts of data quickly and accurately. They can handle structured data, such as numbers and categories, as well as unstructured data, such as text, images, and video. This versatility allows AI-DSS to analyze a wider range of data sources than traditional DSS, leading to more comprehensive insights and better-informed decision-making. For instance, ML can analyze social media data to gauge consumer sentiment or process satellite images to monitor environmental changes.
- **Automating Decision Processes**: One of the key advantages of incorporating ML into DSS is the automation of routine and complex decision-making processes. ML algorithms can analyze real-time data streams to make instant decisions without human intervention. This capability is particularly beneficial for operational decisions that require speed and accuracy, such as fraud detection in banking transactions or real-time bidding in digital advertising.
- **Customizing Recommendations**: Machine learning algorithms can tailor recommendations to specific scenarios, users, or objectives by learning from past decisions and their outcomes. This personalization enhances the relevance and effectiveness of the support provided by AI-DSS. In e-commerce, for example, ML-driven recommendation systems suggest products to customers based on their browsing and purchase history, significantly improving user experience and sales.
- **Facilitating Complex Problem-Solving**: Advanced ML techniques, such as deep learning, are capable of handling multifaceted and intricate problems that involve analyzing large datasets with complex patterns. These techniques enable AI-DSS to tackle challenging decision-making scenarios, such as diagnosing diseases from medical images or optimizing complex supply chains. Deep learning's ability to process and learn from unstructured data, such as images and natural language, expands the applicability of DSS to a broader range of fields and problems.

- **Continuous Learning and Improvement**: A defining feature of machine learning is its ability to learn from new data and experiences continuously. This means that AI-DSS powered by ML can adapt and improve over time, becoming more accurate and effective in their decision support. This continuous learning process ensures that DSS remains up-to-date and aligned with changing environments, trends, and user needs.

Natural Language Processing (NLP)

NLP allows computers to understand, interpret, and generate human language. In DSS, NLP is used to analyze unstructured data (for example, text reports, emails, and social media posts) to extract valuable insights and support decision-making.

- **Predictive Analytics**: Predictive analytics involves using statistical models and forecasting techniques to understand the future. In AI-DSS, it is used for predicting trends, demands, and potential future risks.
- **Data Mining and Big Data Analytics**: Data mining involves exploring and analyzing large blocks of information to discover meaningful patterns and rules. Combined with big data analytics, it enables AI-DSS to handle and extract insights from vast and complex datasets.
- **Applications of AI-Enabled DSS**: The integration of AI into DSS has marked a significant evolution in various sectors, streamlining processes, enhancing efficiency, and enabling informed decision-making. AI-enabled DSS leverages the capabilities of machine learning, natural language processing, and data analytics to provide insights and recommendations that assist humans in making complex decisions. This chapter explores the diverse applications of AI-enabled DSS across different domains, illustrating their impact and potential.
- **Healthcare**: In healthcare, AI-enabled DSS are revolutionizing patient care and hospital management. These systems can analyze vast amounts of medical data, including electronic health records (EHR), imaging data, and genetic information, to support diagnostic processes, treatment planning, and patient monitoring. For example, AI algorithms can help radiologists interpret medical images more accurately and efficiently, leading to quicker and more precise diagnoses. Additionally, AI-driven predictive analytics can identify patients at high risk of certain diseases or readmissions, enabling preventative measures and personalized care plans.
- **Finance and Banking**: The finance and banking sector benefits from AI-enabled DSS through enhanced risk management, fraud detection, and customer service. AI models analyze transaction patterns to identify potential fraud in real-time, significantly reducing financial losses. In investment banking, AI-driven systems offer insights into market trends, helping analysts and

investors make informed decisions. Moreover, personalized banking services, such as robo-advisors, use AI to provide customized investment advice to clients based on their financial goals and risk tolerance.

- **Environmental Management**: AI-enabled DSS are instrumental in addressing environmental challenges by analyzing climate data, monitoring biodiversity, and predicting natural disasters. These systems can process and interpret data from satellites, sensors, and other sources to track changes in ecosystems, forecast weather patterns, and assess disaster risks. This capability supports proactive environmental management, including disaster preparedness, resource conservation, and sustainable development initiatives.
- **Manufacturing and Supply Chain**: In the manufacturing sector, AI-enabled DSS optimizes production processes, maintenance, and supply chain management. Predictive maintenance systems analyze data from machinery sensors to predict equipment failures before they occur, minimizing downtime and maintenance costs. AI algorithms also enhance supply chain efficiency by forecasting demand, optimizing inventory levels, and identifying the most efficient logistics routes.
- **E-Commerce and Retail**: AI-enabled DSS transforms the e-commerce and retail industry by personalizing customer experiences and optimizing operations. AI-driven recommendation systems analyze customer data to suggest products, improving customer satisfaction and increasing sales. In retail, AI models predict consumer trends and inventory needs, assisting in stock management and marketing strategies.
- **Urban Planning and Smart Cities**: AI-enabled DSS contributes to the development of smart cities, improving urban planning, traffic management, and public services. These systems analyze data from various sources, including traffic cameras, sensors, and social media, to optimize traffic flow, reduce congestion, and enhance public safety. Additionally, AI-driven models support sustainable urban development by analyzing patterns of energy consumption, waste production, and resource distribution.

***Figure* 5.3:** NLP

AI and Electronic Health Records

The integration of AI into the healthcare ecosystem, especially within EHRs, represents a pivotal advancement in medical informatics. This chapter aims to elucidate the transformative role of AI in enhancing EHR systems, thereby improving patient care, clinical outcomes, and healthcare operations. We will navigate through the foundational concepts, applications, challenges, and the future outlook of AI in the realm of EHRs, providing a comprehensive overview for new readers.

- **Introduction to EHRs:** Electronic Health Records (EHRs) are digital versions of patients' paper charts, accessible in real-time and containing a patient's medical history, diagnoses, medications, treatment plans, immunization dates, allergies, radiology images, and laboratory test results. EHRs have revolutionized how healthcare information is shared and managed, offering benefits, such as improved patient care, increased efficiency, and reduced healthcare costs. However, the vast amount of data generated by EHRs also presents challenges, including data overload and the need for sophisticated data analysis techniques, where AI steps in as a powerful tool.
- **The Role of AI in Enhancing EHRs:** AI is revolutionizing the healthcare industry by significantly enhancing the functionality and utility of EHRs. By applying sophisticated AI methodologies such as machine learning, natural language processing, and deep learning, the healthcare sector is witnessing

unprecedented improvements in data management, patient care, and clinical decision-making. This section delves into the multifaceted role of AI in augmenting EHR systems, highlighting its impact on data analysis, patient outcome prediction, clinical documentation, and decision support systems.

- **Automated Data Analysis and Insights:** AI excels in sifting through vast amounts of data to detect patterns, trends, and correlations that might not be immediately evident. In the context of EHRs, AI algorithms can analyze historical patient data, including vital signs, laboratory results, and medication histories, to uncover insights that inform clinical decisions. For instance, by identifying patterns in data from patients with similar conditions, AI can help predict disease progression and suggest effective treatment protocols. This capability not only enhances the quality of care but also supports personalized medicine approaches by tailoring treatments to individual patient characteristics.
- **Predictive Modeling for Patient Outcomes:** One of the most significant contributions of AI to EHRs is in predictive modeling. AI models can forecast patient outcomes by evaluating risk factors and current health statuses, thereby enabling early interventions for diseases with high morbidity and mortality rates. For example, AI tools can predict the likelihood of patient readmission, the risk of developing chronic conditions such as diabetes or heart disease, and the prognosis of diseases based on existing patient data. These predictions help healthcare providers focus their efforts on high-risk patients, potentially reducing hospital readmission rates and improving patient outcomes.
- **Natural Language Processing (NLP) for Unstructured Data:** A substantial portion of EHR data is unstructured, including clinical notes, radiology reports, and discharge summaries. NLP technologies enable the extraction and analysis of valuable information hidden in this unstructured data. By converting text into structured data that AI algorithms can process, NLP facilitates a deeper understanding of patient histories and clinical narratives. This not only aids in accurate diagnosis and treatment planning but also streamlines the documentation process, reducing the administrative burden on healthcare professionals.
- **Enhancing CDSS**: AI-powered CDSS are advanced tools that provide healthcare professionals with evidence-based clinical guidance tailored to the specific characteristics of each patient. These systems leverage AI to analyze EHR data in real-time, offering recommendations, flagging potential drug interactions, and alerting clinicians to abnormal test results. By integrating AI with CDSS, healthcare providers receive actionable insights at the point of care, enhancing decision-making processes and patient safety.
- **Data Analysis and Insight Generation**: AI algorithms excel at analyzing large datasets to identify patterns, trends, and anomalies that may not be apparent to human analysts. In EHRs, AI can predict patient outcomes, identify high-

risk patients, and suggest personalized treatment plans by analyzing historical patient data, clinical notes, and medical imaging.

Figure 5.4: *AI and EHRs*

Clinical Decision Support Systems (CDSS)

AI-powered CDSS enhances clinical practice by providing clinicians with evidence-based decision support tools that can offer recommendations, alert them to potential medication errors, and highlight critical laboratory results, thus improving patient safety and healthcare quality.

Challenges in Integrating AI with EHRs

Despite the potential benefits, the integration of AI into EHRs faces several challenges:

- **Data Privacy and Security**: Ensuring the privacy and security of patient data is paramount. AI systems must comply with healthcare regulations, such as the Health Insurance Portability and Accountability Act (HIPAA) in the United States, to protect sensitive health information.
- **Interoperability**: EHR systems from different vendors often have issues with interoperability, making it difficult to share and analyze data across systems. Standardizing data formats and protocols is essential for the effective use of AI.

- **Data Quality and Bias**: AI models are only as good as the data they are trained on. Inaccurate, incomplete, or biased data can lead to erroneous outcomes, underscoring the need for high-quality, representative data.

Future Outlook

The future of AI in EHRs is promising, with ongoing advancements aimed at overcoming current limitations and unlocking new possibilities. Potential directions include:

- **Predictive Analytics for Preventive Care**: Leveraging AI to analyze EHR data for predictive analytics can enable healthcare providers to offer more proactive and preventive care, identifying health risks before they develop into serious conditions.
- **Enhanced Patient Engagement**: AI can personalize patient experiences by providing tailored health recommendations, monitoring patient health remotely, and offering virtual health assistants, thereby fostering greater patient engagement in their care.
- **Advanced Interoperability Solutions**: Efforts to improve data standardization and develop more sophisticated AI models can enhance interoperability among disparate EHR systems, facilitating seamless data exchange and integration.

Challenges and Ethical Dilemmas

The advent of AI in healthcare, particularly in CDSS, marks a pivotal shift towards more data-driven, personalized, and efficient care. However, this integration is fraught with challenges and ethical dilemmas. This chapter aims to explore these complexities, offering insights into navigating the balance between innovation and ethical responsibility.

- **The Evolution of AI in CDSS**: Briefly recount the history of CDSS and the introduction of AI into these systems, emphasizing the transition from rule-based engines to sophisticated machine learning and deep learning models. Highlight key milestones and the potential of AI to revolutionize healthcare delivery.
- **Data Quality and Integrity**: The foundation of effective and ethical AI in CDSS lies in the quality and integrity of the data these technologies analyze. High-quality data are essential for training robust AI models that accurately predict outcomes, provide personalized treatment recommendations, and enhance patient care. However, achieving and maintaining high data quality and integrity in healthcare poses significant challenges, stemming from various sources and impacting AI applications in nuanced ways.

Challenges in Data Quality and Integrity

- **Incompleteness and Missing Data**: Healthcare datasets often have missing values, whether due to non-collection of certain information, loss of data during transfer between systems, or patient refusal to provide details. AI models trained on incomplete datasets may develop biases or inaccuracies, leading to suboptimal clinical recommendations.
- **Inaccuracy and Errors**: Data entry errors, misdiagnoses, and inaccuracies in patient records can significantly distort the training of AI algorithms. The propagation of these inaccuracies can lead to erroneous AI-driven decisions, potentially compromising patient safety.
- **Inconsistency and Variability**: Variability in how data are recorded across different healthcare systems–ranging from differences in terminology to differences in measurement units–can lead to inconsistencies in the data. Such inconsistencies pose a significant challenge for AI systems, which rely on standardized inputs to function correctly.
- **Temporal Changes**: The dynamic nature of healthcare data, where patient conditions and treatment protocols evolve over time, adds another layer of complexity. Ensuring data integrity means continuously updating AI models to reflect current clinical knowledge and patient information.

***Figure* 5.5**: *Data Quality and Integrity*

Strategies for Enhancing Data Quality and Integrity

- **Data Cleaning and Preprocessing**: Implementing rigorous data cleaning and preprocessing pipelines is crucial. These processes involve identifying and correcting errors and inconsistencies, imputing missing values, and standardizing data formats. Automated tools, alongside manual review by clinical experts, can enhance the accuracy and consistency of healthcare datasets.
- **Robust Data Governance**: Establishing comprehensive data governance policies is essential for maintaining data quality and integrity. These policies should cover data collection, storage, processing, and sharing practices, ensuring that all data handling processes uphold high standards of accuracy, privacy, and security.
- **Use of Interoperable Standards**: Adopting interoperable data standards, such as HL7 FHIR (Health Level Seven Fast Healthcare Interoperability Resources), can help reduce variability and ensure that data from different sources are compatible. Standardization facilitates the integration of diverse datasets, enhancing the reliability of AI-driven insights.
- **Continuous Monitoring and Updating**: Given the evolving nature of medical knowledge and patient information, continuous monitoring and regular updating of AI models are vital. AI systems should be designed to adapt to new data, incorporating the latest clinical guidelines and research findings to maintain their accuracy and relevance.
- **Engagement of Multidisciplinary Teams**: Involving a multidisciplinary team–including data scientists, healthcare professionals, and ethicists–in the development and oversight of AI systems can help identify and address data quality issues. Clinicians can provide crucial insights into the context and significance of data, while ethicists ensure that data-handling practices respect patient rights and equity.
- **Complexity of Healthcare Data**: The complexity of healthcare data presents significant challenges for the integration and effective utilization of AI in CDSS. This complexity arises from several inherent characteristics of the data, each adding layers of difficulty for AI algorithms designed to process, analyze, and derive meaningful insights from healthcare datasets.
- **Multidimensional Nature**: Healthcare data are inherently multidimensional, encompassing a wide range of information types, including patient demographics, clinical notes, laboratory results, imaging studies, and genomics. Each data type has its own format, standards, and level of structure, ranging from highly structured (for example, lab results) to unstructured (for example, clinician notes). AI models must navigate this multidimensionality

to integrate and interpret these disparate data sources effectively, a task that requires sophisticated preprocessing and feature engineering techniques.

- **Heterogeneity and Variability**: Data heterogeneity in healthcare extends beyond the diversity of data types to include variability in healthcare practices, patient populations, and disease manifestations. The same condition may present differently across patients due to factors, such as age, gender, genetic background, and comorbidities, making it challenging for AI systems to identify patterns that generalize well across diverse patient groups. Additionally, variations in clinical practices and treatment protocols across institutions introduce further variability, complicating the development of universally applicable AI models.
- **Temporal Dynamics**: Healthcare data are characterized by temporal dynamics, with patient conditions and treatment responses evolving over time. Longitudinal patient records capturing the progression of diseases, treatment interventions, and outcomes over time are crucial for developing predictive models in CDSS. However, modeling these temporal relationships requires advanced AI techniques that can handle sequential data, account for time-dependent variations, and predict future health trajectories, adding complexity to the AI development process.
- **High-Dimensional Data and the Curse of Dimensionality**: The vast amount of data collected in healthcare, particularly with the advent of big data technologies, introduces the challenge of high dimensionality. As the number of features in a dataset increases, the computational resources and complexity of the models needed to process and analyze the data also grow. This high dimensionality can lead to the "*curse of dimensionality*," where the performance of AI algorithms degrades due to the sparsity of high-dimensional space, making it difficult to extract meaningful patterns without overfitting.
- **Semantic Ambiguity**: Clinical notes and other textual data in healthcare records are rich sources of patient information but are fraught with semantic ambiguity. Natural language processing (NLP) techniques applied to extract information from these texts must contend with synonyms, homonyms, abbreviations, and domain-specific jargon. Moreover, the context often plays a critical role in interpreting these texts accurately, necessitating sophisticated NLP models that can understand and process the nuances of clinical language.

Strategies for Addressing the Complexity

To effectively leverage AI in CDSS amidst these complexities, several strategies can be employed:

- **Advanced Data Integration Techniques**: Employing sophisticated data integration techniques that can handle the multidimensionality and heterogeneity of healthcare data is crucial. This includes the use of ontologies and common data models to standardize and harmonize disparate data sources.

- **Temporal Modeling**: Leveraging AI techniques specialized in temporal data, such as recurrent neural networks (RNNs) and transformer models, can help in accurately modeling the dynamics of patient data over time.
- **Dimensionality Reduction**: Techniques such as principal component analysis (PCA), autoencoders, and feature selection algorithms can reduce the dimensionality of the data, mitigating the curse of dimensionality and enhancing model performance.
- **Contextual NLP Models**: Implementing advanced NLP models that can understand the context and disambiguate clinical text is essential for extracting accurate and meaningful information from unstructured data.
- **Collaborative and Iterative Development**: Engaging clinicians, data scientists, and domain experts in a collaborative and iterative development process ensures that AI models are tailored to the nuances of healthcare data and clinical contexts.

Integration with Healthcare Systems

The integration of Artificial Intelligence (AI) into Clinical Decision Support Systems (CDSS) and broader healthcare systems is a critical step toward realizing the potential of AI to enhance patient care. However, this integration presents a multifaceted challenge, encompassing technical, operational, and cultural dimensions. Successfully addressing these challenges requires a concerted effort to ensure that AI tools not only coexist with existing healthcare IT ecosystems but also complement and enhance clinical workflows.

Technical and Operational Challenges

- **Interoperability**: One of the primary technical challenges in integrating AI with healthcare systems is ensuring interoperability between disparate IT systems and data formats. Healthcare data are stored across various platforms, including Electronic Health Records (EHRs), Picture Archiving and Communication Systems (PACS), and Laboratory Information Systems (LIS), each potentially using different standards and formats. Effective AI integration requires these systems to communicate seamlessly, necessitating the adoption of interoperable standards and protocols such as HL7 FHIR.
- **Data Accessibility and Privacy**: AI systems require access to large volumes of data to train and operate effectively. Ensuring this access while maintaining patient privacy and complying with regulations such as HIPAA (Health

Insurance Portability and Accountability Act) and GDPR (General Data Protection Regulation) is a significant challenge. Solutions must be found that allow AI systems to learn from vast datasets without compromising individual privacy rights.

- **Scalability**: Healthcare systems vary widely in their infrastructure and capabilities, from large academic medical centers to small, rural clinics. AI solutions must be scalable and flexible enough to be deployed across these varied settings without requiring extensive customization or significant infrastructure upgrades.
- **Clinical Workflow Integration**: AI tools must fit into existing clinical workflows to be effective. This means they must be designed not only to provide valuable insights but to do so in a manner that is timely and integrates smoothly with clinicians' decision-making processes. The challenge lies in designing AI applications that are intuitive, require minimal additional input from healthcare professionals, and deliver actionable insights without disrupting the flow of patient care.

Addressing Integration Challenges

- **Standards and Frameworks for Interoperability**: Adopting and promoting the use of international standards for data exchange and interoperability is crucial. Initiatives like FHIR provide a framework for exchanging healthcare information electronically, facilitating easier integration of AI systems.
- **Privacy-preserving Techniques**: Leveraging advanced data analytics techniques, such as federated learning and differential privacy, can enable AI systems to learn from data without needing direct access to sensitive information, helping to maintain privacy and compliance.
- **Modular and Adaptable AI Solutions**: Developing AI applications as modular, adaptable systems that can be easily integrated into different healthcare environments can help overcome scalability challenges. Cloud-based solutions offer scalability and flexibility, allowing for easier updates and maintenance.
- **User-centered Design**: Involving clinicians and healthcare professionals in the design and development process ensures that AI tools are user-friendly and meet the real needs of end-users. Tailoring AI applications to fit seamlessly within existing clinical workflows can enhance adoption and efficacy.
- **Continuous Evaluation and Feedback Loops**: Once integrated, AI systems should be continuously monitored and evaluated within the clinical setting to assess their impact on patient care and clinical workflows. Feedback from healthcare professionals should be used to refine and improve AI applications, ensuring they remain aligned with clinical needs and priorities.

Scalability and Adaptability

In the context of AI in CDSS, scalability and adaptability are critical factors that determine the extent to which these technologies can be effectively and efficiently deployed across diverse healthcare settings. Scalability refers to the capability of AI systems to handle increasing amounts of work or to be capable of enlargement, allowing them to support a wide range of healthcare institutions, from small clinics to large hospitals. Adaptability, on the other hand, denotes the ability of AI systems to adjust to changes or to be tailored to different clinical scenarios, workflows, or patient populations.

***Figure* 5.6**: *Scalability and Adaptability*

Challenges in Scalability and Adaptability

- **Diverse Healthcare Environments**: Healthcare settings vary significantly in terms of size, infrastructure, resources, patient demographics, and clinical focus. An AI system designed for a large urban hospital may not be suitable for a small rural clinic due to differences in technological capabilities, patient populations, and types of care provided.
- **Evolving Clinical Practices**: Clinical guidelines and practices evolve as new research findings emerge and as healthcare policies change. AI systems must be adaptable to incorporate the latest evidence and guidelines to remain relevant and effective.
- **Technological Heterogeneity**: The technology landscape within healthcare is highly heterogeneous, with various institutions using different Electronic

Health Record (EHR) systems, diagnostic tools, and IT infrastructure. Scalability and adaptability are required to ensure AI systems can integrate with this wide array of technologies.

- **Regulatory and Ethical Considerations**: As AI systems scale across regions and countries, they encounter diverse regulatory environments and ethical standards. Adapting to these varied requirements while ensuring compliance and ethical integrity poses a significant challenge.

Strategies for Enhancing Scalability and Adaptability

- **Modular Design**: Developing AI systems with modular architectures can facilitate scalability and adaptability. Modules can be added, removed, or replaced without affecting the overall system, allowing for easy customization and scaling to meet the needs of different healthcare settings.
- **Cloud-based Deployment**: Leveraging cloud computing for AI deployment can significantly enhance scalability. Cloud platforms can dynamically allocate resources based on demand, ensuring that AI systems remain responsive and efficient regardless of the volume of data or number of users. Cloud-based solutions also facilitate the deployment of updates and new features, aiding adaptability.
- **Federated Learning**: Federated learning is a machine learning approach that enables AI models to learn from decentralized data sources without moving the data itself. This technique not only addresses privacy concerns but also allows AI systems to learn from diverse datasets across different institutions, enhancing their adaptability to varied clinical environments.
- **Continuous Learning and Updating Mechanisms**: Incorporating mechanisms for continuous learning and updating within AI systems ensures they remain current with the latest clinical practices and guidelines. This adaptability is crucial for maintaining the relevance and effectiveness of AI-driven CDSS over time.
- **User-centered Development**: Engaging healthcare professionals, patients, and other stakeholders in the development process ensures that AI systems are designed with real-world clinical workflows and patient care needs in mind. This participatory approach enhances the adaptability of AI tools to specific clinical settings and user requirements.
- **Interoperability Standards**: Adhering to and promoting interoperability standards, such as HL7 FHIR, enables AI systems to integrate seamlessly with diverse EHR systems and healthcare IT infrastructure, supporting scalability and adaptability across healthcare settings.

Ethical Considerations

Ethical considerations for Clinical Decision Support Systems (CDSS) are paramount to ensuring these technologies benefit patients without compromising their rights or safety. Key ethical concerns include patient privacy and data security, where sensitive health information must be protected from unauthorized access and breaches. Informed consent is another critical factor, as patients should be aware of how their data is used and the implications of algorithm-driven medical decisions. Transparency and explainability of the CDSS are essential to maintaining trust, enabling healthcare professionals and patients to understand how decisions are made. Bias and fairness must also be addressed, ensuring that CDSS algorithms do not perpetuate inequalities or discrimination in healthcare delivery.

Bias and Fairness

The integration of AI into CDSS holds immense potential for transforming healthcare delivery, improving diagnostic accuracy, and personalizing treatment plans. However, this innovation comes with significant ethical responsibilities, particularly concerning bias in AI and its potential impact on healthcare equity. Bias in AI can arise from various sources and, if unaddressed, may perpetuate or even exacerbate existing health disparities, undermining the ethical imperative to ensure equitable healthcare for all.

Sources of Bias in AI

- **Biased Training Data**: AI algorithms learn to make predictions or decisions based on training data. If this data is unrepresentative of the broader population or contains historical biases, the AI system will likely replicate or amplify these biases. For example, if a dataset predominantly includes information from certain demographic groups, the AI system may perform poorly for underrepresented groups, leading to misdiagnosis or inappropriate treatment recommendations.
- **Algorithmic Biases**: Beyond the data, biases can also stem from the algorithms themselves. The choice of algorithm, feature selection, and model parameters can introduce bias. For instance, certain machine learning models might inadvertently give more weight to variables that correlate with social determinants of health, such as ethnicity or income level, without direct clinical relevance, thus skewing outcomes.
- **Interpretation and Implementation Bias**: The way AI outputs are interpreted and implemented by healthcare providers can also introduce bias. This includes potential biases in clinical judgment when integrating AI recommendations into patient care plans, potentially influenced by the provider's conscious or unconscious biases.

Impact on Healthcare Equity

The consequences of bias in AI are far-reaching, particularly regarding healthcare equity. Biased AI systems can lead to unequal treatment recommendations, diagnostic accuracy, and patient outcomes across different populations. This not only undermines trust in AI and healthcare systems but also exacerbates existing health disparities. For populations already experiencing healthcare inequities, biased AI systems can further limit access to appropriate, timely, and effective care.

Ethical Imperative to Address AI Bias

Addressing bias in AI is not merely a technical challenge; it is an ethical imperative. Ensuring that AI in CDSS promotes healthcare equity requires concerted efforts across multiple dimensions:

- **Diverse and Representative Data**: Ensuring training datasets are diverse and representative of the population is crucial. This involves collecting and utilizing data from varied demographic groups and healthcare settings, reflecting the diversity of patient populations.
- **Transparent and Explainable AI**: Developing AI systems that are transparent and explainable can help identify and mitigate biases. Transparency in how AI models make decisions enables scrutiny and validation of their fairness and equity.
- **Regular Auditing for Bias**: Implementing regular audits of AI systems for bias and equity implications is essential. This should involve both internal and external evaluations, including feedback from diverse stakeholders, to continuously assess and improve AI systems.
- **Multidisciplinary Collaboration**: Combating AI bias requires collaboration across disciplines, including data scientists, healthcare professionals, ethicists, and patient advocates. This multidisciplinary approach ensures that diverse perspectives inform the development and deployment of AI in healthcare.
- **Regulatory and Policy Frameworks**: Developing and enforcing regulatory and policy frameworks that mandate fairness, transparency, and accountability in AI systems is crucial. Such frameworks can guide the ethical development and deployment of AI technologies in healthcare.

Patient Autonomy and Consent

The incorporation of Artificial Intelligence (AI) into Clinical Decision Support Systems (CDSS) represents a paradigm shift in healthcare, offering unprecedented capabilities in diagnostics, treatment optimization, and patient care management. However, this integration also raises complex ethical considerations, particularly concerning patient autonomy and the challenges of obtaining informed consent. Patient autonomy, a fundamental principle of medical ethics, requires that patients are fully informed and voluntarily consent to their care choices. The complexity of AI technologies, however, poses significant challenges to this principle, especially in ensuring that patients understand and consent to the use of AI in their healthcare.

Challenges in Obtaining Informed Consent

- **Complexity of AI Systems**: The technical complexity and opacity of AI algorithms (often referred to as "*black boxes*") make it difficult for patients and sometimes even healthcare providers to understand how AI recommendations are generated. This complexity challenges the traditional informed consent process, which is predicated on patients' understanding of their treatment options.
- **Perception and Understanding of AI**: Patients' varying levels of literacy, particularly digital literacy, can affect their understanding of AI and its implications for their healthcare. Misconceptions and a lack of familiarity with AI technologies can hinder informed consent, as patients may not fully grasp what consent entails in the context of AI-assisted decision-making.
- **Trust and Reliability Concerns**: Trust in the reliability and objectivity of AI recommendations is crucial for informed consent. Patients may have concerns about the accuracy of AI systems, biases in decision-making, and the potential for errors, raising questions about the dependability of AI in critical healthcare decisions.

Strategies for Ensuring Informed Consent

To address these challenges and ensure that patients are adequately informed and consent to the use of AI in their care, several strategies can be employed:

- **Simplifying Complex Information**: Developing materials and consent processes that simplify complex AI concepts without oversimplifying or omitting critical information is essential. This includes using plain language, visual aids, and analogies to explain how AI is used in decision-making and what it means for the patient's care.
- **Enhanced Communication Training for Providers**: Healthcare providers play a critical role in the informed consent process. Providing them with training on how to communicate effectively about AI, including its benefits, risks, and limitations, can help ensure that patients receive comprehensible and relevant information.
- **Patient-Centered Consent Processes**: Tailoring the informed consent process to the individual patient's needs, concerns, and comprehension levels is crucial. This personalized approach may involve additional consultations, Q&A

sessions, and the use of decision aids designed to help patients understand the implications of AI in their care.

- **Transparency and Accountability**: Ensuring transparency about the AI systems' functioning, including data sources, decision-making processes, and any known limitations or biases, can build trust and aid in informed consent. Additionally, clearly outlining accountability for AI-driven recommendations reinforces trust in the decision-making process.
- **Ongoing Consent**: Given the evolving nature of AI technologies and their applications in healthcare, consent should be considered an ongoing process rather than a one-time event. Regular updates and discussions about the use of AI in a patient's care can ensure that consent remains informed and voluntary over time.
- **Public Education and Engagement**: Broadly educating the public about AI in healthcare through media, public forums, and patient advocacy groups can raise awareness and understanding, making informed consent more meaningful and effective.

Navigating the Challenges: Toward Ethical AI in CDSS

Developing Ethical Guidelines: As Artificial Intelligence (AI) becomes increasingly integrated into Clinical Decision Support Systems (CDSS) and other healthcare applications, the establishment of robust ethical guidelines is paramount. These guidelines serve multiple critical functions: ensuring patient safety and privacy, promoting fairness and equity, maintaining public trust in healthcare systems, and preventing misuse or unintended consequences of AI technologies. In the context of healthcare, where decisions can have profound implications for patient outcomes, ethical guidelines are not merely recommendations but essential guardrails that guide the development and deployment of AI in a manner that respects human dignity, autonomy, and rights.

Challenges Addressed by Ethical Guidelines

- **Preventing Bias and Ensuring Equity**: Ethical guidelines aim to prevent biases in AI algorithms that could lead to unequal treatment or outcomes for different patient groups, thereby promoting healthcare equity.
- **Protecting Patient Privacy and Data Security**: With AI systems relying heavily on vast amounts of personal health data, ethical guidelines emphasize the importance of safeguarding patient privacy and ensuring robust data security measures.
- **Ensuring Transparency and Explainability**: Ethical AI in healthcare necessitates transparency about how AI systems make decisions, as well as

ensuring that these decisions can be explained in understandable terms to patients and healthcare providers.

- **Promoting Accountability**: Guidelines highlight the need for clear accountability in AI-driven decisions, ensuring that there are mechanisms for recourse and correction of AI-driven errors in patient care.

Initiatives and Frameworks Guiding Ethical AI Practices in CDSS

Several initiatives and frameworks have been developed globally to guide ethical AI practices in healthcare, underscoring the international consensus on the importance of ethics in AI.

- **World Health Organization (WHO) Guidance on Ethics and Governance of Artificial Intelligence for Health**: The WHO has released comprehensive guidance that outlines six ethical principles to ensure AI works to the public benefit of all people. These principles include protecting human autonomy, promoting human well-being and safety, ensuring transparency, inclusiveness, and responsiveness and promoting AI that is sustainable and equitable.
- **The Asilomar AI Principles**: Developed during a 2017 conference involving leading AI researchers, these principles cover research issues, ethics and values, and longer-term issues. While not healthcare-specific, they provide a broad ethical framework that includes beneficence, non-maleficence, autonomy, justice, and explicability.
- **The IEEE Global Initiative on Ethics of Autonomous and Intelligent Systems**: This initiative offers detailed recommendations for ethically aligned design, including a section specifically on Affective Computing and Healthcare/Wellbeing. It emphasizes prioritizing human well-being in the development and implementation of AI technologies.
- **The European Commission's Ethics Guidelines for Trustworthy AI**: These guidelines outline seven key requirements for AI systems, including human agency and oversight, technical robustness and safety, privacy and data governance, transparency, diversity, non-discrimination and fairness, environmental and societal well-being, and accountability. Although broader than healthcare, these principles are directly applicable to AI in CDSS.
- **The Montreal Declaration for Responsible AI**: This declaration emphasizes the principles of well-being, autonomy, justice, privacy, knowledge, democracy, and responsibility as fundamental to the development of AI systems, including those in healthcare.

Fostering Multidisciplinary Collaboration

The integration of Artificial Intelligence (AI) in Clinical Decision Support Systems (CDSS) offers transformative potential for healthcare, promising to enhance diagnostic accuracy, improve treatment outcomes, and personalize patient care. However, realizing these benefits while navigating the ethical complexities inherent in AI requires a collaborative approach that transcends traditional disciplinary boundaries. Collaboration among healthcare professionals, computer scientists, ethicists, and patients is paramount in developing and deploying AI technologies that are not only innovative but also ethical and aligned with the core values of healthcare.

Addressing Ethical Challenges through Multidisciplinary Teams

- **Comprehensive Understanding of Ethical Implications**: Ethicists and healthcare professionals bring a deep understanding of the ethical considerations in patient care, including patient autonomy, consent, privacy, and equity. Their insights can guide the development of AI technologies that respect these principles, ensuring that ethical considerations are embedded from the outset.
- **Technical Expertise and Innovation**: Computer scientists and AI developers possess the technical expertise necessary to innovate while considering the ethical constraints and aspirations communicated by ethicists and healthcare professionals. They can implement technical solutions that respect ethical guidelines, such as privacy-preserving algorithms or fairness-oriented machine learning models.
- **Patient-Centered Design**: Engaging patients in both the development and implementation of AI technologies is essential to creating solutions that truly reflect their needs, preferences, and values. By prioritizing patient autonomy and involving them directly in the process, AI systems become more trustworthy, relevant, and widely accepted. This participatory model shifts the narrative from building technologies *for* patients to building them *with* patients – fostering inclusion, empathy, and better outcomes.
- **Diverse Perspectives on Ethical Challenges**: Multidisciplinary teams bring diverse perspectives to ethical challenges, fostering a more holistic and nuanced understanding of the implications of AI in healthcare. This diversity of thought is critical in identifying potential ethical pitfalls and devising comprehensive strategies to address them.
- **Regulatory and Policy Guidance**: Collaboration between these diverse stakeholders can also inform the development of regulatory and policy frameworks that govern the use of AI in healthcare. By providing insights into the practical, ethical, and technical challenges of AI in CDSS, multidisciplinary teams can guide policymakers in creating regulations that promote innovation while protecting patient welfare.

Strategies for Effective Multidisciplinary Collaboration

- **Establishing Common Goals**: Define clear, shared objectives that align with healthcare values, such as improving patient outcomes, ensuring equitable access to care, and maintaining patient trust in healthcare systems.

- **Fostering Open Communication**: Encourage open lines of communication among team members, ensuring that all voices are heard and valued. This includes creating spaces where technical jargon is demystified, and ethical considerations are clearly articulated.
- **Building Mutual Respect and Understanding**: Develop mutual respect and understanding among team members by facilitating knowledge exchange sessions where each discipline can share its perspectives, methodologies, and concerns.
- **Continuous Education and Training**: Implement continuous education and training programs that allow team members to stay updated on advancements in AI technologies, ethical considerations, and healthcare needs.
- **Patient Engagement**: Actively involve patients and patient advocacy groups in the development process through consultations, focus groups, and feedback sessions. This ensures that AI technologies are designed with the patient's best interest in mind.

Emerging Trends in AI for CDS and EHR

The integration of AI into CDS systems and EHRs is revolutionizing the healthcare industry. By harnessing the power of AI, healthcare providers can deliver more personalized, efficient, and effective patient care. This evolution is driven by several emerging trends that leverage AI technologies to enhance the capabilities of CDS and EHR systems. Here, we explore these trends and their implications for the future of healthcare.

- **Natural Language Processing (NLP) for Enhanced Data Interpretation**: One of the most significant trends is the application of NLP technologies to interpret and analyze unstructured data within EHRs. NLP algorithms can understand, interpret, and generate human language in a way that is valuable for extracting patient information from doctors' notes, discharge summaries, and imaging reports. This capability allows for a more comprehensive understanding of a patient's history and condition, leading to more informed clinical decision-making.
- **Predictive Analytics for Proactive Healthcare**: AI-driven predictive analytics are being increasingly used in CDS systems to forecast patient outcomes, identify at-risk patients, and recommend preventive measures. By analyzing historical and real-time data, AI models can identify patterns and predict trends related to diseases, hospital readmissions, and potential complications. This proactive approach enables healthcare providers to intervene early, improving patient outcomes and reducing healthcare costs.

- **Personalized Medicine and Treatment Recommendations**: AI is facilitating the shift towards personalized medicine, where treatment plans are tailored to the individual characteristics of each patient. By analyzing vast amounts of data from EHRs, including genetic information, AI algorithms can identify the most effective treatments for specific patient profiles. This personalized approach not only enhances the efficacy of treatments but also minimizes the risk of adverse reactions.
- **Enhanced Interoperability and Data Integration**: Interoperability among different healthcare systems and EHR platforms remains a significant challenge. Emerging AI solutions are addressing this issue by enhancing data integration and sharing capabilities. AI can automate the translation and mapping of data across diverse systems, facilitating seamless data exchange. This interoperability is crucial for comprehensive patient records and supports coordinated care strategies.
- **Image Recognition and Analysis for Diagnostics**: AI-driven image recognition and analysis technologies are revolutionizing diagnostic processes, particularly in radiology, pathology, and dermatology. AI models trained on vast datasets of medical images can identify patterns and anomalies that may be invisible to the human eye. This capability not only improves diagnostic accuracy but also accelerates the diagnostic process, enabling quicker treatment decisions.
- **Chatbots and Virtual Health Assistants**: The use of AI-powered chatbots and virtual health assistants is on the rise, providing patients with instant access to health information and support. These AI tools can guide patients through symptom checkers, offer health and wellness advice, and facilitate appointment scheduling. By automating routine interactions, healthcare providers can improve patient engagement and satisfaction while focusing human resources on more complex tasks.
- **Real-time Monitoring and Alerting Systems**: Wearable devices and IoT (Internet of Things) technologies integrated with AI are enabling real-time monitoring of patient health metrics outside traditional healthcare settings. AI algorithms analyze this data in real-time, providing CDS systems with continuous updates on patient conditions. This trend supports remote patient monitoring, early detection of potential health issues, and timely interventions.
- **Ethical and Explainable AI**: As AI technologies become more ingrained in healthcare, there is a growing emphasis on developing ethical and explainable AI systems. Ethical AI involves designing AI technologies that respect patient privacy, ensure data security, and promote equity in healthcare. Explainable AI refers to AI systems designed to provide transparent explanations of their decision-making processes, enhancing trust among clinicians and patients.

The integration of AI into CDS and EHR systems is transforming healthcare delivery, offering opportunities to improve patient outcomes, enhance efficiency, and personalize care. As these emerging trends evolve, it is crucial for healthcare organizations to embrace these technologies responsibly, ensuring they are implemented ethically and with a patient-centered approach. The future of healthcare lies in leveraging AI to its full potential while navigating the associated challenges and ethical considerations.

Conclusion

The integration of Artificial Intelligence into Clinical Decision Support Systems represents a significant advancement in the realm of healthcare. By leveraging AI's computational power, these systems offer unparalleled accuracy, efficiency, and personalization in patient care. They enable healthcare professionals to make better-informed decisions, thereby improving patient outcomes and optimizing healthcare delivery. However, as we embrace these technological advancements, it is crucial to navigate the challenges they bring, including ethical considerations, data privacy, and the need for human oversight. The evolution of AI in CDSS marks a transformative era in medicine, one that holds great promise for the future of healthcare.

In the next chapter, "*Diagnosis and Imaging Using AI*," we will delve into how artificial intelligence is revolutionizing the fields of medical diagnosis and imaging. We will explore the impact of AI on enhancing the accuracy, speed, and efficiency of diagnosing diseases, as well as its role in advancing imaging techniques that provide deeper insights into the human body. This chapter promises to shed light on the transformative potential of AI in shaping the future of medical diagnostics and patient care.

Points to Remember

For a concise summary that captures the essence of each detailed point in the chapter on "*Emerging Trends in AI for Clinical Decision Support (CDS) and Electronic Health Records (EHR)*," here are the key takeaways to remember:

- **NLP in EHRs**: Natural Language Processing (NLP) is crucial for extracting valuable patient information from unstructured data, enhancing clinical decision-making.
- **Predictive Analytics in Healthcare**: AI-driven predictive analytics can forecast patient outcomes and identify at-risk patients, allowing for early intervention and improved healthcare delivery.
- **Personalized Medicine via AI**: AI enables the customization of treatment plans to individual patient profiles, optimizing treatment efficacy and safety.
- **AI-Enhanced Interoperability**: AI technologies address interoperability

challenges by automating data integration and facilitating seamless data exchange across healthcare systems.

- **AI in Diagnostic Imaging**: Advanced image recognition and analysis powered by AI improve diagnostic accuracy and efficiency in fields, such as radiology and pathology.
- **Chatbots and Virtual Assistants**: AI-powered chatbots and virtual health assistants enhance patient engagement by providing instant access to health information and support.
- **Real-Time Monitoring with AI**: The integration of wearable devices and IoT technologies with AI enables continuous monitoring of patient health metrics, supporting proactive healthcare.
- **Ethical and Explainable AI**: The development of AI in healthcare emphasizes ethical considerations and the need for AI systems to be transparent and understandable in their decision-making processes.

Remembering these points will provide a solid foundation for understanding the current and emerging landscape of AI applications within Clinical Decision Support and Electronic Health Records, highlighting the transformative potential of AI in enhancing patient care, improving outcomes, and addressing healthcare challenges.

Further Readings

Academic Journals and Articles

- "*Deep Learning for Electronic Health Records: A Comparative Review of Multiple Deep Neural Architectures*": This review article compares various deep learning architectures and their application in analyzing EHR data, offering insights into the strengths and weaknesses of each approach.
- "*Natural Language Processing in Healthcare: A Unified Framework for Clinical and Research Applications*": This paper discusses how NLP technologies are applied in healthcare, emphasizing their role in interpreting unstructured data within EHRs.
- "*Predictive Analytics in Healthcare: A Survey*": An overview of predictive analytics in healthcare, covering methods, applications, and challenges in the field.
- "*Personalized Medicine and the Power of Electronic Health Records*": This article explores how EHR data can be leveraged for personalized medicine, detailing case studies and potential future directions.
- "*Interoperability in Healthcare: Benefits, Challenges, and Solutions*": A comprehensive review of interoperability issues in healthcare IT systems, including how AI can address these challenges.

- "*AI and Radiology: An Overview of Challenges and Opportunities for the Field*": Focuses on the application of AI in radiology, discussing both the potential and the pitfalls of current image recognition and analysis technologies.

Books

- "*Deep Medicine: How Artificial Intelligence Can Make Healthcare Human Again*" by Eric Topol: A seminal book that explores how AI can transform healthcare, making it more personalized, efficient, and human-centered.
- "*Artificial Intelligence in Healthcare*" by Adam Bohr and Kaveh Memarzadeh: Provides a comprehensive overview of AI applications in healthcare, including case studies and discussions on ethical considerations.
- "*Healthcare Data Analytics and Management*" edited by Nilanjan Dey, et al.: Offers insights into data management and analytics in healthcare, covering topics from data mining techniques to the integration of AI in healthcare systems.

Industry Reports and White Papers

- "*Top Health Industry Issues of 2023: PwC Health Research Institute's Annual Report*": Includes insights into how AI and technology are reshaping healthcare, with a focus on trends and challenges.
- "*Ethics and Artificial Intelligence in Healthcare*" by the World Health Organization (WHO): A report discussing the ethical considerations of AI in healthcare, offering guidelines and recommendations for policymakers and practitioners.
- "*AI in Health and Care Award: Yearbook*": An annual publication showcasing innovative AI projects in healthcare, providing real-world examples of AI's impact on CDS and EHR systems.

CHAPTER 6
Imaging and Diagnosis Using AI

Introduction

Artificial Intelligence (AI) is rapidly transforming various fields, and healthcare is at the forefront of this revolution. One of the most promising applications of AI in healthcare is medical imaging and diagnosis, where AI-driven technologies are enhancing diagnostic accuracy, efficiency, and accessibility. Hospitals and healthcare institutions worldwide are increasingly adopting AI-powered imaging tools to detect diseases earlier, reduce diagnostic errors, and improve patient outcomes.

For instance, Google's DeepMind AI has developed an advanced imaging model that detects breast cancer in mammograms with higher accuracy than human radiologists, reducing false positives and false negatives. Similarly, Zebra Medical Vision, an AI-driven radiology platform, is used in hospitals to automatically detect conditions, such as lung diseases, fractures, and cardiovascular abnormalities, from medical scans. In ophthalmology, IDx-DR, an FDA-approved AI system, autonomously detects diabetic retinopathy in retinal images, providing immediate results without requiring a specialist.

This chapter explores the theoretical foundations, methodologies, and real-world applications of AI in medical imaging and diagnosis, delving into how AI-driven models are transforming radiology, pathology, cardiology, and other medical fields. We will also examine the challenges, ethical considerations, and future trends shaping AI's role in diagnostic imaging, ultimately paving the way for more accurate, cost-effective, and accessible healthcare.

Structure

In this chapter, we will discuss the following topics:

- Overview of Medical Imaging
- AI in Medical Imaging

- AI Applications in X-ray Imaging in Hospitals and Clinics
  - AI-assisted Diagnosis
  - Image Guided Therapy
  - AI in Radiology
- AI Applications in Magnetic Resonance Imaging (MRI)

Overview of Medical Imaging

Medical imaging is a crucial component of modern healthcare. It allows clinicians to visualize the internal structures of the body, providing essential information for diagnosis, treatment planning, and monitoring of diseases. Common modalities include:

- **X-rays:** Widely used for diagnosing fractures, infections, and tumors.
- **Computed Tomography (CT):** Provides detailed cross-sectional images of the body, useful for detecting cancers, cardiovascular diseases, and more.
- **Magnetic Resonance Imaging (MRI):** Uses magnetic fields and radio waves to produce detailed images of organs and tissues, particularly useful in neurology and musculoskeletal imaging.
- **Ultrasound:** Employs high-frequency sound waves to visualize soft tissues, commonly used in obstetrics and cardiology.
- **Positron Emission Tomography (PET):** Visualizes metabolic processes in the body, aiding in cancer diagnosis and management.

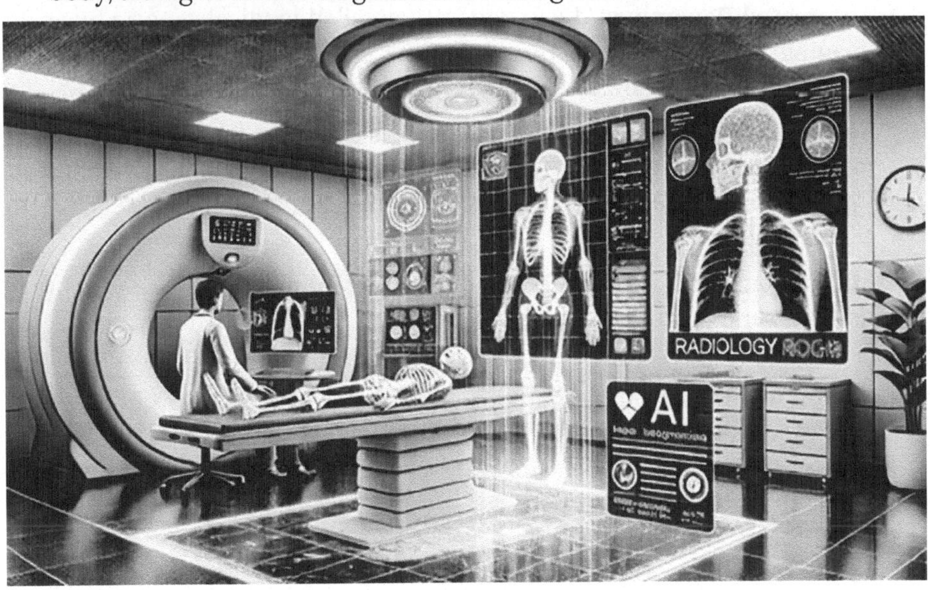

Figure 6.1: *Artificial Intelligence used in Radiology*

AI in Medical Imaging

AI, particularly through machine learning (ML) and deep learning (DL) techniques, has demonstrated significant potential in enhancing medical imaging. The key AI applications in this domain include image preprocessing, segmentation, classification, and anomaly detection. Here are some key AI applications in medical imaging:

- **Disease Detection and Diagnosis**: AI algorithms are capable of detecting diseases such as cancer, pneumonia, and cardiovascular conditions by analyzing medical images. These algorithms can identify patterns and anomalies that might be missed by the human eye, leading to early and more accurate diagnoses.
- **Image Enhancement and Reconstruction**: AI can improve the quality of medical images, especially in low-dose imaging techniques, such as CT scans, by reducing noise and artifacts. This results in clearer images, which are crucial for accurate diagnosis and treatment planning.
- **Workflow Optimization**: AI helps in prioritizing urgent cases, organizing medical images, and generating preliminary reports. This streamlines the workflow in radiology departments, allowing radiologists to focus on more complex cases and reducing overall diagnostic time.
- **Predictive Analytics**: By analyzing historical imaging data, AI can predict the likelihood of disease progression and patient outcomes. This predictive capability assists in creating personalized treatment plans and improving patient management.
- **Automated Reporting**: AI can generate detailed medical reports by analyzing imaging data and identifying key findings. This reduces the burden on radiologists and ensures consistency in reporting.
- **Segmentation and Quantification**: AI tools can segment organs and tissues in medical images and quantify specific features, such as tumor size and volume. This is essential for tracking disease progression and assessing treatment response.
- **3D Imaging and Visualization**: AI enhances 3D imaging techniques, providing detailed and accurate reconstructions of anatomical structures. This is particularly useful in surgical planning and interventional procedures.
- **Radiomics**: AI-driven radiomics involves extracting large amounts of quantitative features from medical images. These features can be used to develop predictive models for various diseases, contributing to precision medicine.

AI Applications in X-ray Imaging in Hospitals and Clinics

X-rays are a cornerstone of diagnostic imaging, widely used in hospitals and clinics for diagnosing various conditions ranging from fractures to infections and tumors. The integration of AI into X-ray imaging enhances diagnostic accuracy, speeds up image analysis, and assists in clinical decision-making. This section explores how AI is being utilized in X-ray imaging, detailing specific applications, benefits, and real-world examples.

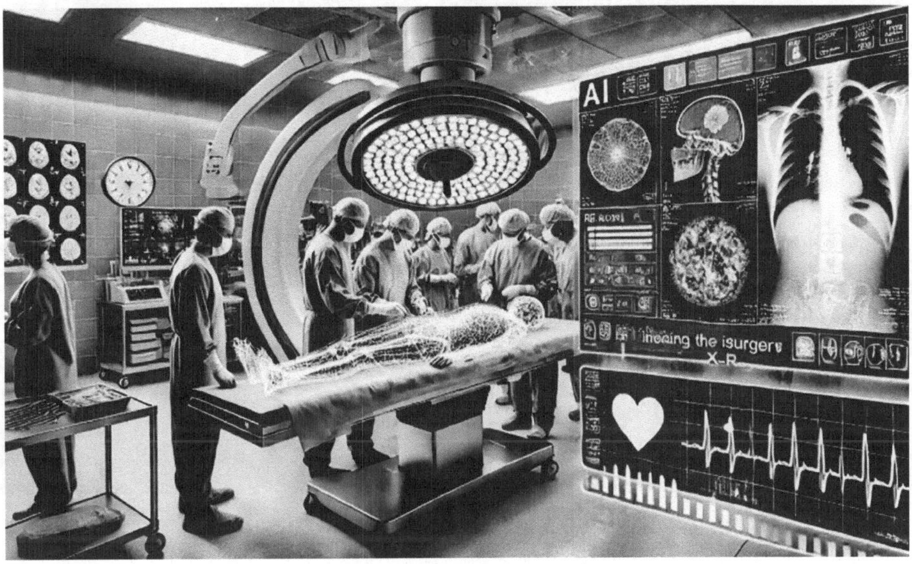

Figure 6.2: *Artificial Intelligence used in X-ray theaters*

AI in X-ray Image Analysis

AI enhances X-ray imaging through several applications:

- Automated Detection and Diagnosis
- Image Enhancement
- Workflow Optimization
- Predictive Analytics

Automated Detection and Diagnosis

AI algorithms, particularly deep learning models, can analyze X-ray images to detect abnormalities with high accuracy. These models are trained on vast datasets of labeled X-ray images to identify patterns indicative of specific conditions.

Example Applications

- **Pneumonia Detection**: AI models can detect signs of pneumonia in chest X-rays, providing an early and accurate diagnosis.
- **Fracture Detection**: AI can identify fractures in bone X-rays, assisting radiologists in diagnosing and treating injuries quickly.
- **Tumor Identification**: AI helps in detecting tumors, such as lung nodules in chest X-rays, which are often challenging to identify in early stages.

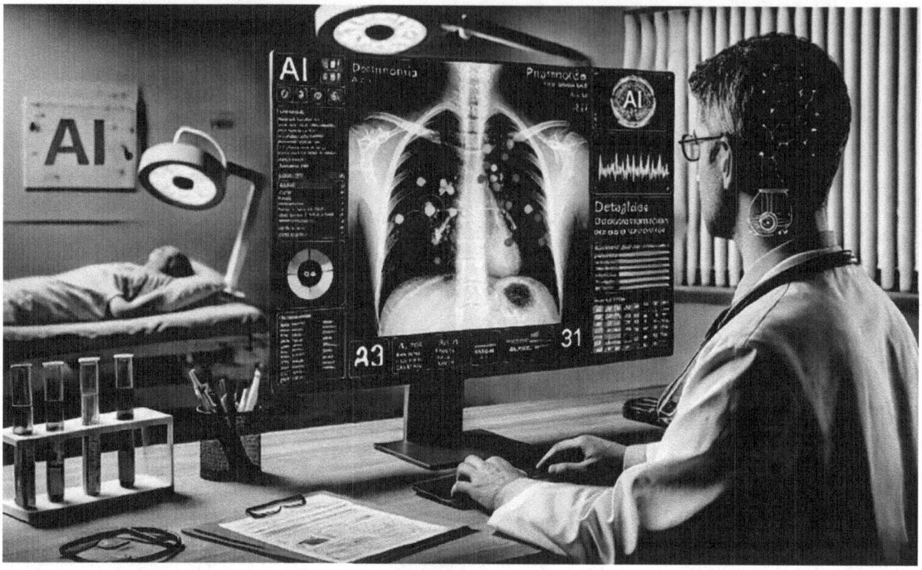

Figure 6.3: *Artificial Intelligence used in detecting Pneumonia*

Example Workflow: Pneumonia Detection

```
from tensorflow.keras.preprocessing.image import ImageDataGenerator
from tensorflow.keras.applications import ResNet50
from tensorflow.keras import layers, models

# Load and preprocess X-ray images
train_datagen = ImageDataGenerator(rescale=1.0/255)
validation_datagen = ImageDataGenerator(rescale=1.0/255)

train_generator = train_datagen.flow_from_directory(
    'chest_xray/train', target_size=(256, 256), batch_size=32,
class_mode='binary')

validation_generator = validation_datagen.flow_from_directory(
    'chest_xray/validation', target_size=(256, 256), batch_
size=32, class_mode='binary')
```

```
# Load a pre-trained ResNet50 model
base_model = ResNet50(weights='imagenet', include_top=False,
input_shape=(256, 256, 3))

# Freeze the base model layers
for layer in base_model.layers:
    layer.trainable = False

# Add custom top layers for pneumonia detection
model = models.Sequential([
    base_model,
    layers.GlobalAveragePooling2D(),
    layers.Dense(256, activation='relu'),
    layers.Dense(1, activation='sigmoid')
])

model.compile(optimizer='adam', loss='binary_crossentropy',
metrics=['accuracy'])

# Train the model on the chest X-ray dataset
model.fit(train_generator, epochs=10, validation_data=validation_
generator)
```

Image Enhancement

AI-based image enhancement techniques improve the quality of X-ray images, making it easier to identify subtle abnormalities.

Techniques

- **Noise Reduction**: AI algorithms can reduce noise in X-ray images, resulting in clearer and more accurate visuals.
- **Contrast Enhancement**: Enhancing the contrast of X-ray images helps in highlighting specific structures, aiding in better diagnosis.
- **Super-Resolution**: AI can generate higher-resolution images from lower-resolution inputs, providing more detailed visuals for analysis.

Example Workflow: Noise Reduction

```
import cv2
import numpy as np
import matplotlib.pyplot as plt

# Load a noisy X-ray image
noisy_image = cv2.imread('noisy_xray.png', cv2.IMREAD_GRAYSCALE)
```

```
# Apply a denoising algorithm (e.g., Non-Local Means Denoising)
denoised_image = cv2.fastNlMeansDenoising(noisy_image, None, 30,
7, 21)

# Display the original and denoised images
plt.figure(figsize=(10, 5))
plt.subplot(1, 2, 1)
plt.title('Original Noisy Image')
plt.imshow(noisy_image, cmap='gray')
plt.subplot(1, 2, 2)
plt.title('Denoised Image')
plt.imshow(denoised_image, cmap='gray')
plt.show()
```

Workflow Optimization

AI streamlines radiology workflows by automating repetitive tasks and prioritizing cases based on urgency.

Applications

- **Triage**: AI systems can triage X-ray images, flagging urgent cases for immediate review by radiologists.
- **Automated Reporting**: AI can generate preliminary reports based on the analysis of X-ray images, saving radiologists time and reducing workload.
- **Quality Control**: AI ensures the quality of X-ray images by detecting issues such as poor positioning or low image quality, prompting retakes if necessary.

Example Workflow: Triage System

```
import numpy as np
# Simulated urgency scores for X-ray images (higher score
indicates higher urgency)
xray_scores = np.random.rand(100) * 10  # Scores between 0 and 10

# Threshold for urgent cases
urgent_threshold = 7.5

# Identify urgent cases
urgent_cases = np.where(xray_scores > urgent_threshold)[0]
# Print urgent case indices
print("Urgent cases indices:", urgent_cases)
```

Predictive Analytics

AI models can predict patient outcomes and the likelihood of disease progression based on X-ray images and other clinical data.

Applications

- **Disease Progression**: Predicts how a disease, such as osteoarthritis, will progress over time based on initial X-ray findings.
- **Risk Stratification**: Identifies patients at high risk of complications or readmission based on X-ray analysis and clinical history.

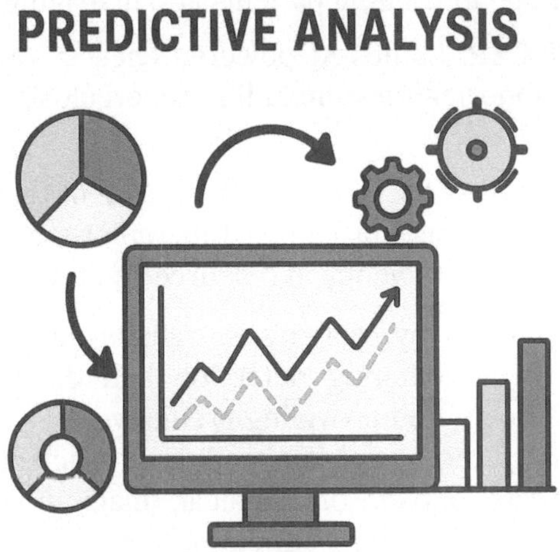

Figure 6.4: *Predictive Analytics*

Example Workflow: Disease Progression Prediction

```
from sklearn.model_selection import train_test_split
from sklearn.linear_model import LogisticRegression

# Simulated dataset of X-ray features and disease progression
labels
# X: Features from X-ray images
# y: Progression labels (0: No progression, 1: Progression)
X = np.random.rand(100, 10)
y = np.random.randint(2, size=100)

# Split the dataset into training and testing sets
X_train, X_test, y_train, y_test = train_test_split(X, y, test_
size=0.2, random_state=42)

# Train a logistic regression model
model = LogisticRegression()
model.fit(X_train, y_train)

# Predict disease progression on the test set
y_pred = model.predict(X_test)

# Evaluate the model
```

```
accuracy = model.score(X_test, y_test)
print("Model Accuracy:", accuracy)
```

Real-World Examples and Case Studies

- **COVID-19 Detection**: During the COVID-19 pandemic, AI models were deployed to analyze chest X-rays for rapid identification of COVID-19 infections, assisting in triaging patients and managing healthcare resources.
- **Lunit INSIGHT CXR**: Lunit's AI-powered chest X-ray analysis software can detect various abnormalities, including tuberculosis and lung nodules, with high accuracy.
- **Qure.ai's qXR**: Qure.ai developed qXR, an AI tool that reads chest X-rays to detect conditions such as lung cancer, tuberculosis, and fractures, significantly improving diagnostic efficiency in resource-limited settings.

The integration of AI into X-ray imaging is transforming diagnostic practices in hospitals and clinics. By automating detection and diagnosis, enhancing image quality, optimizing workflows, and providing predictive analytics, AI helps healthcare professionals deliver faster, more accurate, and more efficient care. As AI technology continues to advance, its impact on medical imaging will only grow, further revolutionizing the field and improving patient outcomes.

Revolutionizing Computed Tomography (CT) with AI

Computed Tomography (CT) has been a cornerstone in medical imaging for decades, providing critical insights into the human body that are essential for diagnosis, treatment planning, and monitoring of diseases. However, the integration of Artificial Intelligence (AI) into CT imaging marks a transformative era, enhancing accuracy, efficiency, and accessibility. This chapter explores the advancements, applications, and future prospects of AI in CT imaging.

The Evolution of CT Imaging

CT imaging, developed in the early 1970s, revolutionized medical diagnostics by enabling detailed cross-sectional images of the body. Over the years, CT technology has advanced significantly, with improvements in image resolution, scanning speed, and dose reduction. However, challenges such as image interpretation, radiation exposure, and data management have persisted.

The Role of AI in CT Imaging

AI, particularly machine learning (ML) and deep learning (DL), has shown immense potential in addressing these challenges. By leveraging large datasets and sophisticated algorithms, AI can enhance various aspects of CT imaging:

- **Image Reconstruction and Enhancement:**
  - Traditional CT reconstruction methods often involve trade-offs between image quality and radiation dose. AI-based reconstruction techniques, such as deep learning algorithms, can produce high-quality images from lower doses, reducing patient exposure to radiation.
  - AI can also enhance image quality by reducing noise and artifacts, leading to clearer and more accurate images for diagnosis.
- **Automated Image Analysis:**
  - AI algorithms can automate the detection and quantification of abnormalities in CT images, such as tumors, fractures, and vascular anomalies. This automation can significantly reduce the workload of radiologists and increase diagnostic accuracy.
  - Machine learning models can be trained to recognize patterns in CT images, enabling early detection of diseases, such as cancer, cardiovascular conditions, and neurological disorders.
- **Workflow Optimization:**
  - AI can streamline the workflow in radiology departments by automating routine tasks, such as image sorting, labeling, and preliminary reporting. This allows radiologists to focus on more complex cases and improves overall efficiency.
  - Predictive analytics can be used to optimize scanner utilization, reduce patient wait times, and improve scheduling.
- **Personalized Medicine:**
  - AI can facilitate personalized treatment planning by integrating CT imaging data with other patient information, such as genetic profiles and electronic health records. This holistic approach can help tailor treatments to individual patients, improving outcomes.

Key Applications of AI in CT Imaging

Here are some key applications of AI in CT imaging:

- **Oncology:** AI-enhanced CT imaging is crucial in oncology for the detection, characterization, and monitoring of tumors. AI algorithms can accurately segment tumors, assess treatment responses, and predict outcomes, aiding in personalized cancer care.
- **Cardiology:** In cardiology, AI can improve the analysis of CT angiography, identifying plaque buildup, stenosis, and other cardiovascular anomalies with

high precision. This aids in early diagnosis and intervention, potentially saving lives.

- **Neurology:** AI applications in neuroimaging include the detection of stroke, traumatic brain injury, and neurodegenerative diseases. AI algorithms can rapidly identify and quantify brain abnormalities, facilitating timely treatment decisions.
- **Pulmonology:** AI can enhance the detection of lung conditions such as pneumonia, chronic obstructive pulmonary disease (COPD), and pulmonary nodules. During the COVID-19 pandemic, AI-assisted CT imaging played a crucial role in the rapid diagnosis and monitoring of affected patients.

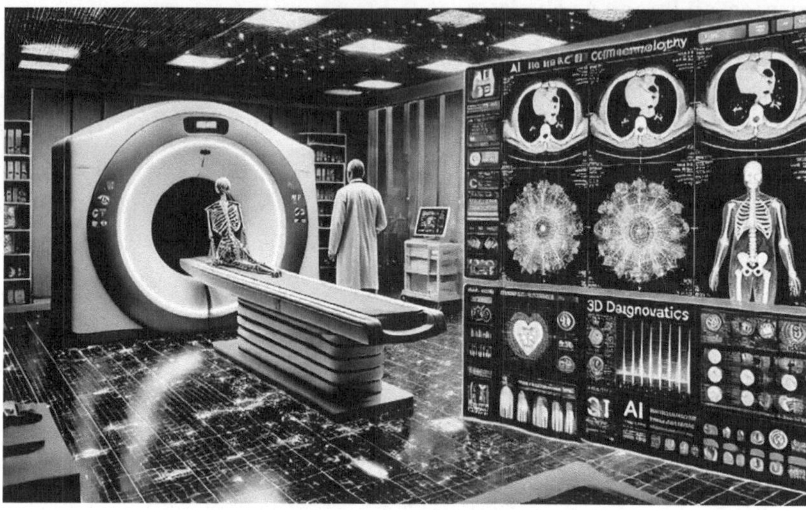

Figure 6.5: *Artificial Intelligence used in CT scans*

Future Prospects

The future of AI in CT imaging is promising, with ongoing research and development focusing on several key areas:

- **Real-time AI:** The development of real-time AI applications that can provide immediate feedback during CT scanning procedures, enhancing the precision of interventions.
- **Multimodal Imaging:** Integrates AI with multimodal imaging techniques, such as combining CT with MRI or PET, to provide comprehensive diagnostic insights.
- **Continuous Learning Systems:** Implements AI systems that continuously learn and improve from new data, ensuring they remain up-to-date with the latest medical knowledge and practices.
- **Global Health Impact:** Leverages AI to make advanced CT imaging accessible

in low-resource settings, addressing global health disparities and improving outcomes in underserved populations.

The integration of AI into CT imaging represents a significant leap forward in medical diagnostics. By enhancing image quality, automating analysis, and personalizing treatment, AI has the potential to revolutionize healthcare delivery. As we navigate the challenges and embrace the opportunities, the collaboration between clinicians, researchers, and technologists will be crucial in realizing the full potential of AI in CT imaging, ultimately improving patient care and outcomes worldwide.

AI Applications in Magnetic Resonance Imaging (MRI)

Magnetic Resonance Imaging (MRI) is a powerful diagnostic tool that uses magnetic fields and radio waves to produce detailed images of the body's internal structures. The integration of Artificial Intelligence (AI) into MRI technology has the potential to transform the field of medical imaging, enhancing image quality, speeding up scan times, and providing deeper insights into various medical conditions. This chapter explores the various applications of AI in MRI, highlighting the advancements, methodologies, and future prospects.

The Role of AI in MRI

AI, particularly through machine learning (ML) and deep learning (DL) techniques, has demonstrated substantial potential in improving MRI's capabilities. Here are some of the key areas where AI is making a significant impact:

- **Image Reconstruction:**
    - Traditional MRI scans can be time-consuming. AI can accelerate this process by reconstructing high-quality images from reduced data, thus reducing scan times. Deep learning models like convolutional neural networks (CNNs) can predict and fill in missing data points, producing high-resolution images from less raw data.
    - AI-based techniques can also help in improving the signal-to-noise ratio (SNR) of MRI images, enhancing image clarity and detail.
- **Image Segmentation and Analysis:**
    - AI can automate the segmentation of MRI images, identifying and delineating various structures and tissues within the body, such as organs, muscles, and lesions. This is particularly useful in brain imaging, where precise segmentation of brain tissues and abnormalities is crucial.
    - Advanced AI algorithms can analyze these segmented images to detect

and quantify abnormalities, such as tumors, cysts, and other pathologies, with high accuracy.

- **Diagnosis and Prognosis:**
    - AI-powered diagnostic tools can assist radiologists by providing automated interpretations of MRI scans. These tools can identify patterns and anomalies that might be missed by the human eye, leading to earlier and more accurate diagnoses.
    - AI can also be used to predict disease progression and patient outcomes by analyzing historical MRI data and identifying trends and risk factors.
- **Quantitative Imaging:**
    - Quantitative MRI (qMRI) involves measuring various physical properties of tissues, such as T1 and T2 relaxation times. AI can enhance the accuracy and efficiency of these measurements, providing valuable quantitative data for diagnosis and treatment planning.
    - AI algorithms can standardize and automate qMRI processes, ensuring consistent and reproducible results across different imaging centers and machines.
- **Workflow Optimization:**
    - AI can streamline MRI workflows by automating routine tasks, such as image sorting, labeling, and preliminary reporting. This reduces the burden on radiologists and allows them to focus on more complex cases.
    - Predictive analytics powered by AI can optimize scanner utilization, reduce patient wait times, and improve scheduling efficiency.

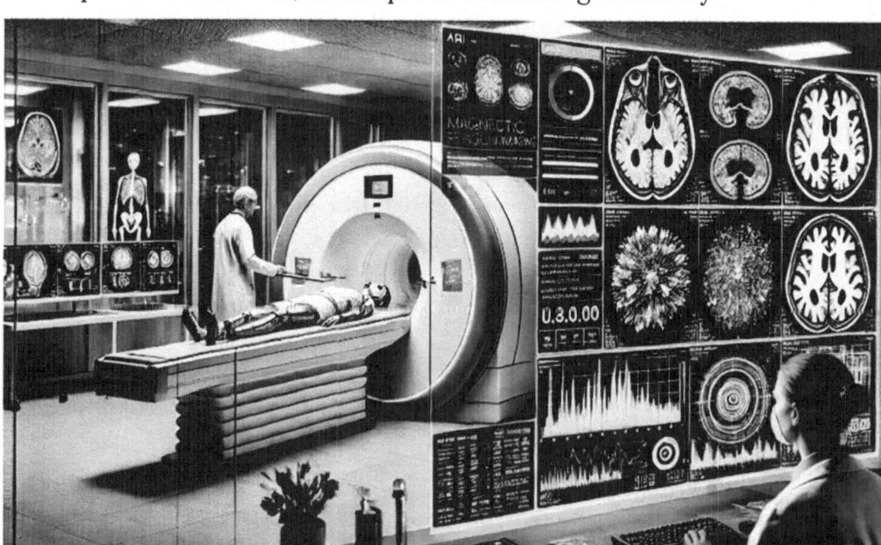

Figure 6.6: *Artificial Intelligence used in MRI theaters*

Key Applications of AI in MRI

Here are some key applications of AI in MRI:

- **Neuroimaging:**
    - In brain imaging, AI can enhance the detection and analysis of neurological conditions, such as Alzheimer's disease, multiple sclerosis, and brain tumors. AI algorithms can accurately segment brain tissues, detect lesions, and monitor disease progression.
    - AI can also be used to analyze functional MRI (fMRI) data, providing insights into brain activity and connectivity patterns, which is valuable for research in neuroscience and psychology.
- **Cardiac Imaging:**
    - AI can improve the accuracy and efficiency of cardiac MRI by automating the segmentation of heart structures and quantifying parameters, such as ventricular volumes, ejection fraction, and myocardial strain.
    - AI algorithms can also detect and assess cardiac abnormalities such as myocardial infarction, fibrosis, and congenital heart defects, aiding in the diagnosis and management of cardiovascular diseases.
- **Musculoskeletal Imaging:**
    - AI applications in musculoskeletal MRI include the automated analysis of joints, muscles, and bones. AI can detect and quantify abnormalities such as tears, fractures, and degenerative changes with high precision.
    - AI can also be used to monitor the response to treatment in conditions such as arthritis and muscle injuries, providing valuable data for personalized treatment planning.
- **Oncology:**
    - In oncology, AI-enhanced MRI can aid in the detection, characterization, and monitoring of tumors. AI algorithms can accurately segment tumors, assess their size and shape, and monitor changes over time, which is crucial for treatment planning and evaluation.
    - AI can also help in differentiating between benign and malignant lesions, improving the accuracy of cancer diagnoses.

Illustrations

To enhance understanding, here are some illustrations of AI applications in MRI:

- **AI-Powered Image Reconstruction:** Illustration showing a traditional MRI scan side-by-side with an AI-reconstructed scan, highlighting the improvements in image quality and reduction in scan time.

- **Automated Image Segmentation:** Diagram depicting the automated segmentation of brain tissues in an MRI scan with labels for different regions, such as gray matter, white matter, and cerebrospinal fluid.
- **Disease Detection and Quantification:** Series of MRI images demonstrating AI's ability to detect and quantify tumors in different stages, with visual markers indicating tumor boundaries and measurements.
- **Workflow Optimization:** Flowchart illustrating the integration of AI into the MRI workflow, showing automated steps such as image sorting, preliminary reporting, and scan scheduling.

The integration of AI into MRI represents a significant advancement in medical imaging. By enhancing image quality, automating analysis, and optimizing workflows, AI has the potential to transform MRI practices, leading to improved diagnostic accuracy, efficiency, and patient outcomes. As the technology continues to evolve, collaboration between clinicians, researchers, and technologists will be essential to overcome challenges and unlock the full potential of AI in MRI.

AI Applications in Ultrasound Imaging

Ultrasound imaging is a widely used diagnostic tool that utilizes high-frequency sound waves to produce real-time images of the body's internal structures. It is particularly valued for its non-invasiveness, safety, and portability. The integration of Artificial Intelligence (AI) into ultrasound technology has the potential to revolutionize this field, enhancing image quality, improving diagnostic accuracy, and streamlining workflows. This chapter explores the various applications of AI in ultrasound imaging, detailing the advancements, methodologies, and future prospects.

The Role of AI in Ultrasound Imaging

AI, especially through machine learning (ML) and deep learning (DL), has made significant strides in enhancing the capabilities of ultrasound imaging. Here are some of the key areas where AI is making an impact:

- **Image Acquisition and Quality Enhancement:**
    - **Automated Image Acquisition**: AI can assist in the acquisition of ultrasound images by guiding the ultrasound probe to the optimal position, ensuring consistent and high-quality images. This is particularly useful in settings where skilled sonographers are not available.
    - **Image Quality Enhancement**: AI algorithms can enhance the quality of ultrasound images by reducing noise and artifacts, improving resolution, and enhancing contrast. This leads to clearer and more detailed images, aiding in accurate diagnosis.

- **Image Interpretation and Analysis:**
  - **Automated Image Analysis**: AI can automate the analysis of ultrasound images, identifying and quantifying structures and abnormalities with high accuracy. This includes detecting lesions, measuring organ sizes, and identifying anatomical landmarks.
  - **Pattern Recognition**: Deep learning models can be trained to recognize patterns in ultrasound images, enabling the early detection of diseases, such as cancer, liver fibrosis, and cardiovascular conditions.
- **Workflow Optimization:**
  - **Automated Reporting**: AI can generate preliminary reports based on the analysis of ultrasound images, highlighting potential abnormalities and measurements. This reduces the workload of radiologists and speeds up the diagnostic process.
  - **Real-Time Assistance**: AI can provide real-time feedback during ultrasound examinations, assisting clinicians in capturing the best possible images and making immediate assessments.
- **Clinical Decision Support:**
  - **Risk Assessment and Prognosis**: AI can analyze ultrasound images in conjunction with other patient data to assess risks and predict outcomes. This is valuable in monitoring pregnancy, managing chronic conditions, and planning surgeries.
  - **Personalized Medicine**: AI can integrate ultrasound data with other clinical information to provide personalized treatment recommendations, improving patient outcomes.

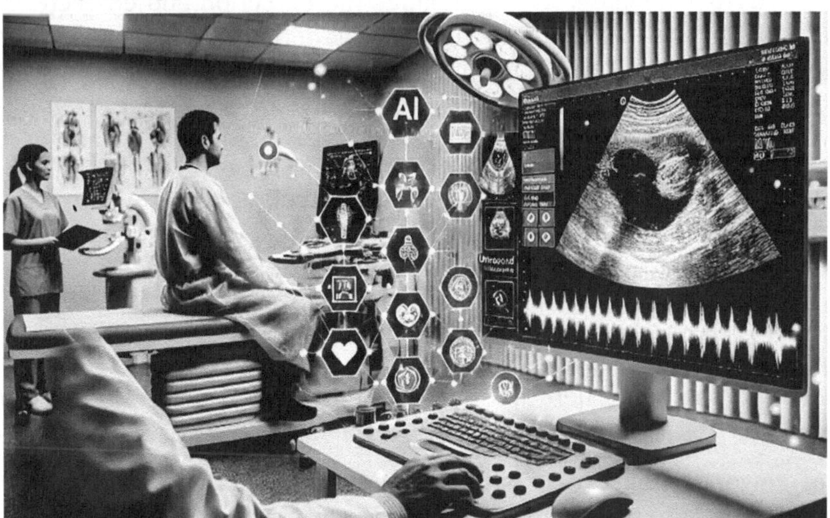

Figure 6.7: *Artificial Intelligence used in Ultrasound arenas*

Key Applications of AI in Ultrasound Imaging

Here are some key applications of AI in ultrasound imaging:

- **Obstetrics and Gynecology:**
    - **Fetal Monitoring:** AI can enhance the accuracy of fetal monitoring by automating the measurement of fetal biometry and detecting abnormalities such as congenital defects. AI can also predict complications such as preterm birth and fetal growth restriction.
    - **Breast Imaging:** AI algorithms can assist in the detection and characterization of breast lesions in ultrasound images, improving the accuracy of breast cancer screening and diagnosis.
- **Cardiology:**
    - **Echocardiography:** AI can automate the analysis of echocardiograms, providing accurate measurements of cardiac function, such as ejection fraction and ventricular volumes. AI can also detect structural heart diseases, such as valve abnormalities and cardiomyopathies.
    - **Vascular Ultrasound:** AI can enhance the detection of vascular conditions such as deep vein thrombosis (DVT), arterial plaques, and aneurysms by analyzing Doppler ultrasound images.
- **Abdominal Imaging:**
    - **Liver and Kidney Assessment:** AI can assist in the evaluation of liver fibrosis, cirrhosis, and tumors by analyzing ultrasound images. AI can also help in detecting kidney stones, cysts, and masses.
    - **Thyroid Imaging:** AI can enhance the detection and characterization of thyroid nodules, aiding in the diagnosis of thyroid cancer and other thyroid disorders.
- **Musculoskeletal Imaging:**
    - **Joint and Muscle Assessment:** AI can automate the analysis of musculoskeletal ultrasound images, detecting conditions such as tendon tears, muscle injuries, and joint effusions. AI can also guide interventions such as injections and biopsies.

Illustrations

To enhance understanding, here are some illustrations of AI applications in ultrasound imaging:

- **AI-Powered Image Acquisition:** Illustration showing an ultrasound probe guided by AI to the optimal position for capturing high-quality images.

- **Automated Image Analysis:** Diagram depicting the automated analysis of a fetal ultrasound image with AI identifying and measuring key structures.
- **Real-Time AI Assistance:** Image showing AI providing real-time feedback during an echocardiography exam, highlighting areas of interest.
- **Automated Reporting:** Flowchart illustrating the process of AI generating a preliminary report based on ultrasound image analysis.

The integration of AI into ultrasound imaging represents a significant advancement in medical diagnostics. By enhancing image acquisition, automating analysis, and optimizing workflows, AI has the potential to transform ultrasound practices, leading to improved diagnostic accuracy, efficiency, and patient outcomes. As the technology continues to evolve, collaboration between clinicians, researchers, and technologists will be essential to overcome challenges and unlock the full potential of AI in ultrasound imaging.

AI Applications in Positron Emission Tomography (PET)

Positron Emission Tomography (PET) is an advanced imaging technique that provides valuable insights into the metabolic processes within the body. By detecting the gamma rays emitted from a positron-emitting radiotracer injected into the patient, PET scans can visualize functional processes, making them a critical tool in oncology, neurology, and cardiology. The integration of Artificial Intelligence (AI) into PET imaging is transforming this field, enhancing image quality, improving diagnostic accuracy, and optimizing workflows. This chapter delves into the various applications of AI in PET imaging, highlighting advancements, methodologies, and future prospects.

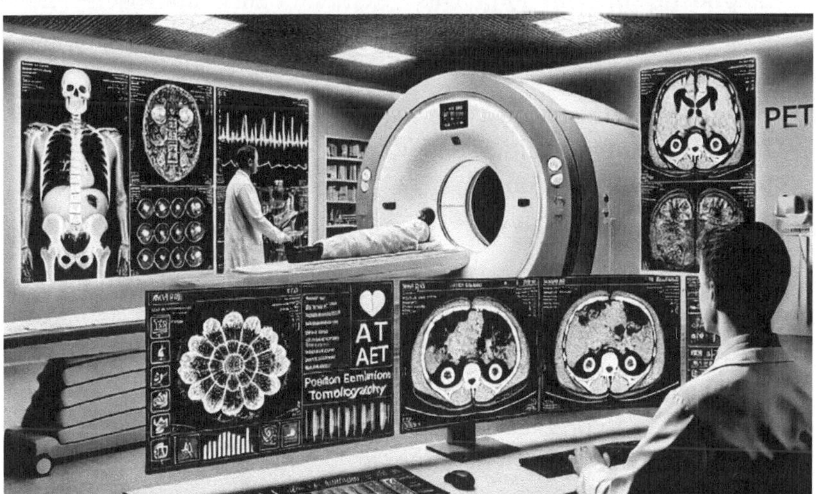

Figure 6.8: *Artificial Intelligence used in PET scans*

The Role of AI in PET Imaging

AI, particularly through machine learning (ML) and deep learning (DL), is enhancing PET imaging in several key areas:

- **Image Reconstruction and Enhancement:**
    - **Accelerated Image Reconstruction**: Traditional PET image reconstruction can be time-consuming and computationally intensive. AI algorithms, such as deep learning models, can accelerate this process, producing high-quality images faster and more efficiently.
    - **Noise Reduction and Resolution Enhancement**: AI techniques can improve the quality of PET images by reducing noise and enhancing resolution. This leads to clearer and more detailed images, which are crucial for accurate diagnosis and assessment.
- **Image Analysis and Quantification:**
    - **Automated Lesion Detection and Segmentation**: AI can automate the detection and segmentation of lesions in PET images. This is particularly useful in oncology, where accurate identification and quantification of tumors are essential for treatment planning and monitoring.
    - **Quantitative Analysis**: AI algorithms can provide quantitative measurements of metabolic activity, such as standardized uptake values (SUVs), enabling precise assessment of disease severity and progression.
- **Multi-Modality Integration:**
    - **Fusion with Other Imaging Modalities**: AI can integrate PET data with other imaging modalities, such as CT or MRI, to provide comprehensive diagnostic information. This multi-modality approach enhances the overall diagnostic accuracy and provides a more complete picture of the patient's condition.
    - **Image Registration**: AI can improve the alignment and fusion of images from different modalities, ensuring accurate correlation of anatomical and functional information.
- **Clinical Decision Support:**
    - **Diagnostic Assistance**: AI can assist clinicians in interpreting PET images by providing automated analyses and highlighting areas of concern. This support can lead to more accurate and timely diagnoses.
    - **Prognostic Predictions**: AI can analyze PET data along with other patient information to predict disease outcomes and treatment responses, aiding in personalized treatment planning.

Key Applications of AI in PET Imaging

Here are some key applications of AI in PET imaging:

- **Oncology:**
  - **Tumor Detection and Characterization**: AI-enhanced PET imaging is vital for detecting and characterizing tumors. AI algorithms can accurately segment tumors, measure metabolic activity, and monitor changes over time, aiding in the diagnosis and management of cancer.
  - **Therapy Response Monitoring**: AI can track changes in tumor metabolism and size, providing early indications of treatment efficacy. This allows for timely adjustments to therapy plans.
- **Neurology:**
  - **Neurodegenerative Diseases**: AI can improve the detection and monitoring of neurodegenerative diseases, such as Alzheimer's disease, Parkinson's disease, and multiple sclerosis. By analyzing PET images, AI can identify patterns of abnormal metabolic activity associated with these conditions.
  - **Epilepsy**: AI can assist in the localization of epileptic foci by analyzing PET scans, aiding in the diagnosis and surgical planning for epilepsy patients.
- **Cardiology:**
  - **Myocardial Perfusion Imaging**: AI can enhance the analysis of PET myocardial perfusion images, providing accurate assessments of blood flow and identifying areas of ischemia. This is crucial for diagnosing and managing coronary artery disease.
  - **Cardiac Sarcoidosis**: AI can detect and quantify inflammatory activity in the heart, aiding in the diagnosis and monitoring of cardiac sarcoidosis.

Illustrations

To enhance understanding, here are some illustrations of AI applications in PET imaging:

- **AI-Enhanced Image Reconstruction:** Illustration showing a comparison between traditional PET image reconstruction and AI-enhanced reconstruction, highlighting improvements in image quality and processing speed.
- **Automated Tumor Segmentation:** Diagram depicting the automated segmentation of a tumor in a PET image, with AI highlighting the tumor boundaries and providing quantitative measurements.
- **Multi-Modality Integration:** Image showing the fusion of PET and CT images, with AI ensuring accurate alignment and integration of anatomical and functional data.

- **Clinical Decision Support:** Flowchart illustrating how AI provides diagnostic assistance and prognostic predictions based on PET image analysis.

Conclusion

The advent of Artificial Intelligence (AI) in imaging and diagnostics marks a transformative era in healthcare, bringing unparalleled accuracy, efficiency, and accessibility to medical practices. This chapter has explored the various dimensions of AI integration into imaging and diagnostic processes, highlighting both the technological advancements and the challenges that accompany them.

AI has revolutionized traditional imaging techniques by enhancing image clarity, facilitating real-time analysis, and enabling early detection of diseases with higher precision. Algorithms, particularly those leveraging deep learning, have shown remarkable capabilities in identifying patterns that often elude human eyes, thus supporting radiologists and clinicians in making more informed decisions.

Moreover, AI-driven diagnostic tools have demonstrated significant potential in predicting disease progression and personalizing treatment plans, thereby improving patient outcomes. The integration of AI in telemedicine has also expanded the reach of quality healthcare services to remote and underserved regions, addressing disparities in healthcare access.

To fully harness the potential of AI in medical imaging, healthcare providers, technology developers, and policymakers must actively commit to:

- **Ethical AI Deployment:** Establishing clear guidelines for the ethical use of AI in diagnostics to ensure fairness, accuracy, and patient safety.
- **Data Privacy and Security:** Implementing robust data protection measures and compliance with HIPAA, GDPR, and other global healthcare regulations to maintain patient confidentiality.
- **Bias Mitigation and Transparency:** Conducting regular audits of AI models to identify and mitigate biases, ensuring AI-driven diagnoses are accurate and equitable for all patient populations.
- **Collaborative AI Development:** Encouraging interdisciplinary collaboration between radiologists, clinicians, data scientists, and policymakers to refine AI tools and improve their clinical applicability.
- **Investment in AI Training and Education:** Equipping healthcare professionals with AI literacy, ensuring that medical practitioners understand and effectively utilize AI-assisted diagnostics in patient care.

By embracing responsible and ethical AI adoption, the healthcare industry can maximize the benefits of AI-driven imaging and diagnostics, ultimately leading to earlier disease detection, enhanced precision in treatments, and improved global health outcomes.

In conclusion, the fusion of AI with imaging and diagnostics heralds a new chapter in medical science, characterized by enhanced diagnostic accuracy, personalized patient care, and broader access to healthcare services. As we navigate this dynamic landscape, it is imperative to balance technological advancements with ethical considerations to ensure that AI serves as a catalyst for positive change in global health. The next chapter will provide an overview of the current challenges and limitations of AI in healthcare, and how these challenges are affecting the development and implementation of AI-based healthcare systems.

Points to Remember

- **Enhanced Accuracy**: AI algorithms, especially deep learning models, significantly improve the accuracy of imaging and diagnostics, enabling early detection and precise identification of diseases.
- **Real-Time Analysis**: AI can analyze medical images in real-time, providing immediate feedback and aiding in quicker clinical decision-making.
- **Pattern Recognition**: AI systems excel in recognizing complex patterns within medical images that may be missed by human observers, supporting more accurate diagnoses.
- **Predictive Analytics**: AI-driven tools can predict disease progression and outcomes, helping in the development of personalized treatment plans and improving patient management.
- **Accessibility**: AI integration in telemedicine and remote diagnostics enhances access to quality healthcare for people in remote and underserved areas, reducing healthcare disparities.
- **Efficiency**: Automation of routine tasks through AI reduces the workload on healthcare professionals, allowing them to focus on more critical aspects of patient care.
- **Data Privacy and Security**: The use of AI in healthcare requires stringent measures to protect patient data privacy and ensure secure handling of sensitive information.
- **Algorithmic Bias**: Addressing biases in AI algorithms is crucial to prevent disparities in healthcare outcomes and ensure fair and equitable treatment for all patients.
- **Ethical Considerations**: Ethical use of AI in healthcare involves maintaining transparency, ensuring informed consent, and fostering trust among patients and healthcare providers.

- **Collaboration**: Successful implementation of AI in imaging and diagnostics requires collaboration between technologists, healthcare professionals, and policymakers to overcome challenges and drive innovation.
- **Regulatory Compliance**: Adhering to regulatory standards and guidelines is essential for the safe and effective deployment of AI technologies in healthcare settings.
- **Continuous Learning**: AI systems should be designed for continuous learning and improvement, incorporating new data and evolving medical knowledge to stay current and effective.
- **Patient-Centric Approach**: AI applications should prioritize patient welfare, focusing on enhancing the quality of care and patient outcomes while respecting patient autonomy and rights.

By keeping these points in mind, stakeholders can effectively harness the potential of AI in imaging and diagnostics to revolutionize healthcare delivery and improve global health outcomes.

Chapter 7
Challenges and Limitations of AI in Healthcare

Introduction

Artificial Intelligence (AI) has been a transformative force in various industries, with healthcare being one of the most promising areas for its application. From enhancing diagnostic accuracy to optimizing treatment plans, AI has the potential to revolutionize healthcare delivery. However, the integration of AI into healthcare systems is not without its challenges and limitations. These issues range from technical and ethical concerns to regulatory and societal impacts. This chapter aims to explore the multifaceted challenges and limitations that impede the widespread adoption of AI in healthcare, providing a comprehensive understanding for healthcare professionals, technologists, and policymakers.

Structure

In this chapter, the following topics will be covered:

- Technical Challenges
- Ethical and Privacy Concerns
- Regulatory and Legal Challenges
- Societal and Cultural Challenges
- Economic and Resource Challenges
- Future Outlook and Recommendations

Technical Challenges

High-quality data is the backbone of any effective AI system. When data is incomplete, inconsistent, or unavailable, it poses serious technical challenges–from model inaccuracies to increased processing overhead. These limitations not only compromise performance but also hinder trust, scalability, and real-world applicability.

Importance of High-Quality Data

The effectiveness of AI in healthcare is fundamentally tied to the quality of data used to train its algorithms. AI models, particularly in healthcare, rely on vast amounts of data to identify patterns, make predictions, and suggest treatments. High-quality data is accurate, complete, and representative of the population it is meant to serve. If the data used to train AI systems is inconsistent, incomplete, or biased, the resulting models will likely make incorrect or even harmful predictions.

- **Inconsistent Data:** Data inconsistency occurs when similar data points are recorded differently across various datasets. For instance, medical records from different healthcare institutions may use different terminologies or formats for the same type of information (for example, "*BP*" versus "*Blood Pressure*" or "*Heart Attack*" versus "*Myocardial Infarction*"). These inconsistencies make it harder for AI systems to generalize across different datasets.
- **Incomplete Data:** Missing data is a common issue in healthcare. Patient records may be incomplete due to missing test results, unrecorded treatments, or patients not providing full medical histories. AI models trained on such data may fail to provide accurate predictions, as they are built on partial information. For example, an AI system trained to predict heart disease might produce incorrect results if key factors such as family history or cholesterol levels are missing from the training data.
- **Biased Data:** Bias in data refers to the underrepresentation or overrepresentation of specific populations or conditions. If AI models are trained on biased data, they are likely to make biased predictions. For instance, if a dataset contains mostly information about middle-aged white males, the AI may not perform well when diagnosing diseases in women, children, or minority populations. This bias can lead to inequitable treatment outcomes, potentially exacerbating health disparities.

In healthcare, even minor inaccuracies in predictions can have severe consequences. For example, a misdiagnosis or incorrect treatment recommendation could jeopardize patient safety. Therefore, ensuring the availability of high-quality, comprehensive data is critical for the success of AI applications in healthcare.

Data Silos

Healthcare data is typically spread across multiple institutions, departments, and systems, often resulting in **data silos**–isolated pockets of information that are difficult to access or integrate. This fragmentation creates significant barriers to AI implementation, as it prevents the creation of large, comprehensive datasets that are essential for training robust AI models.

- **Institutional Fragmentation:** Data silos occur because healthcare data is typically collected and stored in different systems depending on the institution, the department, or the technology platform. Hospitals, clinics, laboratories, pharmacies, and insurance companies often maintain separate records. These systems rarely communicate with one another, making it difficult to create unified datasets.
- **Geographical Fragmentation:** Healthcare data may also be siloed across regions or countries due to differences in healthcare systems and regulations. For example, patient data in the European Union may be governed by GDPR regulations, making it challenging to combine with data from the United States governed by HIPAA.
- **Interoperability Issues:** Many healthcare systems are built on legacy software that does not easily integrate with newer technologies. Even when organizations are willing to share data, technical issues such as differing data formats, coding languages, and software platforms make it difficult to merge datasets into a cohesive whole.

Because AI thrives on large, diverse datasets, data silos significantly hinder the development of effective healthcare AI. An AI system trained only on data from one institution or geographic region may not generalize well to other settings. Overcoming this fragmentation is a major challenge and requires improvements in data sharing and interoperability standards within the healthcare sector.

Data Annotation and Labeling

In the realm of **supervised learning**, which is one of the most common forms of machine learning used in healthcare AI, high-quality data annotation and labeling are critical. Data annotation refers to the process of marking or categorizing data to ensure that AI models can learn from it. For example, annotating medical images with labels such as "*tumor*" or "*no tumor*" helps AI models distinguish between cancerous and non-cancerous tissue.

- **Time-Consuming Process:** The process of annotating and labeling medical data, especially in fields such as radiology or pathology, is highly specialized and time-intensive. It often requires trained professionals, such as radiologists or pathologists, to manually label thousands of images or cases. This can slow down the development of AI models and increase the costs associated with creating high-quality datasets.

- **Cost Implications:** High-quality annotation is expensive. It typically involves hiring skilled medical professionals to meticulously label data. In addition to labor costs, organizations may need to invest in infrastructure and tools to ensure proper data labeling. This cost can be prohibitive, especially for smaller healthcare institutions or research groups that lack the financial resources of large hospitals or corporations.
- **Limited Annotated Datasets:** Because of the high cost and effort involved, healthcare often lacks sufficiently large and well-annotated datasets for training AI models. For instance, creating a labeled dataset for diagnosing rare diseases may be especially challenging, as the cases are infrequent and require highly specialized annotation expertise. As a result, AI systems trained on smaller or inadequately annotated datasets may not perform as accurately or reliably as desired.
- **Quality of Annotations:** The quality of annotations is crucial for AI performance. If annotations are inaccurate or inconsistent, the AI model will learn from flawed data and make incorrect predictions. For example, inconsistent labeling of medical images (for example, if one annotator labels a small abnormality as "*benign*" while another labels it as "*malignant*") could confuse the AI system, leading to misdiagnosis when applied in real-world scenarios.

Figure 7.1: *Data Annotation*

One potential solution to the annotation bottleneck is the use of **semi-supervised learning** or **unsupervised learning** models, which require less human-labeled data. Another option is to develop better tools that assist healthcare professionals in labeling data more efficiently. However, these approaches come with their own challenges and limitations, such as the need for high computational power and the risk of reduced model accuracy.

Model Interpretability and Transparency

Model interpretability refers to how easily humans can understand the decisions or predictions made by an AI model. Transparency involves clearly communicating how the model works, what data it uses, and how decisions are made. Together, they help build trust, enable accountability, support debugging, and ensure that AI systems align with ethical and regulatory standards—especially important in sensitive fields like healthcare.

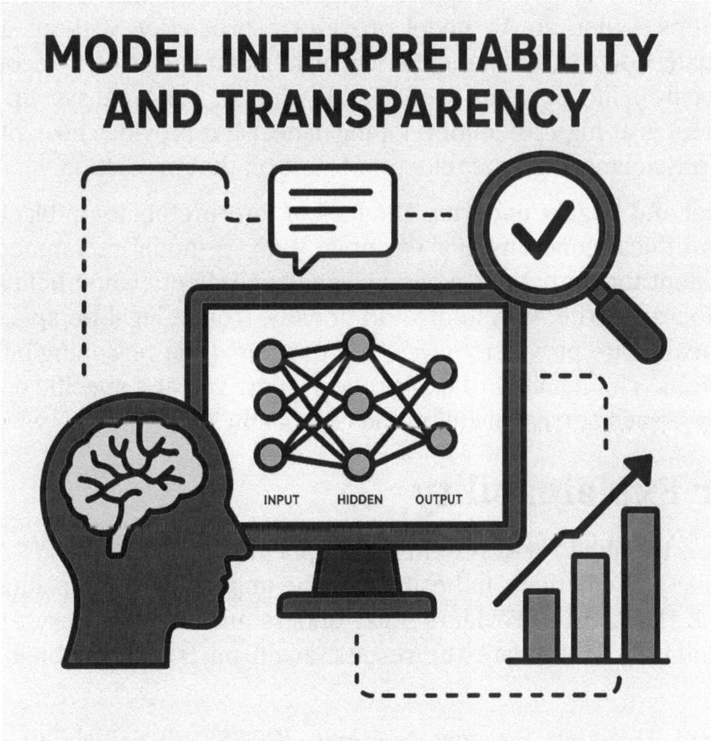

***Figure 7.2**: Model Interpretability and Transparency*

Black Box Models

One of the most significant challenges in deploying AI in healthcare is the issue of **black box models**. These are AI models, particularly those based on deep learning and other advanced machine learning techniques, that make predictions or decisions without offering any insight into how they arrived at those conclusions. Essentially, while these models can provide highly accurate results, the processes and internal logic behind their decision-making are not easily understood, even by experts.

- **Complexity of Deep Learning:** Deep learning models, especially neural networks, are often built with multiple layers of interconnected nodes that perform calculations to arrive at a prediction. Each layer processes data in a way that is not easily interpretable, and as the layers increase, the model's complexity grows exponentially. This complexity makes it nearly impossible to trace how specific input data (such as a patient's symptoms or medical history) leads to an output (such as a diagnosis or treatment recommendation).
- **Risk in Healthcare Contexts:** In the healthcare domain, black box models pose a particularly serious risk. Healthcare professionals rely on clear, understandable explanations for diagnoses and treatments to make informed decisions. When an AI model provides a prediction without a transparent rationale, doctors, and patients may be hesitant to trust the recommendation, especially in life-or-death scenarios. For instance, if an AI system predicts that a patient is at high risk of developing cancer but provides no explanation as to why, physicians might be reluctant to act on that prediction.
- **Ethical and Legal Concerns:** The lack of interpretability in black box models raises ethical concerns. For example, if an AI model recommends a certain treatment and the patient experiences adverse effects, who is held accountable—the doctor or the AI system? Additionally, from a legal perspective, patients and healthcare providers have a right to know the reasoning behind medical decisions. The inability to explain how AI arrived at a specific conclusion can lead to issues of trust, liability, and responsibility.

Need for Explainability

Explainability is the ability of AI systems to provide human-understandable reasons for their decisions or predictions. In healthcare, the importance of explainability cannot be overstated. Healthcare providers must understand how an AI system arrived at its recommendation to validate the results, avoid mistakes, and build trust in the technology.

- **Clinical Decision Support Systems (CDSS):** Explainability is especially crucial in CDSS, which help doctors and healthcare providers make better decisions. For AI systems used in diagnostics, treatment planning, or patient monitoring, clinicians need to know how the system analyzed the data and arrived at a conclusion. For example, in medical imaging, an AI might flag a region in an MRI scan as potentially cancerous. To trust this prediction, a radiologist would want to know why the AI highlighted that region–whether it identified specific abnormal patterns, tissue density differences, or other visual markers.

- **Regulatory Compliance:** Explainability also plays a role in complying with regulatory standards. In many regions, healthcare providers are legally obligated to justify the medical treatments and diagnoses they provide to patients. AI systems that are transparent and explainable can help meet these regulatory requirements, whereas black box models can create legal vulnerabilities. For instance, the European Union's General Data Protection Regulation (GDPR) includes a *"right to explanation,"* where individuals are entitled to explanations about automated decisions that affect them. This right directly impacts AI systems used in healthcare.
- **Gaining Clinician Trust:** Explainability is key to getting healthcare providers to adopt and trust AI. Doctors are trained to rely on clinical evidence, medical reasoning, and patient history when making decisions. If AI can show clear, evidence-based explanations for its decisions, doctors are more likely to integrate AI into their clinical workflows. For example, if an AI system for diagnosing pneumonia highlights specific radiological features in a chest X-ray that match established medical criteria, clinicians are more likely to trust and use the system.

Trust in AI Systems

The ultimate goal of AI systems in healthcare is to assist and enhance human decision-making, but trust is a major barrier to adoption. **Trust** in AI systems is built on transparency, reliability, and the ability to understand how the system works. If healthcare professionals and patients cannot trust the decisions made by AI, its usefulness diminishes significantly.

- **Trust Through Consistency:** One way to build trust in AI is through consistent, reliable performance. If an AI system consistently delivers accurate predictions that align with clinical expertise and outcomes, healthcare professionals are more likely to trust and adopt it. However, without transparency into how the AI system operates, this trust may remain superficial and fragile.
- **Human-AI Collaboration:** AI is not meant to replace doctors but to augment their decision-making capabilities. Trust is critical for effective human-AI collaboration in healthcare. If AI systems are trusted, they can serve as valuable tools to provide a second opinion, flag potential oversights, or offer suggestions for treatments that doctors might not have considered. But when trust is lacking, doctors may ignore AI recommendations or rely solely on their judgment, undermining the potential benefits of AI integration.

Challenges in Achieving Explainability and Transparency

Achieving explainability and transparency in AI systems, especially in the healthcare sector, presents several challenges.

- **Complexity of Models versus Simplicity of Explanations:** There is often a trade-off between the complexity of AI models and their explainability. The most accurate models, such as deep learning models with many layers, tend to be the least explainable. Simpler models, such as decision trees or logistic regression, are much more transparent but may not offer the same level of accuracy or predictive power as more complex models. This trade-off poses a dilemma for healthcare practitioners: should they prioritize explainability over accuracy, or vice versa?
- **Time and Resource Constraints:** Developing explainable AI systems often requires additional resources, time, and expertise. Creating models that can explain their decision-making processes may involve designing interpretable algorithms, developing visualization tools, and building user interfaces that communicate how predictions were made. These additional layers of development can slow down the deployment of AI systems in healthcare.
- **Balancing Interpretability and Performance:** Healthcare AI models that prioritize interpretability might sacrifice performance in terms of speed or predictive power. For instance, if an AI system is optimized to provide real-time decision support during surgeries, adding explainability features could introduce delays or reduce its ability to process data quickly. In critical, time-sensitive medical situations, healthcare providers may prefer a fast, accurate system over one that offers detailed explanations.

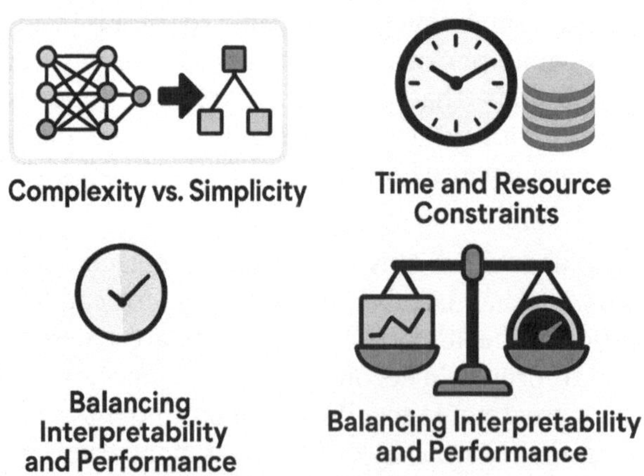

***Figure 7.3**: Challenges in Transparency*

Integration with Existing Systems

The integration of AI into existing healthcare systems is a complex and multifaceted challenge. Healthcare institutions often have well-established processes and technologies, many of which are not designed to accommodate AI's sophisticated needs. Successfully embedding AI into these systems without disrupting care delivery requires overcoming several key barriers.

Legacy Systems

Many healthcare organizations still use outdated systems that are not compatible with modern AI technologies.

- **Compatibility Issues:** AI models require large datasets, computational power, and modern data infrastructures that legacy systems cannot support. For instance, an AI model designed to predict patient outcomes based on electronic health records (EHRs) may require data to be stored in specific formats or processed using modern cloud-based systems. Legacy EHR systems, which may have been implemented a decade ago, are often incompatible with these newer technologies, making AI integration difficult.
- **Inability to Handle Advanced Workflows:** Legacy systems were not built with the flexibility required for AI workflows, such as real-time data analysis, continuous learning, or model updates. This inflexibility limits the ability of AI to deliver its full potential in clinical settings. For example, a hospital's old patient management system may not allow AI to integrate seamlessly and provide instant recommendations for treatment based on up-to-date patient data.
- **Costs and Resources Required for Upgrading:** Upgrading legacy systems is expensive and time-consuming. Many healthcare organizations, especially smaller clinics or rural hospitals, may not have the financial resources or technical expertise needed to replace or update these systems to accommodate AI. As a result, they continue to rely on older technologies that limit the scope and effectiveness of AI.
- **Security Risks:** Legacy systems may also pose significant security risks. They often lack the robust security features of modern systems, leaving them vulnerable to cyberattacks. Integrating AI into these systems without addressing these vulnerabilities can expose sensitive patient data to breaches, leading to privacy violations and regulatory non-compliance.

Interoperability

The lack of standardized data formats and interfaces poses a significant challenge in integrating AI into existing healthcare infrastructures.

- **Fragmented Healthcare Systems:** Healthcare data is stored across multiple departments and organizations (hospitals, clinics, pharmacies, and insurance companies), each using its own system and standards. For example, a radiology department might use one system for imaging, while the pathology department uses a different system for lab results, and these systems may not "*talk*" to each other. AI models that require data from multiple sources, such as a patient's imaging scans, medical history, and lab results, may struggle to access and integrate this fragmented data.
- **Lack of Data Standards:** A major barrier to interoperability is the lack of standardized data formats across the healthcare industry. While initiatives such as Health Level Seven International (HL7) and Fast Healthcare Interoperability Resources (FHIR) are working to standardize data exchange, adoption has been inconsistent. AI systems that are designed to work with one data format may not be able to interpret or process data from another format, further complicating integration efforts.
- **Data Silos and Vendor Lock-In:** Many healthcare organizations are locked into proprietary systems provided by specific vendors, which often do not support data exchange with other systems. This vendor lock-in leads to the creation of data silos, where important patient information is isolated in one part of the healthcare system and inaccessible to other departments or AI tools. For example, if an AI model requires patient records from both a hospital's EHR system and an external laboratory's results, the lack of interoperability may prevent the AI from accessing both datasets.
- **Time and Resource Constraints:** To achieve interoperability, healthcare organizations often need to invest in custom interfaces, middleware, or data transformation tools that can bridge the gaps between disparate systems. This requires both financial investment and technical expertise, which may not be readily available in all healthcare settings.

Workflow Disruption

AI implementation can disrupt existing workflows, leading to resistance from healthcare staff.

- **Introducing New Processes:** AI tools often require healthcare providers to adapt to new ways of working. For example, an AI system used to assist in diagnosis may require doctors to input patient data in specific formats, interpret AI-generated insights, or follow new protocols based on AI recommendations.

This additional workload or change in process can be viewed as a disruption, especially if it does not fit seamlessly into the existing workflow.

- **Learning Curve and Resistance:** Implementing AI tools often requires healthcare professionals to undergo training, which can be time-consuming. Many healthcare providers are already under immense pressure due to staffing shortages, high patient loads, and time constraints. Introducing a new AI system can be perceived as an additional burden, especially if it involves learning new software, changing how they interact with patient data, or trusting AI-generated recommendations over their own expertise. This may lead to resistance from staff who are more comfortable with traditional methods.
- **Fear of Job Displacement:** One of the psychological barriers to AI adoption in healthcare is the fear that AI might replace certain roles, particularly those related to data analysis or diagnostics. For example, radiologists might worry that AI systems for medical imaging analysis could reduce the need for their expertise. This fear of job displacement can create resistance to AI adoption, even when the AI is intended to augment, not replace, human decision-making.
- **Impact on Patient Interaction:** AI systems may also change how healthcare professionals interact with patients. For instance, if doctors spend more time inputting data into AI systems or reviewing AI-generated recommendations, they may have less time for direct patient interaction. This shift could lead to dissatisfaction among healthcare providers who value the personal aspects of patient care and among patients who may feel their interactions are becoming more impersonal.
- **Alignment with Clinical Workflows:** AI tools must be integrated in a way that aligns with existing clinical workflows. Poorly integrated AI can cause inefficiencies or disrupt the flow of patient care. For example, if an AI tool provides diagnostic suggestions that don't fit within the existing process for making treatment decisions, doctors may be reluctant to use it. To avoid such disruptions, AI systems must be designed to work in tandem with the established protocols and processes of healthcare professionals.

Scalability and Generalization

Scalability refers to an AI system's ability to handle growing amounts of data, users, or complexity without performance loss. Generalization is the model's capacity to perform well on unseen data beyond the training environment. Together, these qualities are essential for deploying AI solutions across diverse settings, populations, and real-world conditions—ensuring that models remain robust, efficient, and reliable at scale.

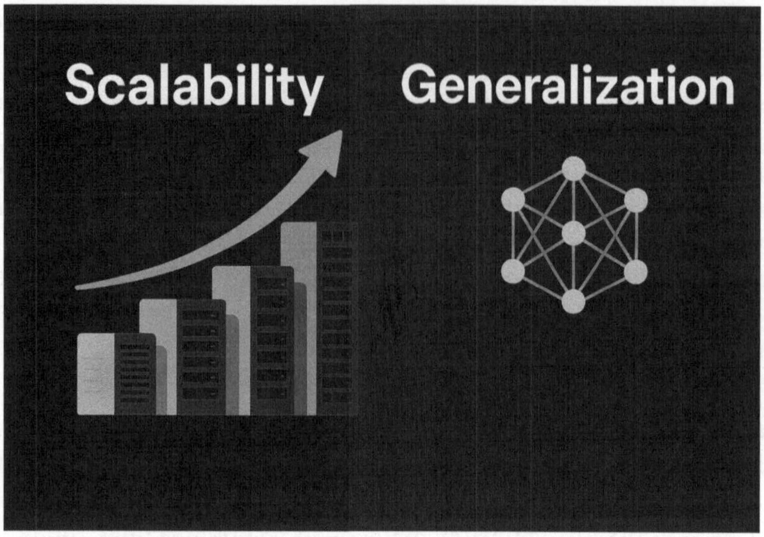

***Figure 7.4**: Scalability and Generalization*

Model Generalization

AI models trained on specific datasets may not perform well when applied to different populations or settings.

What is Generalization? Generalization is the ability of an AI model to apply the knowledge it has learned from a training dataset to new, unseen data. In healthcare, this means that an AI model developed in one hospital, or trained on one group of patients, should be able to perform well when deployed in other hospitals, regions, or patient populations. However, this is often difficult to achieve due to variations in patient demographics, healthcare practices, and data quality across different settings.

- **Diversity in Healthcare Data:** The generalization challenge arises because healthcare data is inherently diverse. Patient populations vary significantly across regions, countries, and even within different healthcare institutions. For example, a model trained to detect pneumonia in a population of middle-aged adults in a developed country may not generalize well when used in a rural clinic in a developing country, where patients might have different risk factors, comorbidities, or access to medical care.
- **Overfitting to Training Data:** AI models are prone to **overfitting**, where the model learns patterns that are specific to the training data but not applicable to new data. This is particularly problematic in healthcare, where patient data can be noisy, incomplete, or biased. For instance, if an AI model is trained primarily on data from patients with specific conditions (such as heart disease in older adults), it may not perform well on younger patients or those with different comorbidities.

- **Bias in Training Data:** If the dataset used to train an AI model is not representative of the broader patient population, the model may produce biased or inaccurate predictions when applied to other groups. For example, an AI model trained on predominantly male patients may not generalize well to female patients, leading to incorrect diagnoses or treatment recommendations for women. This lack of generalization can exacerbate health disparities and reduce the reliability of AI systems in real-world settings.
- **Challenges with Rare Diseases:** Generalization is particularly difficult in the case of rare diseases. AI models typically require large amounts of data to learn patterns, but data for rare diseases is often limited. As a result, AI systems trained on small, specific datasets may struggle to generalize and provide accurate diagnoses or treatments for rare conditions, which further limits the scalability of these models.
- **Differences in Healthcare Systems and Practices:** Variations in healthcare practices between institutions and countries can also affect generalization. For instance, diagnostic protocols, treatment approaches, and medical equipment may differ between hospitals or regions. An AI model trained in a well-resourced urban hospital may not generalize to a rural clinic with fewer resources or different medical protocols. This lack of generalization can make it difficult to deploy AI solutions universally across healthcare systems.

What is Scalability? Scalability refers to an AI system's ability to handle increasing workloads, expand to larger datasets, or be implemented across multiple healthcare settings without a loss in performance or efficiency. In healthcare, scaling AI models from a single department or hospital to a nationwide or global system is a complex process. It requires not only technical capability but also infrastructure, resources, and policy alignment.

- **Infrastructure Requirements:** AI models require substantial computational power, particularly for tasks such as medical imaging analysis, natural language processing, or predictive analytics. This computational demand necessitates robust IT infrastructure, including high-performance servers, cloud computing capabilities, and fast data processing systems. Large hospitals and academic medical centers may have the necessary infrastructure, but smaller clinics, rural hospitals, or healthcare facilities in developing countries often do not, making it difficult to scale AI solutions across the healthcare industry.
- **Cost of Scaling AI:** Deploying AI solutions at scale comes with significant costs, including purchasing the necessary hardware, software, and data storage systems. In addition, scaling AI requires investments in data processing, security measures, and training for healthcare staff. For smaller healthcare institutions or those with limited budgets, these costs can be prohibitive, hindering the widespread adoption of AI.

- **Data Volume and Quality:** As AI systems scale, they must process larger volumes of data. While more data can lead to more accurate predictions, it also introduces challenges. Large datasets are often more complex and may contain errors, inconsistencies, or missing information. Scaling AI systems to handle this volume of data requires sophisticated data management and preprocessing tools, which may not be available in smaller or less-resourced healthcare settings.
- **Cloud and Edge Computing:** One potential solution for scalability is the use of **cloud computing** and **edge computing** technologies. Cloud computing allows AI models to be deployed and accessed remotely, reducing the need for local hardware and computational resources. Edge computing, on the other hand, allows AI processing to happen closer to the source of the data (such as medical devices or local servers), reducing the need for large-scale data transmission and central processing. However, implementing these technologies requires investment in reliable internet connectivity and advanced data processing tools, which may not be feasible in all healthcare settings.
- **Regulatory and Privacy Constraints:** Scaling AI across different regions or countries involves navigating various regulatory frameworks and privacy laws. For example, in Europe, AI systems must comply with GDPR, while in the U.S., they must adhere to HIPAA. These regulations often require that patient data be stored and processed in specific ways, which can complicate the scaling of AI solutions across borders. Ensuring compliance with diverse legal and regulatory requirements is a significant barrier to scalability.
- **Customizing AI for Different Settings:** Scaling AI also involves customizing the system to fit the needs of different healthcare institutions. For example, a model that works well in a large urban hospital may need to be adapted for use in a rural clinic with fewer resources and a different patient population. This customization process can be time-consuming and costly, limiting the scalability of AI across various healthcare environments.

The Importance of Continuous Learning

Healthcare is a rapidly evolving field, with new medical knowledge, treatments, and technologies constantly emerging. AI systems, particularly those used for diagnosis, treatment recommendations, or patient monitoring, must adapt to this changing environment. **Static models**, which are trained once and not updated, quickly become outdated and less effective. For AI to remain accurate and relevant, it must be continuously trained on new, up-to-date data.

- **Dynamic Data in Healthcare:** Healthcare data is dynamic, meaning that new patient records, diagnostic techniques, and treatment outcomes are continuously generated. For AI systems to stay relevant, they must be trained on this new data to ensure they reflect current clinical practices. For example, an AI model used to predict heart disease risk might need to incorporate new findings about risk factors, treatment options, or changes in patient demographics over time.

- **Data Drift:** Over time, the data that AI systems are trained on may no longer represent the current population or clinical environment. This phenomenon, known as **data drift**, can cause the model's performance to degrade. For instance, if an AI system was trained on data from a predominantly young and healthy population but is later used in a population with higher rates of chronic illness, the model's predictions may become inaccurate. Continuously updating the model with new data helps mitigate this risk.
- **Challenges of Continuous Training:** Continuously training AI models requires ongoing access to high-quality data, computational resources, and expertise. This is not always feasible for smaller healthcare institutions or those with limited IT infrastructure. Additionally, updating AI systems involves revalidating their performance to ensure they continue to meet regulatory and ethical standards, which can be resource-intensive.
- **Cost and Resource Implications:** Regularly updating AI systems incurs costs related to data collection, model retraining, and software updates. For healthcare organizations with limited budgets, maintaining and updating AI systems may not be sustainable. This can lead to outdated models being used in clinical practice, which could compromise patient care.
- **Real-World Data vs. Training Data:** AI systems trained in controlled environments or academic settings may struggle to generalize when exposed to real-world clinical data. Real-world data is often noisier, more incomplete, or less standardized than the curated datasets used in AI training. As AI systems are deployed in real-world settings, they need to adapt to these variations by continuously learning from real-time patient data.

AI System Maintenance and Updating

AI systems require continuous maintenance and updates to stay relevant, accurate, and secure over time. This includes monitoring performance, retraining models with new data, fixing bugs, and adapting to changes in user behavior or regulations. Ongoing updates ensure that the AI system evolves with real-world dynamics and maintains its effectiveness in changing environments.

Dynamic Nature of Healthcare Data

Healthcare is an ever-evolving field with constant advancements in medical research, diagnostic techniques, treatment protocols, and patient care standards. As new diseases emerge, medical practices change, and patient demographics shift, AI systems must adapt to these changes to remain effective. For instance, new guidelines for managing chronic diseases such as diabetes or hypertension may emerge, and AI models must be updated to reflect these changes to provide accurate treatment recommendations.

- **Adapting to New Knowledge:** Medical research is advancing rapidly, with new discoveries being made regularly. AI models, which often rely on historical data to make predictions or diagnoses, need to be updated with this new knowledge to stay current. For example, when new medications or therapies are introduced, AI systems need to incorporate this information into their decision-making algorithms to ensure they recommend the most up-to-date treatments.
- **Handling Data Drift:** Over time, the characteristics of the patient population may change, which can affect the performance of AI models. For example, if an AI system was trained on data from a specific patient demographic or region, it might not perform as accurately when used in a different context, such as a new region or among a different population group. This phenomenon, known as **data drift**, can lead to decreased model accuracy and effectiveness. Regular updates to the model are essential to ensure it adapts to the changing data landscape.
- **COVID-19 as a Case Study:** The COVID-19 pandemic highlighted the need for AI systems to adapt quickly. When the pandemic emerged, many AI models in healthcare were not trained to recognize COVID-19 symptoms or predict disease progression. Rapid updates and retraining of AI systems were necessary to incorporate data related to the virus, its symptoms, and effective treatment protocols. This illustrates the importance of continuous learning and updating AI systems to handle unforeseen medical challenges.

Financial Costs

The maintenance and updating of AI systems can be costly, particularly for smaller healthcare institutions with limited budgets. While the initial implementation of AI might involve significant investment, the ongoing costs of keeping the system up-to-date can be even higher. These costs include infrastructure upgrades, hiring or training staff, and ensuring compliance with regulations.

- **Infrastructure Costs:** AI models require considerable computing power and data storage, which means that healthcare organizations must continuously invest in upgrading their IT infrastructure to support AI. This includes not only powerful servers and cloud storage but also the tools needed to manage and update AI models. If the infrastructure is not maintained and improved, the performance of AI systems can degrade over time.
- **Hiring and Training Specialized Personnel:** Maintaining AI systems requires a team of skilled professionals, including data scientists, AI engineers, IT

specialists, and clinical experts, to monitor performance, identify issues, and implement updates. In many cases, healthcare organizations need to invest in training their staff to manage and interact with AI systems effectively. Hiring or contracting AI experts can be expensive, and smaller institutions may struggle to find the necessary talent.

- **Integration Costs:** AI systems must be integrated into existing healthcare workflows and technologies, and this integration needs to be maintained over time. As AI systems evolve and require updates, the process of ensuring they work seamlessly with other clinical systems (such as electronic health records, billing software, or medical devices) can be resource-intensive. If not properly managed, these updates can lead to disruptions in clinical workflows, causing inefficiencies or errors in patient care.
- **Compliance and Regulatory Updates:** AI systems in healthcare must comply with various regulations (for example, HIPAA, GDPR). As these regulations evolve, AI models need to be updated to ensure compliance. This requires not only technical updates but also a thorough understanding of legal frameworks, which adds to the resource burden. Failure to comply with regulations can lead to legal penalties and damage to the healthcare provider's reputation.

Fast-Paced AI Innovation

AI technology is advancing at a rapid pace, with new algorithms, models, and techniques emerging frequently. What was considered cutting-edge AI technology just a few years ago can quickly become outdated. In healthcare, this is particularly challenging because outdated AI systems may provide less accurate or reliable predictions, potentially putting patient safety at risk.

- **New AI Models and Techniques:** Advances in AI, such as new machine learning algorithms or deep learning techniques, offer improved performance in areas such as medical imaging, disease prediction, and patient monitoring. Healthcare providers using older AI systems may find that their models are no longer as accurate or efficient as newer systems. For example, newer AI models may be better at detecting rare diseases or processing large datasets in real-time, making older models obsolete in these contexts.
- **Regular System Upgrades:** To avoid obsolescence, AI systems need to be updated regularly with the latest technology and methodologies. This often requires replacing or upgrading the underlying software and hardware that power these systems. Failing to do so can result in AI models that are slow, inaccurate, or unable to handle modern healthcare challenges. For instance, a diagnostic AI system that has not been updated to account for new diagnostic methods may lag behind human clinicians in terms of accuracy.

- **Vendor Dependency and Lock-In:** Many healthcare organizations rely on AI systems provided by third-party vendors. As AI technology evolves, these vendors may release updated versions of their systems or discontinue support for older versions. This can create a situation where healthcare providers are locked into using a specific vendor's AI system, even if better options become available. Vendor lock-in can make it difficult for organizations to switch to newer, more advanced AI systems without significant disruption or cost.
- **Adapting to New Healthcare Protocols:** AI systems must also keep pace with evolving healthcare protocols. For example, changes in treatment guidelines, diagnostic criteria, or best practices for managing specific diseases must be incorporated into AI systems to ensure they provide relevant recommendations. An AI system that does not update in line with these new protocols risks becoming obsolete or even harmful if it continues to provide outdated advice.

***Figure** 7.5: Fast-Paced AI Innovation*

Monitoring and Performance Evaluation

Ensuring AI systems continue to deliver accurate and safe outcomes requires ongoing monitoring and evaluation.

Performance Monitoring: AI models in healthcare must be continuously monitored to ensure they perform as expected. Healthcare environments are dynamic, and the conditions in which AI systems operate can change, affecting their accuracy and reliability. For example, changes in patient populations, clinical practices, or the types of diseases being treated can all impact the performance of an AI model.

- **Real-Time Monitoring:** Many AI systems, particularly those used in critical applications such as diagnostics or treatment recommendations, require real-time monitoring to detect any deviations in performance. If an AI model begins to produce inaccurate predictions or fails to meet clinical standards, healthcare providers need to intervene quickly. For example, an AI system used in radiology must be regularly assessed to ensure it correctly identifies tumors in medical images. Failure to monitor performance can lead to incorrect diagnoses and harm patient outcomes.
- **Evaluating Accuracy Over Time:** As AI models age, their accuracy may decline, especially if they are not updated with new data. For instance, an AI model trained on a dataset from five years ago may not perform well when applied to today's patients, whose demographics or health conditions may have changed. Regular evaluation and testing of AI models using updated datasets are essential to maintaining high levels of accuracy and safety.
- **Feedback Loops for Continuous Improvement:** One way to ensure the continuous improvement of AI systems is through **feedback loops**. In healthcare, feedback loops involve regularly updating AI models based on new data and feedback from clinicians and patients. For example, if a clinician notices that an AI system is consistently providing inaccurate diagnoses for a particular group of patients, they can report this to the system's developers, who can then retrain the model with additional data to improve its performance.

Ethical and Privacy Concerns

As AI becomes increasingly integrated into healthcare, it brings not only opportunities but also critical ethical and privacy concerns. From protecting sensitive patient data to addressing algorithmic bias and ensuring informed consent, the responsible use of AI requires thoughtful design, transparency, and accountability. Navigating these challenges is essential to building trust, safeguarding patient rights, and delivering equitable, patient-centered care.

Patient Data Privacy

- **Sensitive Information:** Healthcare data contains highly sensitive information, making data privacy a critical concern.
- **Data Breaches:** The risk of data breaches increases with the digitization of healthcare records, posing threats to patient confidentiality.
- **Compliance with Regulations:** Healthcare organizations must comply with strict regulations, such as GDPR and HIPAA, which govern data privacy and security.

Bias in AI Algorithms

- **Algorithmic Bias:** AI algorithms can inherit biases from the data they are trained on, leading to unequal treatment outcomes for different patient groups.
- **Impact on Health Equity:** Bias in AI systems can exacerbate existing health disparities, particularly for marginalized populations.
- **Mitigating Bias:** It is essential to develop strategies for detecting and mitigating bias in AI models to ensure fair and equitable healthcare delivery.

Consent and Autonomy

- **Informed Consent:** Patients must be fully informed about how AI is used in their care, including the potential risks and benefits.
- **Autonomy in Decision-Making:** The use of AI in healthcare raises questions about patient autonomy and the extent to which AI should influence treatment decisions.
- **Transparency in AI Use:** Clear communication with patients about the role of AI in their care is crucial to maintaining trust.

Accountability and Liability

- **Who is Responsible?** The question of accountability in AI-driven healthcare decisions is complex, involving multiple stakeholders, including developers, healthcare providers, and organizations.
- **Legal Implications:** Determining liability in cases where AI systems fail or make errors is a significant challenge.
- **Frameworks for Accountability:** Developing legal and ethical frameworks to address accountability in AI-driven healthcare is essential.

Ethical Dilemmas in AI-Driven Decisions

- **Moral and Ethical Considerations:** AI systems may be faced with ethical dilemmas, such as prioritizing patients in resource-constrained environments.
- **Balancing Human and AI Judgment:** Determining the appropriate balance between human judgment and AI recommendations is an ongoing ethical challenge.
- **Patient-Centered Care:** Ensuring that AI systems align with the principles of patient-centered care is crucial for ethical AI implementation.

Regulatory and Legal Challenges

The integration of AI into healthcare presents a range of regulatory and legal challenges that must be addressed to ensure safe, ethical, and lawful deployment. From navigating fragmented regulatory frameworks and protecting intellectual property to addressing liability in case of AI errors, the legal landscape remains complex and evolving. Additionally, cross-border data sharing and jurisdictional conflicts further complicate global collaboration. Establishing clear, harmonized, and forward-looking legal standards is crucial for unlocking the full potential of AI in healthcare.

- **Regulatory Frameworks and Standards**
  - **Lack of Standardization:** The absence of standardized regulations for AI in healthcare creates uncertainty for developers and healthcare providers.
  - **Regulatory Approvals:** Obtaining regulatory approval for AI-based healthcare solutions can be a lengthy and complex process.
  - **Harmonizing Regulations:** The need for harmonized regulations across different jurisdictions is critical for the global deployment of AI in healthcare.
- **Intellectual Property Rights**
  - **AI-Generated Innovations:** Determining ownership and intellectual property rights for innovations generated by AI systems is a complex issue.
  - **Patentability of AI Solutions:** The patentability of AI-driven healthcare solutions is still a gray area, with ongoing debates about what constitutes a patentable invention.
  - **Protecting AI Innovations:** Developers need to navigate the legal landscape to protect their AI innovations while ensuring compliance with healthcare regulations.
- **Liability and Malpractice Issues**
  - **AI Errors and Malpractice:** The potential for AI systems to make errors raises questions about liability and malpractice in healthcare.
  - **Legal Precedents:** The lack of legal precedents for AI-related malpractice cases creates uncertainty for healthcare providers and patients.
  - **Risk Management:** Healthcare organizations must develop strategies to manage the risks associated with AI-driven care, including liability insurance and legal safeguards.
- **Cross-Border Data Sharing and Jurisdictional Conflicts**
  - **Global Collaboration:** The global nature of AI development and healthcare requires cross-border data sharing, which can lead to jurisdictional conflicts.
  - **Data Sovereignty:** Different countries have varying laws regarding data sovereignty, which can complicate international collaborations.
  - **Resolving Conflicts:** Developing international agreements and frameworks to address jurisdictional conflicts is essential for the future of AI in healthcare.

Societal and Cultural Challenges

The adoption of AI in healthcare is not just a technical endeavor–it also involves navigating deep-rooted societal and cultural dynamics. Trust, public perception, and acceptance play a pivotal role in how AI systems are received. Additionally, issues like job displacement, access inequality, and cultural insensitivity can hinder equitable implementation. Addressing these challenges through inclusive design, public education, and cultural adaptation is essential for ensuring that AI enhances healthcare for all communities, not just a few.

- **Acceptance and Trust in AI**
  - **Public Perception:** The public's perception of AI in healthcare is shaped by factors such as media representation, personal experiences, and cultural attitudes.
  - **Building Trust:** Establishing trust in AI systems is critical for their successful adoption in healthcare.
  - **Addressing Misinformation:** Combating misinformation and educating the public about the benefits and risks of AI in healthcare is essential.
- **Impact on Healthcare Workforce**
  - **Job Displacement:** The automation of certain tasks by AI could lead to job displacement in the healthcare sector.
  - **Reskilling and Upskilling:** Healthcare professionals need to be reskilled and upskilled to work alongside AI systems effectively.
  - **Changing Roles:** The integration of AI may lead to changes in the roles and responsibilities of healthcare workers, requiring adaptation and flexibility.
- **Digital Divide and Access Inequality (continued)**
  - **Over-Reliance on Infrastructure:** AI technologies often rely on high-quality digital infrastructure, such as internet access and computing resources, which may be lacking in rural or underdeveloped regions.
  - **Healthcare Disparities:** The unequal distribution of AI technologies can exacerbate existing healthcare disparities, leaving marginalized communities with limited access to advanced healthcare solutions.
  - **Strategies for Inclusivity:** Policymakers and healthcare providers must work together to ensure that AI-driven healthcare solutions are accessible to all, regardless of geographic or socioeconomic barriers.
- **Cultural Sensitivity in AI Applications**
  - **Cultural Variability:** Healthcare practices and expectations vary across cultures, and AI systems must be designed with cultural sensitivity in mind.

- **Language and Communication Barriers:** AI systems must be capable of understanding and responding to the diverse linguistic and cultural needs of patients to avoid miscommunication.
- **Tailoring AI to Local Contexts:** Developing AI solutions that are adaptable to different cultural and societal contexts is crucial for their successful implementation.

Economic and Resource Challenges

Implementing AI in healthcare demands substantial economic investment and strategic resource planning. From the high initial costs of adoption to the long-term financial commitment for maintenance and updates, these technologies can strain budgets—especially in resource-constrained settings. Measuring ROI, allocating funds amidst competing priorities, and managing dependencies on technology vendors further complicate decision-making. Addressing these challenges is crucial to ensure that AI enhances healthcare delivery without compromising sustainability or equity.

- **Cost of AI Implementation**
  - **Initial Investment:** Implementing AI systems in healthcare requires significant upfront investment in technology, infrastructure, and training.
  - **High Cost of AI Technologies:** Advanced AI technologies, such as machine learning platforms and cloud computing services, can be prohibitively expensive for many healthcare organizations, particularly in low-income settings.
  - **Long-Term Financial Commitment:** Maintaining and updating AI systems requires ongoing financial resources, making it challenging for healthcare providers to sustain these technologies over the long term.
- **Return on Investment (ROI)**
  - **Measuring ROI:** It can be difficult to measure the return on investment for AI technologies in healthcare, particularly when the benefits may not be immediately visible or quantifiable.
  - **Balancing Costs and Benefits:** Healthcare providers must balance the cost of implementing AI systems with the potential benefits, such as improved patient outcomes and operational efficiency.
  - **Realizing Long-Term Benefits:** While AI can offer significant long-term benefits, such as reduced costs and improved patient care, these benefits may take time to materialize, creating financial uncertainty.
- **Resource Allocation and Prioritization**
  - **Competing Priorities:** Healthcare organizations must prioritize their resources and decide whether to allocate funds to AI technologies over

other pressing healthcare needs, such as staffing, medical equipment, and patient care.

 - **Opportunity Costs:** Investing in AI may come at the expense of other critical areas of healthcare, potentially leading to difficult trade-offs.
 - **Strategic Resource Planning:** Effective resource planning is essential to ensure that AI investments align with the broader goals of healthcare organizations and contribute to overall patient care.

- **Dependency on Technology Vendors**
  - **Vendor Lock-In:** Healthcare organizations may become dependent on specific AI technology vendors, limiting their ability to switch providers or adopt new technologies in the future.
  - **Monopolization Risks:** The concentration of AI expertise and technology in a small number of companies could lead to monopolization, reducing competition and innovation.
  - **Collaboration with Vendors:** Healthcare organizations must develop collaborative relationships with AI vendors to ensure that technologies are customized to meet their unique needs while retaining flexibility.

Future Outlook and Recommendations

Invest in high-quality data, explainable AI models, and robust privacy frameworks to overcome current limitations. Foster collaboration among healthcare providers, technologists, policymakers, and patients, while leveraging public-private partnerships and federated learning. Build trust through ethical guidelines and regulatory harmonization to enable sustainable AI integration in healthcare.

- **Potential Solutions to Address Challenges**
  - **Improving Data Quality:** Investing in high-quality, diverse, and well-annotated datasets is essential for improving the accuracy and generalizability of AI models in healthcare.
  - **Enhancing Model Interpretability:** Research and development efforts should focus on creating AI models that are more interpretable and transparent, allowing healthcare providers to understand and trust AI-driven decisions.
  - **Strengthening Privacy Protections:** Developing robust data protection frameworks that ensure patient privacy and security is critical for the safe deployment of AI in healthcare.
- **Collaborative Efforts between Stakeholders**
  - **Multi-Stakeholder Collaboration:** Addressing the challenges of AI

in healthcare requires collaboration between healthcare providers, technologists, policymakers, and patients.

- **Cross-Disciplinary Expertise:** Bringing together experts from fields such as medicine, AI, ethics, and law is essential for creating well-rounded and effective AI solutions.
- **Public-Private Partnerships:** Public-private partnerships can help drive innovation in AI while ensuring that healthcare organizations have access to the necessary resources and expertise.

- **Innovations to Overcome Limitations**
  - **Advances in Explainable AI (XAI):** The development of explainable AI models that provide clear and understandable insights into their decision-making processes can help address issues of transparency and trust.
  - **Federated Learning Models:** Federated learning, which allows AI models to be trained on decentralized data without sharing sensitive information, offers a solution to data privacy and access challenges.
  - **Adaptive AI Systems:** Developing AI systems that can adapt to new data and environments without requiring frequent retraining will improve scalability and generalization.
- **Roadmap for Future AI Integration in Healthcare**
  - **Building Trust and Awareness:** Raising awareness about the benefits and limitations of AI in healthcare through education and public engagement is crucial for its widespread adoption.
  - **Developing Ethical Guidelines:** Establishing clear ethical guidelines for the use of AI in healthcare will help address concerns related to bias, privacy, and accountability.
  - **Regulatory Harmonization:** Working towards regulatory harmonization at the national and international levels will enable the safe and effective deployment of AI across healthcare systems worldwide.

Conclusion

AI holds immense potential to revolutionize healthcare by improving diagnostic accuracy, streamlining treatment processes, and optimizing patient care. From enabling earlier disease detection through predictive analytics to assisting in complex surgeries and personalizing treatment plans, AI has already begun to reshape the landscape of modern healthcare. However, this transformative power comes with significant challenges that must be addressed before AI can fully realize its potential.

One of the most pressing issues is the quality and availability of healthcare data. AI systems require vast, high-quality datasets to function effectively, yet healthcare data often suffers from fragmentation, inconsistency, and inaccessibility. These challenges are compounded by issues of bias in AI models, which arise when datasets do not adequately represent diverse populations. This can lead to AI systems that perform well for certain groups but poorly for others, exacerbating existing health disparities.

Furthermore, the lack of interoperability between AI systems and existing healthcare infrastructure, such as electronic health records (EHRs), remains a significant hurdle. The absence of standardized data formats across institutions impedes the seamless integration of AI into healthcare workflows, limiting its effectiveness. This technical complexity is exacerbated by the "*black box*" nature of many AI algorithms, particularly in deep learning models. The opacity of these systems raises concerns among healthcare professionals about the reliability and trustworthiness of AI-driven recommendations, creating a barrier to widespread adoption.

Ethical and legal concerns also loom large in the conversation about AI in healthcare. Issues related to patient privacy, data security, and the potential for AI errors are critical to address. Determining who is accountable for mistakes made by AI systems remains a gray area, and without clear regulations and guidelines, healthcare institutions may be reluctant to fully embrace AI technologies. Additionally, the high costs of implementing AI systems present another limitation, particularly for low-resource healthcare settings, where the infrastructure may not be adequate to support such advanced technology.

Despite these challenges, AI's future in healthcare is promising. The successful integration of AI will require collaboration across multiple stakeholders, including technologists, healthcare professionals, policymakers, and regulatory bodies. Efforts must focus on creating AI systems that are transparent, equitable, and easy to integrate into existing healthcare practices. Moreover, robust training programs will be essential to equip healthcare professionals with the necessary skills to effectively use AI tools and interpret their outputs.

Importantly, AI should be viewed as a tool to augment human decision-making, rather than replace it. Human oversight and collaboration will remain critical, especially in life-or-death scenarios where AI systems may lack the contextual understanding or empathy that human practitioners provide. With responsible development and deployment, supported by comprehensive regulatory frameworks, AI has the potential to significantly improve healthcare outcomes, reduce disparities, and enhance the overall efficiency of healthcare systems.

Ultimately, while AI's challenges in healthcare are formidable, they are not insurmountable. By addressing these limitations through thoughtful and ethical approaches, AI can play a crucial role in shaping the future of global healthcare, making it more efficient, accessible, and effective for all.

As AI continues to evolve, its transformative potential in healthcare grows stronger, offering new possibilities for diagnosis, treatment, and system efficiency.

The next chapter explores the future trajectory of AI in healthcare, highlighting emerging trends, innovations, and the path forward for responsible adoption.

Points to Remember

- AI models rely on vast, high-quality data, but healthcare data is often fragmented, incomplete, or inconsistent, limiting the accuracy of AI-driven solutions.
- AI models trained on biased or unrepresentative datasets can perpetuate healthcare inequalities, especially for underrepresented populations, leading to inaccurate or harmful outcomes.
- Integrating AI into healthcare systems is complicated by differing data standards, formats, and legacy systems, making seamless AI integration difficult.
- Many AI algorithms, especially in deep learning, lack transparency in how they arrive at decisions, causing trust issues among clinicians and patients.
- AI's reliance on personal healthcare data raises significant concerns about patient privacy, consent, and data security. Clarifying accountability in cases of AI errors is also crucial.
- AI technologies in healthcare face slow regulatory approvals due to unclear guidelines, leading to delays in deployment and usage.
- For AI to be successful in healthcare, it must be developed with a focus on fairness, transparency, and accountability. Continuous research and regulatory oversight are essential to ensure AI aligns with ethical standards.
- AI models often struggle to generalize across diverse populations, medical conditions, or healthcare environments, which limits their widespread applicability.
- AI implementation varies widely across countries, with low-resource settings facing significant barriers in terms of cost, infrastructure, and technological readiness.

Further Readings

Here are some recommended further readings on the challenges and limitations of AI in healthcare:

Books:

- **"Artificial Intelligence in Healthcare"** by Adam Bohr and Kaveh Memarzadeh (2020): Provides an in-depth overview of AI applications in healthcare, including the challenges and ethical considerations of using AI technologies in clinical settings.

- **"Deep Medicine: How Artificial Intelligence Can Make Healthcare Human Again"** by Eric Topol (2019): Focuses on how AI can improve healthcare by enhancing, rather than replacing, the role of human caregivers. Discusses AI's potential while addressing its limitations.
- **"AI in Healthcare: A Critical Analysis of the Legal, Ethical, and Social Implications"** by Nathalie Burkert and Ruth Müller (2022): This book delves into the regulatory, ethical, and societal challenges surrounding AI in healthcare.
- **"Artificial Intelligence and Machine Learning in Healthcare: A Systematic Review of Their Impact on Healthcare, Cost, and Outcomes"** by Ankur Teredesai and Neal Chawla (2019): A thorough examination of the impact of AI and ML on healthcare systems, with a particular focus on the limitations and obstacles to its implementation.

Research Articles:

- **"Ethical and Legal Challenges of Artificial Intelligence-Driven Healthcare"** by Tanuj Kancherla and Amit Chhabra, published in *Healthcare* (2021): Discusses the legal, regulatory, and ethical challenges AI faces in the healthcare sector.
- **"Opportunities and Challenges for Artificial Intelligence in Healthcare"** by Andrew Beam and Isaac Kohane, published in JAMA (2018): A well-cited article that outlines both the promise of AI in healthcare and the hurdles related to data quality, integration, and scalability.
- **"Artificial Intelligence in Healthcare: Opportunities, Risks, and Ethical Considerations"** by Jovana Jovanović et al., published in *Journal of Medical Ethics* (2020): This paper covers the ethical considerations of using AI in healthcare, from patient privacy to accountability for AI-driven medical decisions.
- **"Artificial Intelligence in Medical Practice: The Question of Accountability"** by Gabrielle Samuel and Barbara Prainsack, published in *Journal of Medical Ethics* (2019): Explores the accountability concerns and regulatory challenges associated with AI-driven healthcare technologies.

Reports:

- **"The Future of AI in Healthcare: The Road to AI Maturity"** by *Deloitte Insights* (2020): A detailed industry report discussing AI maturity in healthcare, the roadblocks to adoption, and strategies for overcoming these challenges.
- **"Artificial Intelligence in Global Health: Defining a Collective Path Forward"** by USAID *and* WHO (2021): This report looks at the global implications of AI in healthcare, especially in low-resource settings, with a focus on ethical, regulatory, and practical challenges.

CHAPTER 8
Future of AI in Healthcare

Introduction

As we step into an era marked by rapid advancements in artificial intelligence, the healthcare sector is undergoing a profound transformation. AI's potential to revolutionize healthcare has moved beyond theoretical discussions to real-world applications, impacting how we prevent, diagnose, treat, and manage diseases. From predictive analytics in population health to AI-driven robotic surgeries and personalized medicine, the future of healthcare is increasingly intertwined with intelligent technologies.

This chapter delves into the evolving landscape of AI in healthcare, examining the current innovations and emerging trends that are shaping its future. We explore how AI is augmenting medical professionals, enhancing patient outcomes, and addressing some of the most pressing challenges in the industry, such as the global shortage of healthcare workers, rising costs, and the need for equitable access to quality care.

However, with great promise comes significant challenges. The integration of AI into healthcare systems is fraught with ethical, legal, and technical complexities. Issues such as data privacy, algorithmic bias, and the need for regulatory frameworks are critical factors that will influence how AI is adopted and scaled in healthcare.

In this chapter, we investigate how these factors interplay with the advances in AI technologies, offering insights into the future trajectory of AI in healthcare and the potential to redefine patient care, research, and medical innovation for generations to come.

Structure

In this chapter, the following topics will be covered:

- AI-Driven Diagnostics: Early Detection and Accuracy
- Personalized Treatment and AI in Precision Medicine

- AI-Enabled Remote Monitoring and Telemedicine
- Robotics and AI-Assisted Surgeries
- AI in Drug Discovery and Development
- AI for Administrative Efficiency
- The Road Ahead: AI as a Collaborative Tool

AI-Driven Diagnostics: Early Detection and Accuracy

One of the most transformative aspects of artificial intelligence in healthcare is its ability to significantly enhance the accuracy and speed of medical diagnostics. Traditionally, the process of diagnosing diseases, especially complex conditions, relies on the expertise and experience of healthcare professionals who manually analyze patient symptoms, medical images, and lab results. Despite the high skill level of medical practitioners, human error is inevitable, and the manual nature of this process can be time-consuming, leading to delays in diagnosis and treatment. AI promises to revolutionize this space by improving diagnostic precision, speeding up the detection of diseases, and, often, identifying conditions that might be missed by human observation alone.

Image Recognition and Radiology

AI's role in diagnostics is perhaps most visible in the field of medical imaging and radiology. Machine learning algorithms, particularly those based on deep learning, have been developed to analyze medical images such as X-rays, MRIs, CT scans, and mammograms. These AI-powered systems can identify abnormalities such as tumors, fractures, and lesions with a level of precision that sometimes surpasses that of experienced radiologists.

For example, AI systems in mammography can detect early signs of breast cancer in imaging, often identifying subtle changes that human radiologists might overlook, especially in dense breast tissue. Similarly, in dermatology, AI algorithms trained on thousands of images of skin lesions are showing promise in detecting melanoma with accuracy levels comparable to that of dermatologists. This early detection is crucial for improving survival rates, as many cancers are more treatable when caught in their early stages.

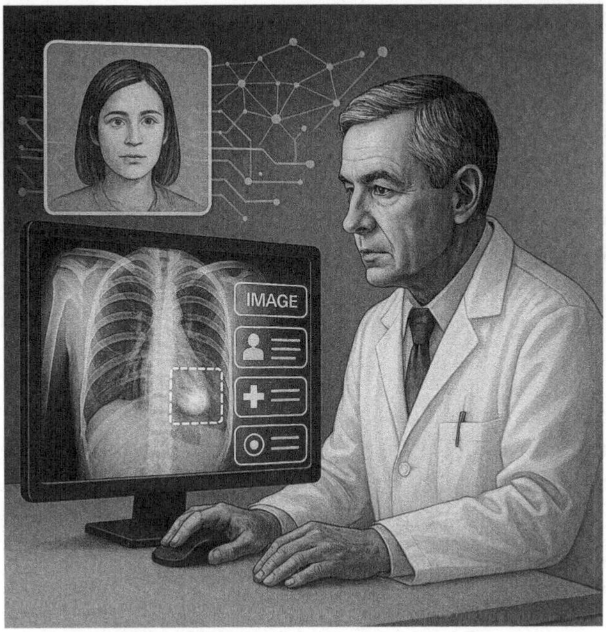

***Figure 8.1**: Image Recognition and Radiology*

The future of AI in radiology extends beyond merely flagging potential issues for human review. AI systems are expected to perform real-time image interpretation, helping radiologists make faster and more informed decisions. These systems will also reduce the workload of radiologists by automatically triaging cases, allowing them to focus on the most urgent or complex cases while routine diagnoses are handled by AI.

Predictive Analytics in Diagnostics

AI's power to analyze vast datasets and detect patterns makes it an invaluable tool in predictive diagnostics. AI algorithms can sift through a patient's medical history, genetics, lifestyle, and environmental data to identify risk factors and predict the likelihood of developing certain diseases. This type of predictive analytics enables proactive, rather than reactive, healthcare.

For instance, AI is being used to predict the onset of conditions such as diabetes, heart disease, and Alzheimer's disease. In cardiology, AI systems can analyze electrocardiograms (ECGs) or echocardiograms to predict the risk of a heart attack or other cardiovascular events well before they occur. By providing this early warning, AI enables healthcare providers to implement preventive measures and treatments that can reduce the risk of these life-threatening conditions.

In diabetes care, AI can predict when patients are likely to experience complications such as hypoglycemia or hyperglycemia by analyzing data from continuous glucose monitors and other wearable devices. This predictive power not only improves patient safety but also enhances the quality of life for those living with chronic conditions, as they can take preventive action before a medical emergency occurs.

AI in Genomics and Personalized Diagnostics

The application of AI in genomics represents a leap forward in personalized diagnostics. Genomic data contains valuable information that can help identify genetic predispositions to various diseases, but the sheer volume and complexity of genomic data make it challenging to analyze. AI, particularly deep learning algorithms, is capable of processing massive amounts of genomic data and identifying genetic mutations or patterns linked to specific diseases.

For instance, AI is being used in cancer genomics to analyze tumor DNA and identify mutations that may be driving the growth of cancer cells. By understanding the genetic makeup of a tumor, AI can help oncologists select the most appropriate targeted therapies, which can lead to better outcomes with fewer side effects. This level of precision in cancer treatment is known as precision oncology, and it is expected to become a cornerstone of cancer care in the future.

AI's role in genomics is not limited to cancer. It is also being used to identify genetic markers for diseases such as cystic fibrosis, Huntington's disease, and hereditary breast and ovarian cancer. As AI continues to advance, it will likely become an essential tool in early disease detection, allowing for earlier and more personalized interventions.

AI in Pathology

Pathology is another area where AI is making a significant impact. Pathologists traditionally diagnose diseases by examining tissue samples under a microscope to identify abnormalities. However, this process is labor-intensive and subject to human interpretation, which can introduce variability and error. AI-powered pathology tools can automate the analysis of tissue samples, identifying cancerous cells or other abnormalities with a high degree of accuracy.

Digital pathology, powered by AI, is already being used to assist in diagnosing cancers, such as prostate and breast cancer. AI algorithms can analyze tissue slides, detect patterns, and identify malignant cells faster than a pathologist working manually. In some studies, AI systems have been shown to outperform pathologists in terms of accuracy, especially in cases where the differences between healthy and cancerous cells are subtle.

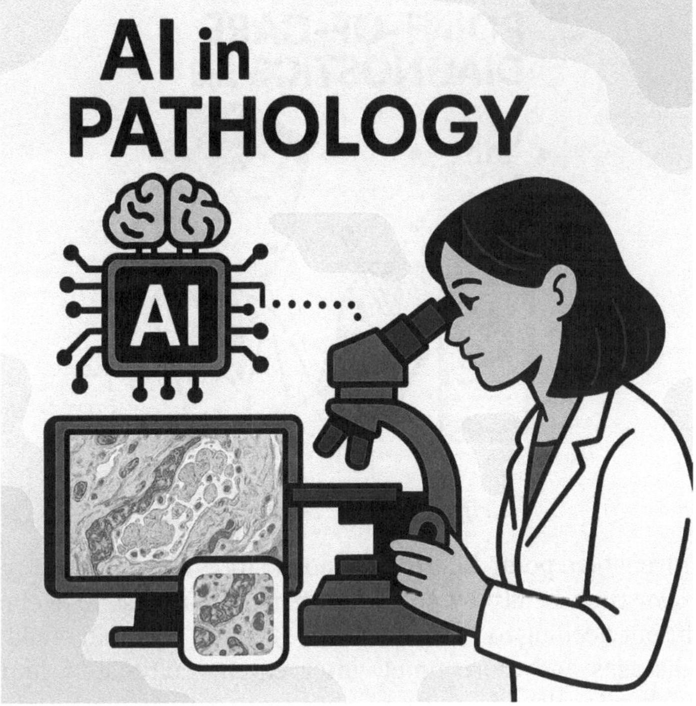

Figure 8.2: *AI in Pathology*

Looking to the future, AI in pathology could lead to fully automated diagnostic systems capable of performing routine analyses without human intervention. This would not only improve the speed and accuracy of diagnoses but also make pathology services more accessible, particularly in regions where there is a shortage of skilled pathologists.

Point-of-Care Diagnostics and AI

As AI technologies continue to evolve, their integration into point-of-care diagnostics is expected to grow, bringing diagnostic capabilities closer to the patient. AI-powered diagnostic tools can now be deployed on mobile devices, allowing for real-time, on-the-spot diagnostics in settings such as primary care offices, remote clinics, and even patients' homes.

For instance, AI is being used in portable ultrasound devices that can be operated by non-experts. These devices guide users through the imaging process and use AI to interpret the results, providing immediate diagnostic feedback. Similarly, AI-driven smartphone apps are being developed to diagnose conditions such as skin cancer, diabetic retinopathy, and respiratory diseases by analyzing images captured with the phone's camera.

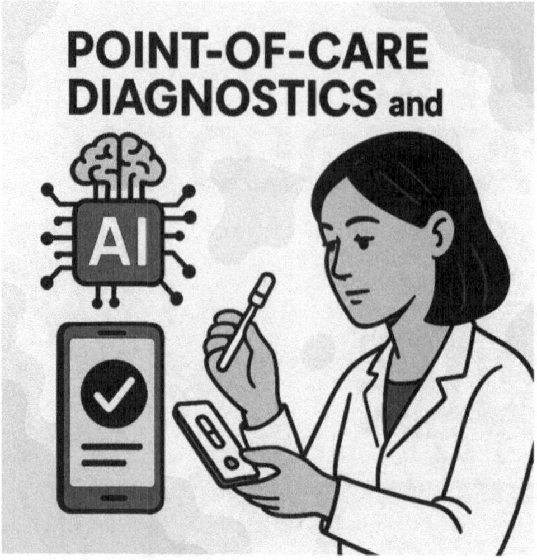

Figure 8.3: *POC Diagnostics*

In the future, AI-enabled point-of-care diagnostic tools will empower patients to take more control over their health by providing them with access to accurate, real-time diagnostics without needing to visit a healthcare facility. This shift could lead to earlier detection of diseases and more timely interventions, ultimately improving health outcomes on a global scale.

Challenges and Limitations in AI-Driven Diagnostics

While the potential of AI in diagnostics is immense, there are challenges that must be addressed to fully realize its benefits. One of the key challenges is the quality of the data used to train AI models. AI algorithms require large, high-quality datasets to learn from, and if the data is incomplete, biased, or unrepresentative, the AI's diagnostic accuracy can be compromised. Ensuring that AI models are trained on diverse datasets that account for variations in patient demographics, including age, gender, and ethnicity, is essential for developing AI systems that can serve all patients effectively.

Another challenge is the need for regulatory oversight. As AI systems take on greater responsibility in diagnosing diseases, robust regulatory frameworks will be required to ensure that these systems are safe, effective, and transparent. Currently, regulatory agencies such as the FDA are working to establish guidelines for the approval of AI-based medical devices, but the rapid pace of AI development presents a challenge in keeping regulations up to date.

Finally, there are ethical concerns related to the use of AI in diagnostics, particularly around issues of data privacy and security. AI systems rely on vast amounts of personal health data, and ensuring that this data is protected and used responsibly is crucial for maintaining patient trust.

Personalized Treatment and AI in Precision Medicine

The future of healthcare is moving toward a more personalized approach, where treatments are tailored to individual patients rather than relying on a one-size-fits-all model. Artificial intelligence (AI) is at the heart of this transformation, enabling the practice of precision medicine–a medical model that takes into account an individual's genetic, environmental, and lifestyle factors to develop personalized treatment plans. By leveraging AI's ability to process large amounts of data and uncover complex patterns, precision medicine offers the potential for more effective therapies with fewer side effects, optimized for each patient's unique characteristics.

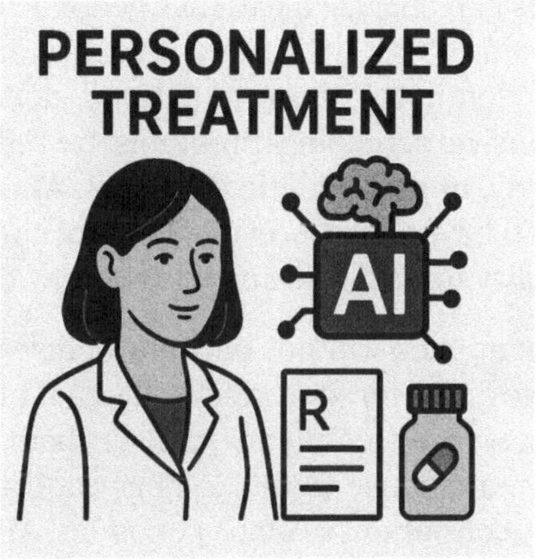

Figure 8.4: *Personalized Treatment*

The Shift from Generalized to Personalized Healthcare

Traditionally, medical treatments have been designed based on average responses across broad patient populations. For instance, most drugs and therapies are tested in clinical trials involving thousands of participants, and the results inform standard treatment protocols that are applied across diverse patient groups. While this approach has been successful in treating many conditions, it does not account for the vast variability in how individuals respond to the same treatments. Factors such as genetics, age, gender, ethnicity, and underlying health conditions can all influence the effectiveness of a treatment and its potential side effects.

AI is changing this by enabling a shift from generalized treatment plans to ones that are personalized to each patient's unique biology. By analyzing data from genomics, proteomics, and metabolomics, along with a patient's medical history and real-time health data, AI can predict how a person will respond to specific treatments, allowing doctors to choose therapies that are more likely to be effective and safe for that individual.

AI's Role in Analyzing Genomic Data

Genomic medicine plays a central role in precision medicine, and AI is proving to be a critical tool for analyzing the vast amounts of genomic data generated during genetic testing. The human genome contains over 3 billion base pairs, and interpreting the variations within this sequence to understand their implications for health is a monumental task. AI, particularly machine learning algorithms, can process this data at a scale and speed far beyond human capabilities, identifying genetic mutations and variations that are associated with specific diseases.

For example, AI algorithms can analyze a patient's genomic data to identify mutations in genes such as BRCA1 and BRCA2, which are linked to an increased risk of breast and ovarian cancers. By identifying these mutations, doctors can offer preventive treatments or more intensive screening programs to reduce the patient's risk of developing cancer. Similarly, in rare genetic disorders, AI is helping to identify novel mutations that might not have been previously associated with certain diseases, thereby improving the ability to diagnose and treat these conditions.

In the future, AI-driven genomics will not only aid in disease prevention but also in selecting the most effective drugs for individual patients. This is particularly important in fields such as oncology, where treatments such as chemotherapy often come with severe side effects, and the response to these drugs can vary greatly from patient to patient. By analyzing a cancer patient's tumor genomics, AI can recommend targeted therapies that are more likely to work based on the genetic makeup of the tumor while avoiding treatments that are less likely to be effective.

Predictive Analytics for Personalized Treatment Plans

AI's predictive analytics capabilities allow for the development of treatment plans tailored to a patient's unique needs by predicting how they will respond to different therapeutic options. These predictive models can be based on a wide range of factors, including genetic data, lifestyle factors, environmental exposures, and previous medical history. By analyzing these data points, AI can help clinicians determine the most effective course of treatment and anticipate potential complications.

For instance, in the field of cardiology, AI is being used to predict which patients are at higher risk of heart failure based on their medical history and real-time health data, such as heart rate and blood pressure from wearable devices. With this predictive insight, doctors can recommend lifestyle changes, medications, or even surgical interventions to prevent the onset of heart failure, all tailored to the individual patient.

In oncology, AI can predict how a tumor will respond to various chemotherapy agents, allowing oncologists to choose the treatment with the highest probability of success. This reduces the trial-and-error approach that often accompanies cancer treatment, where patients may have to undergo multiple rounds of different therapies before finding one that works. By using AI to personalize the treatment plan from the outset, patients can experience better outcomes with fewer side effects.

AI and Drug Matching in Precision Medicine

Another critical application of AI in precision medicine is drug matching, where AI helps to determine which medications will be most effective for a specific patient. Traditionally, prescribing medications has been based on general population averages, but patients can have widely varying responses due to factors such as genetic differences in how they metabolize drugs.

Pharmacogenomics, the study of how genes affect a person's response to drugs, is an area where AI is making significant strides. AI can analyze a patient's genetic profile to determine how they will metabolize certain medications, allowing doctors to choose the right drug and the correct dosage from the start. For example, patients with certain genetic variations might metabolize common pain medications such as codeine either too quickly, leading to overdose, or too slowly, making the drug ineffective. By using AI to guide drug prescriptions, doctors can minimize adverse reactions and improve treatment efficacy.

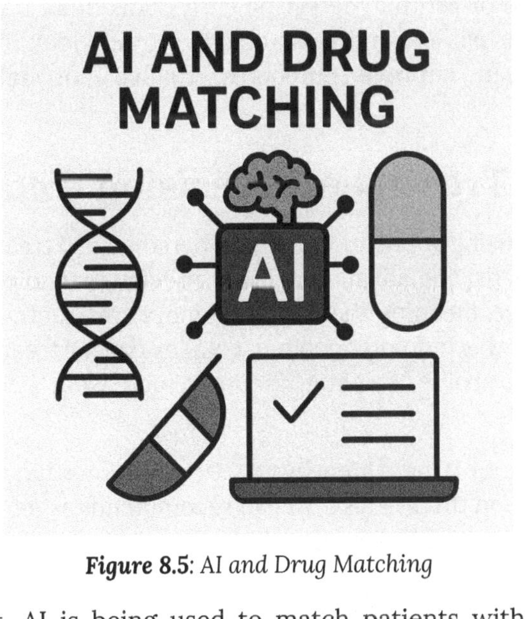

Figure 8.5: *AI and Drug Matching*

In cancer treatment, AI is being used to match patients with the most effective immunotherapies, which harness the body's immune system to fight cancer. AI algorithms analyze a patient's tumor characteristics and immune system markers to identify which immunotherapy drugs are likely to produce the best results. This targeted approach reduces unnecessary treatments and improves the chances of success.

Dynamic Personalization Through Real-Time Monitoring

One of the most exciting possibilities for AI in precision medicine is the ability to dynamically adjust treatment plans in real-time based on continuous monitoring of a patient's health. Wearable devices, such as smartwatches and fitness trackers, are becoming increasingly sophisticated, capturing data on heart rate, blood pressure, sleep patterns, physical activity, and even blood glucose levels. AI systems can analyze this data in real-time to detect subtle changes in a patient's health, allowing for early interventions or adjustments to their treatment plan before a condition worsens.

For example, in diabetes management, AI systems can analyze data from continuous glucose monitors to predict when a patient's blood sugar levels are likely to spike or drop, allowing for real-time adjustments to insulin doses. In the future, AI systems could automatically administer insulin or adjust medication dosages based on a patient's real-time health data, optimizing their treatment without the need for constant physician oversight.

Similarly, in chronic disease management, AI can monitor patients with conditions such as heart disease or asthma, detecting early signs of an impending health crisis and alerting both the patient and their healthcare provider. This kind of dynamic, personalized care can improve outcomes, reduce hospitalizations, and lower healthcare costs.

AI in Cancer Treatment: Precision Oncology

One of the most promising applications of AI in personalized treatment is in the field of oncology, where AI is driving advancements in precision oncology. Cancer is a highly heterogeneous disease, meaning that no two tumors are exactly alike, even within the same type of cancer. AI is helping oncologists tailor cancer treatments to the specific molecular and genetic profile of a patient's tumor, increasing the chances of treatment success.

AI systems analyze tumor DNA to identify genetic mutations that are driving the growth of cancer cells. Based on this analysis, AI can recommend targeted therapies designed to attack these mutations. For instance, in breast cancer, AI can identify whether a tumor is driven by overexpression of the HER2 protein and suggest treatments such as trastuzumab, a drug that specifically targets HER2-positive cancers.

Moreover, AI can help identify patients who are likely to respond to cutting-edge treatments such as immunotherapy, which has revolutionized cancer treatment in recent years. By analyzing biomarkers in a patient's immune system, AI can predict which patients are most likely to benefit from immunotherapy, sparing others from undergoing costly and potentially ineffective treatments.

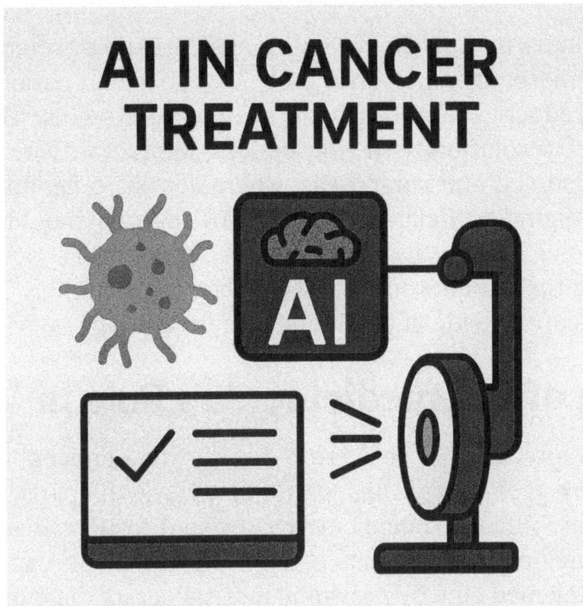

Figure 8.6: *Ai in Cancer Treatment*

Challenges and Limitations in AI-Driven Personalized Medicine

While the potential of AI in personalized medicine is vast, several challenges must be addressed to fully realize its benefits. One of the primary challenges is data integration. Personalized medicine relies on data from a wide variety of sources, including genetic information, electronic health records (EHRs), wearable devices, and environmental factors. Integrating and analyzing these diverse data types in a meaningful way remains a complex task.

Data privacy is another critical concern. AI systems need access to large amounts of sensitive personal health data to function effectively, raising questions about how this data is stored, shared, and protected. Ensuring compliance with privacy regulations such as HIPAA and GDPR is essential for maintaining patient trust.

Additionally, the cost of implementing AI-driven personalized medicine can be high, particularly in terms of genomic sequencing and advanced diagnostic tests. While the cost of these technologies is decreasing over time, making them more accessible to broader populations will be crucial for ensuring that personalized medicine does not exacerbate existing healthcare disparities.

AI-Enabled Remote Monitoring and Telemedicine

As healthcare continues to evolve in the digital age, AI-enabled remote monitoring and telemedicine are emerging as powerful tools for enhancing patient care, improving accessibility, and reducing the burden on healthcare systems. These technologies offer the potential to revolutionize the way patients interact with healthcare providers, especially in underserved and rural areas, where access to healthcare services may be limited. By leveraging artificial intelligence (AI) and real-time data from wearable devices, telemedicine platforms, and remote monitoring systems, healthcare providers can monitor patients more effectively, provide timely interventions, and offer personalized care outside of traditional clinical settings.

The Growth of Telemedicine: AI's Role in Virtual Care

Telemedicine, the practice of delivering healthcare services remotely through telecommunications technology, has seen rapid growth, particularly during the COVID-19 pandemic. While telemedicine has existed for decades, the combination of AI and telemedicine platforms has greatly expanded the capabilities of virtual care. AI enhances telemedicine by providing more accurate diagnostics, personalized treatment recommendations, and real-time monitoring, all of which can be delivered through virtual channels.

AI-powered telemedicine platforms can assist healthcare providers by analyzing patient data during virtual consultations, offering clinical decision support, and even diagnosing common conditions based on the patient's symptoms. For instance, AI chatbots are being used to conduct preliminary assessments by asking patients questions about their symptoms, medical history, and lifestyle before they speak with a healthcare provider. These chatbots can flag potential health issues and direct patients to the appropriate level of care, whether it is scheduling an in-person visit or connecting with a specialist.

In the future, telemedicine platforms will likely incorporate more sophisticated AI algorithms that can interpret medical images, analyze lab results, and provide personalized treatment plans, all within the context of a virtual consultation. This would allow healthcare providers to offer high-quality care remotely, improving access for patients who live in areas with limited healthcare infrastructure or those who have difficulty traveling to medical facilities.

AI in Remote Patient Monitoring: Real-Time Insights

One of the most impactful applications of AI in healthcare is remote patient monitoring (RPM), which uses AI to track a patient's health status in real-time, allowing for continuous care outside the clinical setting. RPM technologies typically rely on wearable devices, such as smartwatches, fitness trackers, and other health sensors, to collect vital signs like heart rate, blood pressure, glucose levels, and oxygen saturation. These devices generate vast amounts of data that AI systems can analyze to detect abnormalities, predict health events, and alert both patients and healthcare providers to potential issues.

For example, patients with chronic conditions such as heart disease, diabetes, or hypertension can benefit from AI-enabled RPM systems. In diabetes management, continuous glucose monitors (CGMs) equipped with AI algorithms can track blood sugar levels throughout the day and predict when a patient is at risk of hyperglycemia (high blood sugar) or hypoglycemia (low blood sugar). These AI systems can notify the patient to take corrective action, such as adjusting their insulin dose or consuming a carbohydrate-rich snack, thereby preventing dangerous health events before they occur.

Similarly, AI-driven RPM systems can monitor patients with heart disease by analyzing data from wearables that track heart rate, blood pressure, and activity levels. If the AI detects any signs of cardiac distress, such as arrhythmias or a sudden spike in blood pressure, it can send an alert to the patient's healthcare provider, enabling a timely intervention. This real-time monitoring reduces the need for frequent in-person visits, improves patient outcomes, and reduces the likelihood of hospital readmissions.

Chronic Disease Management and AI-Driven Remote Care

Chronic diseases, such as diabetes, hypertension, heart disease, and respiratory conditions, account for a significant portion of healthcare costs and patient morbidity worldwide. Effective management of these conditions often requires frequent monitoring, medication adjustments, and lifestyle interventions, which can be difficult for patients to maintain without constant guidance. AI-enabled remote care offers a solution by continuously monitoring patients with chronic diseases and providing personalized recommendations based on real-time data.

For example, in respiratory diseases such as chronic obstructive pulmonary disease (COPD), AI systems can analyze data from wearable devices and home-based monitoring equipment, such as pulse oximeters and spirometers, to track lung function and oxygen levels. If the AI detects a decline in lung function or a drop in oxygen saturation, it can prompt the patient to adjust their medication, seek medical attention, or take preventive actions such as using supplemental oxygen. This type of proactive care can reduce the risk of complications and hospitalizations.

In hypertension management, AI-powered blood pressure monitors can track a patient's blood pressure throughout the day and use predictive analytics to identify trends that may indicate worsening hypertension. If a patient's blood pressure begins to rise, the AI system can suggest lifestyle modifications, such as reducing salt intake or increasing physical activity, or prompt the patient to consult their healthcare provider for potential medication adjustments.

By using AI to provide personalized, real-time insights, remote care systems can empower patients to take control of their health and make informed decisions about their care, leading to better outcomes and reducing the burden on healthcare systems.

AI and Wearable Devices: Expanding Healthcare Access

Wearable devices, such as smartwatches and fitness trackers, are becoming increasingly sophisticated and are now equipped with a wide range of sensors capable of tracking various health metrics. These devices, combined with AI, are playing a crucial role in expanding access to healthcare by enabling continuous monitoring and early detection of potential health issues. The data collected by these wearables can be analyzed by AI algorithms to detect patterns and predict health events, providing both patients and healthcare providers with actionable insights.

For instance, the latest generation of smartwatches can monitor heart rate, detect irregular heart rhythms, and even perform electrocardiograms (ECGs). AI algorithms can analyze this data to identify early signs of atrial fibrillation (AFib), a common heart condition that increases the risk of stroke. By detecting AFib early, AI-enabled wearables can prompt users to seek medical attention before a serious event such as a stroke occurs.

Wearables are also being used to monitor patients with sleep disorders. AI can analyze data from sleep trackers to detect patterns of disrupted sleep, such as sleep apnea, and provide recommendations for improving sleep quality. In some cases, the AI can recommend lifestyle changes or suggest further diagnostic testing for sleep disorders.

In the future, AI-enabled wearables could be used to monitor a broader range of health metrics, such as hydration levels, stress, and mental health, providing a more holistic view of a patient's health. By democratizing access to continuous health monitoring, these devices can help identify health issues earlier, improve patient outcomes, and reduce healthcare disparities, particularly in remote or underserved areas.

AI-Driven Decision Support in Remote Care

AI-powered decision support systems are enhancing the effectiveness of remote care by helping healthcare providers make informed decisions based on real-time data. These systems analyze the data collected from remote monitoring devices and wearable technology, providing actionable insights that can guide treatment decisions.

AI can identify trends, predict outcomes, and recommend interventions, allowing healthcare providers to deliver timely and personalized care.

For example, an AI system monitoring a patient with congestive heart failure (CHF) can analyze data from wearable sensors and predict when the patient is at risk of fluid retention, a common complication of CHF. The AI can then recommend increasing the patient's diuretic dosage or adjusting their diet to prevent hospitalization. By providing these recommendations in real-time, AI-driven decision support systems can help healthcare providers stay ahead of disease progression and deliver more proactive care.

In telemedicine, AI decision support tools can assist healthcare providers during virtual consultations by analyzing patient data and offering diagnostic suggestions or treatment recommendations. For example, if a patient presents with symptoms of a respiratory infection during a virtual visit, the AI system can analyze their medical history, current symptoms, and environmental factors (such as local flu outbreaks) to suggest potential diagnoses, such as the flu or COVID-19. This allows the healthcare provider to make more accurate and informed decisions, even in a remote setting.

The Impact of AI on Healthcare Accessibility

One of the most significant benefits of AI-enabled remote monitoring and telemedicine is the potential to improve healthcare accessibility for underserved populations. In many parts of the world, particularly rural and remote areas, access to healthcare is limited by a shortage of medical professionals, long travel distances to healthcare facilities, and financial constraints. AI-driven telemedicine and remote monitoring can bridge this gap by providing virtual care options and enabling continuous monitoring without the need for in-person visits.

For example, patients in rural areas can use AI-powered telemedicine platforms to consult with specialists who may be located hundreds of miles away. AI-enabled diagnostic tools can assist healthcare providers in making accurate diagnoses during virtual consultations, reducing the need for patients to travel to larger cities for specialized care. Additionally, AI-driven RPM systems allow patients in remote areas to receive continuous monitoring for chronic conditions, reducing the likelihood of complications and hospitalizations.

By reducing geographic and financial barriers to care, AI-enabled remote monitoring and telemedicine can help address healthcare disparities and improve health outcomes for underserved populations.

Challenges and Considerations for AI in Remote Monitoring and Telemedicine

While the potential of AI-enabled remote monitoring and telemedicine is vast, several challenges must be addressed to fully realize its benefits. One of the key challenges is ensuring the accuracy and reliability of AI systems. AI algorithms must be trained on diverse datasets that account for variations in patient demographics, such as age, gender, ethnicity, and underlying health conditions, to avoid biases and ensure that the AI performs effectively for all patients.

Data privacy and security are also major concerns in remote monitoring and telemedicine. The data collected by wearable devices and telemedicine platforms is highly sensitive, and ensuring that it is protected from breaches and misuse is critical for maintaining patient trust. Healthcare providers and technology companies must comply with privacy regulations, such as the Health Insurance Portability and Accountability Act (HIPAA) in the United States and the General Data Protection.

Robotics and AI-Assisted Surgeries

Robotic surgery, guided by artificial intelligence (AI), is one of the most transformative developments in modern healthcare, offering unprecedented precision, efficiency, and safety in surgical procedures. By combining the strengths of robotics and AI, surgical outcomes are improving across a range of specialties, from minimally invasive procedures to complex surgeries that were previously deemed high-risk. AI-assisted surgeries are reducing human error, enhancing surgeon capabilities, and making surgeries safer, faster, and more accessible to patients globally.

The Rise of Robotic-Assisted Surgery

Robotic-assisted surgery (RAS) systems have been in use for several decades, with the **da Vinci Surgical System**, developed by Intuitive Surgical, being one of the most well-known. These systems allow surgeons to perform minimally invasive surgeries with high precision, using robotic arms controlled by the surgeon via a console. The robotic arms, equipped with surgical instruments, offer greater dexterity, range of motion, and stability than the human hand, allowing surgeons to perform intricate procedures with smaller incisions and less tissue damage.

AI has further enhanced these systems by providing real-time guidance and insights during surgery. While the surgeon remains in control, AI can assist by analyzing intraoperative data, anticipating the next steps, and providing feedback to optimize the surgical procedure. For example, AI algorithms can analyze imaging data to identify the exact location of tumors or blood vessels, helping surgeons avoid critical structures and reduce the risk of complications.

In the future, robotic-assisted surgeries are expected to become even more advanced, with AI playing a larger role in decision-making, improving surgical precision, and potentially performing autonomous surgeries in certain scenarios.

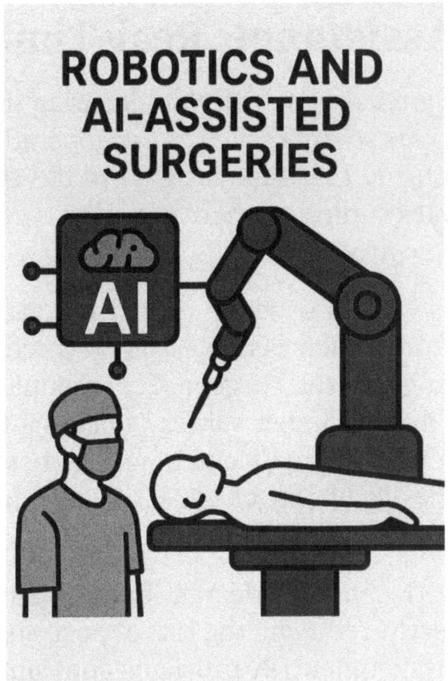

***Figure 8.7**: AI and Robotic Surgery*

AI-Powered Preoperative Planning

One of the key applications of AI in robotic surgery is in **preoperative planning**. Surgeons traditionally rely on imaging data, such as MRIs and CT scans, to plan surgical procedures. This planning process can be time-consuming and complex, as the surgeon must manually interpret the data and decide on the best approach for the surgery.

AI can automate much of this process by analyzing preoperative imaging data and generating a detailed, personalized surgical plan. Machine learning algorithms can segment anatomical structures, identify potential risks, and recommend the optimal surgical approach based on the patient's unique anatomy and medical condition. This reduces the time required for preoperative planning and ensures that the surgery is tailored to the patient's specific needs.

For instance, in orthopedic surgeries such as joint replacements, AI can analyze the patient's bone structure and recommend the best placement and alignment of the artificial joint to ensure a more natural range of motion post-surgery. Similarly, in neurosurgery, AI can assist in planning the safest route to access brain tumors while avoiding critical areas that control motor or cognitive functions.

In the future, AI systems could integrate even more data, such as a patient's genetic information or previous medical history, to create highly personalized and optimized surgical plans that improve both short- and long-term outcomes.

Intraoperative Assistance: Real-Time AI Guidance

During surgery, real-time guidance is critical to ensuring the procedure's success. AI can analyze data from various sources, such as intraoperative imaging, patient vitals, and robotic sensors, to provide real-time insights to the surgeon. This assistance is particularly useful in complex surgeries where precision is essential, such as in cardiac, neurosurgery, and oncologic procedures.

AI algorithms can process images or video feeds from cameras inside the patient's body to identify key structures, such as nerves, blood vessels, or tumors, and provide visual overlays or alerts to guide the surgeon. For example, AI can help identify the exact margins of a tumor during cancer surgery, ensuring that the surgeon removes all malignant tissue while preserving as much healthy tissue as possible. This real-time feedback reduces the likelihood of cancer recurrence and improves patient outcomes.

In orthopedic surgeries, AI can provide real-time guidance to ensure that joint implants are aligned correctly, reducing the risk of post-surgical complications such as implant loosening or misalignment. By providing constant feedback to the surgeon, AI systems help ensure that every movement is precise, minimizing the risk of human error.

Autonomous and Semi-Autonomous Surgical Systems

One of the most exciting areas of research in AI-assisted surgery is the development of **autonomous and semi-autonomous surgical systems**. While fully autonomous surgeries, where AI performs a procedure without human intervention, are still in the experimental phase, there have already been successful demonstrations of semi-autonomous surgical systems.

For example, in 2016, researchers at Johns Hopkins University demonstrated a semi-autonomous robotic system capable of suturing soft tissue with minimal human oversight. The system, known as the **Smart Tissue Autonomous Robot (STAR)**, used advanced imaging and AI algorithms to guide its movements and perform precise suturing that rivaled or even exceeded the accuracy of experienced human surgeons.

Semi-autonomous systems, where AI handles certain aspects of the surgery while the surgeon oversees the procedure, are likely to be implemented in the near future. These systems could perform routine tasks such as suturing, drilling, or cutting, freeing up the surgeon to focus on more complex parts of the procedure. By automating these repetitive tasks, AI can reduce the length of surgeries, minimize fatigue for the surgeon, and improve patient outcomes.

In the longer term, fully autonomous surgical systems could be developed for certain procedures, such as those involving highly standardized tasks or in situations where human surgeons are unavailable, such as in remote or battlefield locations. These systems could be particularly valuable in providing surgical care in regions with a shortage of skilled surgeons.

Minimally Invasive Surgery and Faster Recovery Times

One of the main benefits of robotic-assisted surgery, particularly when combined with AI, is the ability to perform **minimally invasive surgeries** (MIS), which involve smaller incisions, less tissue damage, and faster recovery times compared to traditional open surgeries. AI-enhanced robotic systems can make smaller, more precise incisions, reducing the trauma to the surrounding tissues and allowing for quicker healing.

Minimally invasive surgeries are associated with numerous benefits for patients, including reduced postoperative pain, lower risk of infection, shorter hospital stays, and faster return to normal activities. AI's ability to assist in these procedures by providing real-time guidance, improving precision, and minimizing errors is helping to expand the range of procedures that can be performed using minimally invasive techniques.

For example, in gastrointestinal surgeries, AI-enhanced robotic systems can navigate the small, delicate structures of the digestive tract with high precision, reducing the need for large incisions. Similarly, in urologic surgeries, such as prostatectomies, AI-assisted robotics can perform complex procedures with minimal impact on surrounding tissues, leading to better outcomes and quicker recovery times.

As AI continues to improve, the range of procedures that can be performed using minimally invasive techniques will likely expand, making surgery less invasive and more accessible to a broader range of patients.

Robotic Surgery in Remote and Underserved Areas

AI-powered robotic surgery has the potential to address healthcare disparities by bringing advanced surgical capabilities to remote and underserved areas where access to skilled surgeons is limited. **Telesurgery**, the practice of performing surgery remotely using robotic systems controlled by a surgeon in another location, is becoming increasingly feasible thanks to advancements in AI and telecommunications technologies.

In telesurgery, the surgeon operates a robotic system from a remote location, while AI assists with real-time image processing, decision support, and precision guidance. This allows highly skilled surgeons to perform complex procedures on patients located in rural or underserved areas without the need for the patient to travel to a major medical center. AI's ability to assist in controlling the robotic system ensures that the procedure is performed with high precision, even across long distances.

For example, in 2001, the **Lindbergh Operation** marked the first transatlantic robotic surgery, where a team of surgeons in New York City successfully removed a gallbladder from a patient in Strasbourg, France. Since then, advances in AI, robotics, and telecommunications have made such remote surgeries more practical and reliable. In the future, AI-assisted robotic systems could enable surgeons to perform life-saving procedures in areas affected by natural disasters, conflict zones, or space missions, where access to healthcare is limited.

AI-Assisted Training and Surgical Education

AI is also playing a transformative role in **surgical education and training**. Traditionally, surgeons have learned through a combination of classroom instruction, simulation, and hands-on experience in the operating room. AI is enhancing this process by providing virtual reality (VR) and augmented reality (AR) simulations that allow surgeons to practice procedures in a risk-free environment, receiving real-time feedback from AI systems.

For example, AI-powered surgical simulators can recreate complex surgical scenarios, allowing trainees to practice and refine their skills. These simulators can track the surgeon's movements, analyze their performance, and provide detailed feedback on areas that need improvement. AI can also recommend specific exercises to help trainees address their weaknesses and improve their skills over time.

Moreover, AI can analyze data from actual surgeries performed by experienced surgeons and create detailed models of optimal surgical techniques. These models can then be used to train surgical residents, helping them learn the best practices for performing specific procedures. As AI continues to advance, it will play an increasingly important role in training the next generation of surgeons, ensuring that they are equipped with the skills needed to perform complex surgeries with precision and confidence.

Challenges and Considerations for AI-Assisted Surgery

While the potential benefits of AI-assisted surgery are immense, several challenges need to be addressed to fully integrate these technologies into routine clinical practice. One of the key challenges is **regulation and safety**. AI systems in surgery must be rigorously tested and validated to ensure they perform safely and effectively. Regulatory agencies, such as the U.S. Food and Drug Administration (FDA), are still developing frameworks to evaluate the safety of AI-driven surgical technologies, and ensuring that these systems meet high standards of safety is critical.

Another challenge is the **cost** of AI-assisted robotic systems. While these technologies offer significant benefits, the high cost of acquiring and maintaining robotic surgical systems can be a barrier for many hospitals, particularly in low- and middle-income countries. As AI and robotic systems become more widespread, it will be important to address the cost barriers to ensure that these advanced surgical tools are accessible to a broader range of healthcare providers and patients.

There are also **ethical considerations** related to AI in surgery, particularly as we move toward more autonomous systems. Questions about liability, decision-making authority, and patient consent will need to be addressed as AI takes on a larger role in the operating room. Ensuring that AI systems are transparent and that patients are fully informed about the role of AI in their surgeries will be essential for maintaining trust.

AI in Drug Discovery and Development

The process of drug discovery and development is one of the most critical yet time-consuming and costly aspects of healthcare. On average, it takes over a decade and billions of dollars to bring a new drug from the research phase to market approval. AI is revolutionizing this process by significantly speeding up drug discovery, optimizing clinical trials, and reducing the overall costs associated with developing new treatments. By leveraging vast amounts of biomedical data, AI can identify promising drug candidates, predict their safety and efficacy, and streamline the entire process of drug development.

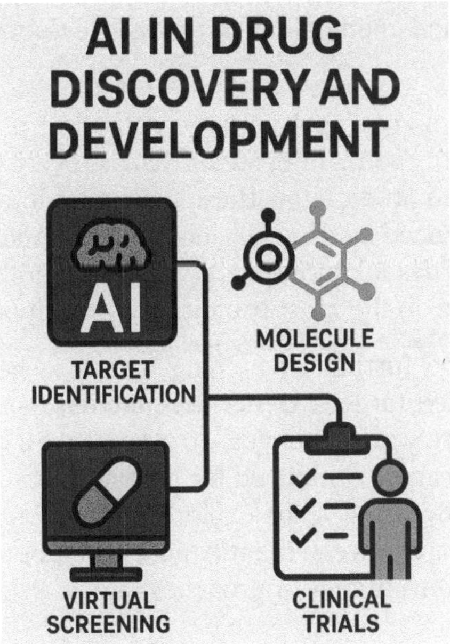

Figure 8.8: *AI in Drug Discovery*

The Traditional Challenges of Drug Discovery

Traditionally, the process of discovering and developing a new drug involves several key stages: **target identification, hit identification, lead optimization, preclinical testing, clinical trials**, and finally **regulatory approval**. Each of these stages is complex and fraught with challenges. For example, target identification, which involves discovering a biological molecule or pathway involved in a disease, is often time-consuming and difficult due to the complexity of human biology. Similarly, the process of identifying drug candidates that can interact with these targets requires screening thousands, sometimes millions, of compounds, followed by iterative optimization and testing.

Even after a promising candidate is identified, preclinical testing in laboratory settings and animal models may not always predict the drug's behavior in humans. Clinical trials, which are required to test the safety and efficacy of the drug in humans, are often expensive, slow, and have high failure rates. AI is transforming these stages by providing more accurate predictions, reducing time, and improving the likelihood of success, thus accelerating the overall drug discovery pipeline.

AI in Target Identification and Drug Design

AI's ability to process massive datasets and identify hidden patterns is revolutionizing **target identification**, the first step in drug discovery. In this phase, researchers seek to identify molecular targets–such as proteins or genes–that are associated with a particular disease. Traditionally, this required a deep understanding of biology and extensive laboratory research. AI, however, can analyze complex biological data from genomics, proteomics, and metabolomics to uncover potential drug targets more efficiently.

For example, AI algorithms can analyze large datasets from **genomic research** and patient databases to identify genes or proteins that are overexpressed in disease states, such as cancer. AI can also predict how these molecules interact with each other and how they might be influenced by drug-like compounds. Machine learning algorithms can then simulate how drugs might interact with these targets at the molecular level, helping researchers focus on the most promising candidates.

In drug design, AI can go further by helping to create new molecules tailored to interact with the identified targets. **Generative models**, such as those used in deep learning, can design entirely new chemical structures with desired properties. These AI-generated molecules can be optimized for characteristics such as binding affinity, solubility, and stability. By using AI to explore a much larger chemical space than traditional methods, researchers can identify novel compounds that would have taken years to discover using conventional approaches.

Virtual Screening and AI-Driven Compound Discovery

One of the most significant contributions of AI in drug discovery is **virtual screening**, a process that uses AI and computational models to evaluate millions of chemical compounds for their potential as drug candidates. Virtual screening allows researchers to predict how different compounds will interact with biological targets, reducing the need for costly and time-consuming laboratory experiments.

AI-driven virtual screening models can rapidly analyze vast chemical libraries to identify "hits," or compounds that show promise in binding to the target of interest. These models use machine learning algorithms to predict the interactions between the compound and the target based on the molecular structure, potentially identifying compounds that human researchers might overlook.

For instance, deep learning models such as **convolutional neural networks (CNNs)** can be trained on known drug-target interaction data to predict how a new compound will bind to a target. These predictions allow researchers to prioritize the most promising compounds for further investigation in laboratory experiments, speeding up the hit identification process.

Additionally, AI is enhancing **de novo drug design**, where algorithms are used to generate entirely new molecules with properties optimized for specific targets. Instead of relying on existing chemical libraries, AI can create new compounds that meet specific criteria, such as high binding affinity and low toxicity, offering the potential to discover drugs that are more effective and safer than those identified through traditional methods.

Predicting Drug Safety and Efficacy

One of the major reasons for failure in drug development, particularly during clinical trials, is the **toxicity** or lack of efficacy of a drug. AI is playing a pivotal role in addressing these issues by predicting potential safety concerns and therapeutic efficacy early in the drug development process.

AI models can analyze **toxicological data** from preclinical studies, as well as historical clinical trial data, to predict whether a drug candidate is likely to cause adverse side effects in humans. For example, AI can predict potential off-target effects, such as interactions with unintended proteins or pathways that could lead to toxic outcomes. Machine learning algorithms are also being used to predict whether a drug will pass through the blood-brain barrier or how it will be metabolized by the liver, giving researchers early insights into how the drug might behave in the human body.

By identifying potential safety risks early, AI can help eliminate unsuitable drug candidates before they enter clinical trials, saving time and resources. Additionally, AI can predict which patient populations are most likely to benefit from a particular drug, allowing for more targeted clinical trials and increasing the chances of success.

In terms of **efficacy**, AI can simulate how a drug will interact with its intended target, allowing researchers to refine the drug's molecular structure to improve its therapeutic effects. These simulations can also be used to predict how different doses of the drug will impact the patient, helping to optimize dosing regimens for clinical trials.

AI in Clinical Trial Optimization

AI is transforming the notoriously complex and expensive process of clinical trials, where drugs are tested for safety and efficacy in human populations. Clinical trials can take years to complete, cost millions of dollars, and often have high failure rates. AI is helping to streamline this process by improving **patient recruitment, trial design, and data analysis**.

Patient recruitment is one of the most challenging aspects of clinical trials, as finding the right patients who meet specific inclusion and exclusion criteria can be time-consuming. AI can speed up this process by analyzing electronic health records (EHRs), genomic data, and patient registries to identify individuals who are most likely to benefit from a particular treatment. This targeted recruitment approach reduces the time needed to enroll patients and increases the likelihood of trial success by ensuring that the study population is well-matched to the drug being tested.

AI can also improve **trial design** by analyzing historical trial data and predicting which endpoints, patient populations, and dosage levels are most likely to yield successful outcomes. For example, AI can suggest adaptive trial designs, where the trial protocol is modified in real-time based on interim results. This allows for more efficient use of resources and can lead to faster approvals if the drug demonstrates early signs of efficacy.

Moreover, AI can streamline **data analysis** during clinical trials by automating the process of monitoring patient outcomes, detecting adverse events, and analyzing complex datasets. Machine learning algorithms can analyze patient responses to treatment in real-time, allowing researchers to make faster decisions about whether a trial should continue or be halted. By providing real-time insights, AI reduces the risk of trial failures due to unforeseen complications and helps bring effective drugs to market more quickly.

AI and Personalized Medicine in Drug Development

AI is also playing a key role in the development of **personalized medicine**, where treatments are tailored to the specific genetic, environmental, and lifestyle factors of individual patients. In the context of drug development, AI is helping to identify biomarkers that can be used to predict how different patients will respond to a particular drug, allowing for more targeted therapies and reducing the likelihood of adverse reactions.

For example, AI can analyze genomic data to identify genetic mutations that affect how patients metabolize certain drugs. By understanding these genetic differences, pharmaceutical companies can develop personalized treatments that are more effective for specific subgroups of patients. In oncology, AI is being used to identify **biomarkers** that predict how patients with certain types of cancer will respond to targeted therapies, enabling more precise and effective treatment options.

Personalized medicine is particularly important in fields such as **immunotherapy**, where AI can help match patients with the most appropriate treatments based on their unique immune system profiles. By using AI to develop drugs that are tailored to individual patients, pharmaceutical companies can improve treatment outcomes, reduce the risk of side effects, and increase the likelihood of drug approval.

AI in Repurposing Existing Drugs

Another exciting application of AI in drug discovery is **drug repurposing**, where existing drugs developed for one condition are tested for effectiveness in treating other diseases. Drug repurposing can significantly reduce the time and cost of drug development because the safety profile of the drug is already well understood, allowing researchers to bypass many of the early-stage trials.

AI can accelerate drug repurposing by analyzing large datasets of clinical trial results, patient outcomes, and molecular interactions to identify existing drugs that may be effective for new indications. For example, during the COVID-19 pandemic, AI was used to identify potential antiviral drugs by analyzing the molecular structure of the virus and comparing it to existing drugs that had similar molecular targets.

In oncology, AI has been used to identify drugs originally developed for conditions such as hypertension or diabetes that may have anticancer properties. By finding new uses for existing drugs, AI can bring treatments to patients more quickly and at a lower cost, potentially opening up new therapeutic options for diseases with limited treatment options.

Challenges and Considerations for AI in Drug Development

While AI holds immense potential to revolutionize drug discovery and development, several challenges remain. One of the primary challenges is **data quality and availability**. AI algorithms rely on large amounts of high-quality data to make accurate predictions, and in some cases, this data may be incomplete, inconsistent, or biased.

Ensuring that AI systems are trained on diverse, high-quality datasets is essential for producing reliable results.

Another challenge is **regulatory approval**. AI is still a relatively new technology in drug development, and regulatory agencies such as the **FDA** are still developing frameworks for evaluating AI-generated drug candidates. Ensuring that AI systems are transparent, interpretable, and meet regulatory standards for safety and efficacy is critical for their widespread adoption.

Additionally, there are **ethical considerations** related to the use of AI in drug discovery, particularly around issues of data privacy and ownership. As AI systems analyze sensitive patient data, it is important to ensure that this data is handled responsibly and that patients' privacy is protected.

AI for Administrative Efficiency in Healthcare

While the clinical applications of artificial intelligence (AI) often capture headlines, the role of AI in improving administrative efficiency in healthcare is equally transformative. Administrative tasks—ranging from scheduling appointments to processing insurance claims—consume a significant portion of healthcare resources and time. AI has the potential to streamline these processes, reduce administrative burdens on healthcare staff, and improve the overall efficiency of healthcare systems. By automating routine tasks, optimizing workflows, and reducing human error, AI can save time and money, allowing healthcare providers to focus more on patient care.

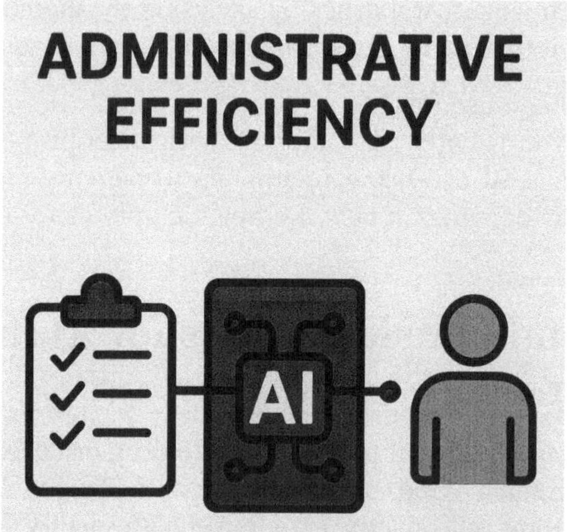

Figure 8.9: *Administrative Efficiency*

Automating Scheduling and Patient Management

One of the most time-consuming administrative tasks in healthcare is **appointment scheduling**. Traditionally, scheduling involves coordinating the availability of healthcare providers, facilities, and patients, which can lead to inefficiencies such as overbooked or underutilized resources, long wait times, and missed appointments. AI-powered scheduling tools can automate and optimize this process, leading to better utilization of resources and improved patient satisfaction.

AI-based systems can analyze data on patient demand, provider availability, and facility constraints to create optimal scheduling solutions. These tools can suggest appointment times that minimize patient wait times and maximize provider efficiency. For instance, an AI system can track when certain appointments, such as follow-up visits or routine check-ups, are more likely to be canceled or rescheduled and adjust the schedule accordingly to reduce gaps in provider availability.

Additionally, AI can offer personalized scheduling options for patients by taking into account their preferences, such as preferred times of day or locations. AI chatbots and virtual assistants can communicate directly with patients to schedule, reschedule, or cancel appointments, reducing the need for human intervention. This reduces the administrative burden on healthcare staff and improves the overall patient experience by offering greater flexibility and convenience.

Optimizing Hospital and Clinic Operations

Beyond scheduling, AI can play a crucial role in **optimizing hospital and clinic operations**. Hospitals and clinics must manage a wide range of resources, including staff, medical equipment, operating rooms, and hospital beds. Inefficient management of these resources can lead to bottlenecks, long wait times, and increased costs. AI-driven systems can analyze historical data, real-time patient flow, and operational trends to optimize resource allocation and streamline workflows.

For example, AI systems can predict patient admission rates based on historical data and external factors such as seasonal trends, population health data, or even weather conditions. These predictions allow hospitals to better prepare for fluctuations in demand, ensuring that they have the appropriate number of staff and resources available at any given time. AI can also predict when certain hospital resources, such as operating rooms or diagnostic equipment, are likely to be in high demand and allocate them accordingly to reduce patient wait times and prevent bottlenecks.

In the emergency department (ED), AI can help triage incoming patients based on the severity of their conditions, reducing wait times for critical cases. By analyzing patient data in real-time, AI can assign priority levels and direct patients to the appropriate care, improving the overall efficiency of the ED.

Furthermore, AI-driven **workflow optimization** tools can identify inefficiencies in day-to-day operations and suggest improvements. For example, AI systems can track how long each step in a patient's care journey takes and identify areas where delays frequently occur, such as during diagnostic testing or in transferring patients between departments. By highlighting these inefficiencies, AI allows hospital administrators to make data-driven decisions that improve operational efficiency and patient outcomes.

Reducing Administrative Burdens with Natural Language Processing (NLP)

One of the most labor-intensive tasks for healthcare providers is handling documentation and administrative paperwork. Healthcare professionals spend a significant portion of their time on tasks such as writing clinical notes, entering patient information into electronic health records (EHRs), and coding medical procedures for billing and insurance purposes. AI-powered **natural language processing (NLP)** technologies are helping to reduce these burdens by automating much of the documentation process.

NLP systems can automatically transcribe and analyze conversations between doctors and patients, converting spoken language into structured data that can be entered directly into EHRs. For example, an AI system can listen to a physician's verbal notes during a patient consultation and automatically generate a clinical summary, complete with relevant medical codes for billing purposes. This allows healthcare providers to focus more on patient care and less on administrative tasks.

NLP is also being used to **extract relevant information** from unstructured data sources, such as medical records, research papers, and insurance claims. By automating the extraction and analysis of medical information, NLP can streamline processes such as insurance claims processing, clinical research, and regulatory reporting. For instance, instead of manually reviewing long medical histories or research papers, healthcare professionals can use NLP-powered tools to quickly find the information they need, improving both efficiency and accuracy.

AI in Billing and Revenue Cycle Management

Another major area where AI is making a significant impact is in **billing and revenue cycle management (RCM)**. Healthcare billing is a complex process that involves coding medical procedures, submitting insurance claims, processing payments, and handling disputes. Mistakes in medical coding or claims submission can lead to delays in reimbursement, denied claims, and financial losses for healthcare providers. AI is helping to automate and streamline these processes, improving accuracy and reducing administrative burdens.

AI-powered billing systems can analyze clinical notes and automatically assign the correct **medical codes** based on the procedures and services provided. This reduces the likelihood of errors and ensures that claims are submitted correctly the first time, leading to faster reimbursement. AI can also detect discrepancies in billing and flag potential issues, such as undercoding or overcoding, which can result in revenue loss or compliance violations.

Additionally, AI-driven systems can monitor the status of insurance claims and identify patterns in claim denials, allowing healthcare providers to take proactive steps to resolve issues. For example, AI can analyze historical claims data to predict which types of claims are most likely to be denied by certain insurers and suggest ways to improve claims submission. By automating these processes, AI reduces the administrative burden on billing staff, increases revenue for healthcare providers, and shortens the time it takes to receive payments.

Fraud Detection and Prevention

AI is also playing an important role in **fraud detection and prevention** in healthcare. Healthcare fraud, including billing fraud and false insurance claims, costs the industry billions of dollars each year. AI's ability to analyze vast amounts of data and identify unusual patterns makes it an effective tool for detecting fraudulent activities.

For example, AI algorithms can analyze billing data to identify patterns that suggest fraudulent behavior, such as upcoding (billing for more expensive services than were provided) or billing for services that were not performed. By flagging these anomalies in real-time, AI can help healthcare providers and insurers detect and prevent fraud before it leads to significant financial losses.

AI can also be used to identify suspicious patterns in **insurance claims**, such as multiple claims for the same procedure from different providers or patterns of unnecessary tests and treatments. By analyzing data from multiple sources, AI systems can detect potential fraud even in complex schemes that involve multiple providers, insurers, and patients.

In addition to detecting fraud, AI can help **prevent fraud** by analyzing patient and provider data to assess the risk of fraudulent activities. For example, AI can flag providers with a history of billing inconsistencies or patients with unusual healthcare utilization patterns, allowing healthcare organizations to take preventive measures before fraud occurs.

Enhancing Patient Communication and Support with AI

AI-powered **virtual assistants** and **chatbots** are increasingly being used to improve patient communication and support, further enhancing administrative efficiency.

These AI tools can handle routine inquiries, provide appointment reminders, answer frequently asked questions, and even assist patients in navigating their treatment plans. By automating these tasks, AI reduces the workload for administrative staff and improves the patient experience by providing faster, more consistent responses.

For example, AI chatbots can be integrated into healthcare websites or patient portals to assist patients in scheduling appointments, accessing medical records, or understanding their treatment plans. These virtual assistants can also help patients manage chronic conditions by sending medication reminders, tracking symptoms, and providing educational resources. By offering 24/7 support, AI-powered tools ensure that patients receive the help they need, even outside of regular office hours.

In more complex cases, AI virtual assistants can triage patient inquiries and escalate them to human staff when necessary. For example, if a patient has a question about a potential medical emergency, the AI assistant can direct them to contact their healthcare provider immediately or visit an emergency room. This hybrid approach allows AI to handle routine administrative tasks while ensuring that more critical issues receive the attention of healthcare professionals.

AI in Managing Electronic Health Records (EHRs)

The management of **electronic health records (EHRs)** is one of the most data-intensive tasks in healthcare, and AI is helping to streamline this process. EHR systems contain a vast amount of patient data, including medical histories, test results, prescriptions, and treatment plans. Manually managing and updating this data can be time-consuming and prone to errors. AI is automating many aspects of EHR management, making it easier for healthcare providers to access, update, and analyze patient data.

For instance, AI can automatically update EHRs based on real-time data from patient monitoring systems, wearable devices, and other medical technologies. This ensures that patient records are always up-to-date, reducing the risk of errors and improving the continuity of care. AI can also analyze EHR data to identify trends in patient health, such as changes in vital signs or lab results, and alert healthcare providers to potential issues before they become serious.

Furthermore, AI can help healthcare providers search and retrieve specific information from EHRs more quickly. Natural language processing (NLP) algorithms can analyze unstructured data in EHRs, such as clinical notes, and extract relevant information, making it easier for providers to find the data they need without manually searching through long records. This improves the efficiency of patient care and allows healthcare providers to make more informed decisions based on comprehensive, up-to-date information.

Challenges and Considerations for AI in Healthcare Administration

While AI has the potential to greatly improve administrative efficiency in healthcare, there are several challenges and considerations that must be addressed to fully realize its benefits. One of the main challenges is **data privacy and security**. Healthcare data is highly sensitive, and the use of AI in managing this data raises concerns about how it is stored, shared, and protected. Ensuring that AI systems comply with data privacy regulations, such as the **Health Insurance Portability and Accountability Act (HIPAA)** in the United States, is essential for maintaining patient trust and preventing data breaches.

Another challenge is **integration with existing healthcare systems**. Many healthcare organizations use legacy systems for scheduling, billing, and EHR management, and integrating AI technologies with these systems can be difficult. Healthcare providers must invest in the infrastructure and training necessary to implement AI solutions effectively, which can be a barrier for smaller organizations with limited resources.

Additionally, there is the issue of **human oversight and accountability**. While AI can automate many administrative tasks, it is important to ensure that human staff remain involved in overseeing critical decisions, such as billing disputes or patient communications. Ensuring that AI systems are transparent and explainable so that healthcare providers understand how decisions are being made is essential for maintaining trust and accountability.

The Road Ahead: AI as a Collaborative Tool in Healthcare

The future of artificial intelligence (AI) in healthcare is not one where machines replace human healthcare providers, but one where AI and humans work in close collaboration to enhance patient care. AI's role in healthcare is evolving toward augmenting the capabilities of clinicians, improving decision-making, and creating a more efficient and effective healthcare system. The key to success lies in leveraging AI as a **collaborative tool**—one that supports healthcare professionals by providing data-driven insights, automating routine tasks, and enabling more personalized and precise care for patients. This collaborative approach, which combines human intuition and expertise with the processing power and speed of AI, has the potential to revolutionize healthcare in the years to come.

AI as a CDSS

One of the most promising areas of AI as a collaborative tool is its role in **Clinical Decision Support Systems (CDSS)**. CDSS tools are designed to assist healthcare professionals by providing evidence-based recommendations and real-time data insights during the diagnostic and treatment processes. Rather than replacing doctors, these AI-powered systems enhance a clinician's decision-making ability by processing large amounts of patient data, clinical research, and medical guidelines to offer actionable insights.

For example, AI-driven CDSS can analyze a patient's medical history, lab results, and imaging data to suggest potential diagnoses that a clinician might consider. In cases where multiple treatment options are available, AI can evaluate the likely outcomes based on patient-specific factors and recommend the most effective course of action. This collaboration between AI and clinicians ensures that decisions are made with the most up-to-date information, reducing the risk of errors and improving patient outcomes.

Additionally, CDSS tools can help clinicians stay informed about the latest developments in medical research, which is especially important in fast-moving fields such as oncology, where new treatments and protocols are constantly emerging. By integrating AI into clinical workflows, healthcare providers can make more informed decisions while reducing the cognitive load on physicians, allowing them to focus on patient care.

AI-Assisted Diagnostics: Enhancing Human Expertise

AI is proving to be an invaluable partner in **diagnostics**, where its ability to analyze medical images, lab results, and patient data with high precision can augment the expertise of healthcare professionals. In specialties such as radiology, pathology, and dermatology, AI has already demonstrated its potential to improve diagnostic accuracy, reduce human error, and enable earlier detection of diseases.

For instance, AI-powered tools are being used in radiology to assist with the interpretation of medical images such as X-rays, MRIs, and CT scans. These tools can highlight abnormalities such as tumors, fractures, or lesions that may not be immediately visible to the human eye. While the final diagnosis remains in the hands of the radiologist, AI acts as a second pair of eyes, ensuring that nothing is missed. This collaborative approach not only improves diagnostic accuracy but also helps radiologists manage their workloads more effectively, as AI can quickly screen normal cases, allowing clinicians to focus on more complex cases.

Similarly, in **pathology**, AI is being used to analyze tissue samples and identify cancerous cells with high precision. By collaborating with AI, pathologists can enhance their ability to detect early-stage cancers, leading to better patient outcomes. In dermatology, AI-driven tools are assisting clinicians in identifying skin cancers by analyzing images of skin lesions and comparing them to vast databases of known conditions. These AI tools help dermatologists make more informed decisions, especially in cases where subtle differences between benign and malignant lesions are difficult to detect.

AI and Robotics: Augmenting Surgical Precision

The integration of AI and **robotic surgery** is another area where collaboration between humans and AI is proving transformative. Robotic-assisted surgery allows surgeons to perform minimally invasive procedures with greater precision and control, and AI is enhancing this capability by providing real-time guidance and decision support during operations.

AI systems in robotic surgery can analyze intraoperative data, such as imaging and sensor data, to provide surgeons with real-time feedback and recommendations. For example, AI can help guide the surgeon's instruments to avoid critical structures such as nerves or blood vessels, reducing the risk of complications. AI can also analyze the surgical site and suggest the best path for making incisions or removing tumors. This type of collaboration between AI and surgeons enhances the precision of the surgery, leading to fewer complications, shorter recovery times, and better patient outcomes.

Importantly, AI-driven robotic systems do not replace surgeons but rather **augment** their abilities. The surgeon remains in control of the procedure, while AI acts as a tool that enhances their accuracy and decision-making. This collaborative approach ensures that human expertise and judgment are still central to the surgical process, while AI provides additional support to improve outcomes.

AI in Personalized Medicine: Tailoring Treatment Plans

One of the most exciting frontiers for AI in healthcare is its role in **personalized medicine**, where treatments are tailored to the unique genetic, environmental, and lifestyle factors of each patient. AI's ability to process vast amounts of data, including genomic data, patient medical histories, and real-time health data from wearable devices, allows healthcare providers to create more personalized treatment plans that are optimized for individual patients.

For example, in oncology, AI can analyze a patient's **tumor genetics** to identify specific mutations driving the growth of cancer cells. This information can then be used to recommend targeted therapies that are more likely to be effective based on the patient's genetic profile. Similarly, AI can predict how a patient will respond to different chemotherapy agents, helping oncologists select the most appropriate treatment regimen and avoid therapies that are less likely to be effective.

Beyond cancer treatment, AI is also being used to personalize care for patients with chronic conditions such as diabetes, heart disease, and asthma. AI-driven tools can analyze real-time health data from wearable devices and recommend personalized interventions based on the patient's current health status. This type of collaboration between AI and healthcare providers ensures that patients receive treatments that are tailored to their individual needs, improving outcomes and reducing the risk of adverse reactions.

AI-Driven Predictive Analytics for Preventive Care

Another important aspect of AI's collaboration with healthcare providers is its role in **predictive analytics** for preventive care. By analyzing large datasets from electronic health records (EHRs), wearable devices, and population health data, AI can identify patients who are at risk of developing chronic conditions or experiencing health complications in the future. This allows healthcare providers to intervene early and prevent the progression of disease.

For example, AI can analyze patterns in a patient's lab results, medical history, and lifestyle data to predict their risk of developing heart disease or diabetes. If the AI detects that a patient is at high risk, it can recommend preventive measures such as lifestyle changes, medication adjustments, or more frequent monitoring. This type of collaboration between AI and healthcare providers enables more proactive care, reducing the need for costly interventions later on.

In the field of **mental health**, AI-driven predictive analytics are being used to identify patients at risk of conditions such as depression or anxiety based on their medical history and real-time data from wearable devices. By detecting early warning signs, healthcare providers can intervene with appropriate therapies or counseling before the condition worsens.

AI in Administrative Efficiency: Streamlining Workflows

AI's collaborative role is not limited to clinical settings; it also extends to **administrative tasks**, where it helps to reduce the burden on healthcare staff by streamlining workflows and automating routine tasks. From managing appointment scheduling to processing insurance claims, AI is improving the efficiency of healthcare operations, allowing providers to focus more on patient care.

For instance, AI-powered scheduling systems can automatically assign patients to available slots based on their preferences and provider availability, reducing no-shows and optimizing clinic schedules. AI can also automate tasks such as billing and claims processing, reducing administrative errors and ensuring that providers are reimbursed more quickly. By handling these routine tasks, AI allows healthcare staff to spend more time interacting with patients and less time on paperwork.

AI's ability to **analyze data** and provide actionable insights also extends to resource management. For example, AI can predict patient admission rates based on historical data and external factors such as seasonal trends or population health data. This allows hospitals to allocate staff and resources more effectively, reducing wait times and improving patient flow.

AI and Human Intuition: The Perfect Partnership

While AI excels at processing data, identifying patterns, and making predictions, there are still areas where **human intuition, empathy, and creativity** remain essential. The collaborative model between AI and healthcare providers ensures that AI handles data-driven tasks, while clinicians apply their judgment, experience, and understanding of the patient's individual circumstances to make the final decisions.

For example, in complex cases where a patient's symptoms are not straightforward or where multiple treatment options are available, the healthcare provider can use AI as a tool to evaluate the options but ultimately rely on their own expertise and knowledge of the patient's preferences to choose the best course of action. This partnership between AI and humans allows for a morc holistic approach to patient care, combining the strengths of both technology and human insight.

Challenges and the Human-AI Relationship

Despite the many benefits of AI in healthcare, there are challenges to ensuring that AI and healthcare providers can collaborate effectively. One key challenge is the need for **trust and transparency**. For AI to be fully integrated into healthcare workflows, clinicians must trust that the AI's recommendations are reliable and based on sound data. Ensuring that AI systems are **explainable**—meaning that healthcare providers can understand how the AI arrived at its conclusions—is essential for building this trust.

Another challenge is ensuring that healthcare providers receive the necessary **training** to work effectively with AI systems. As AI becomes more prevalent in healthcare, providers will need to develop new skills in interpreting AI-generated insights, understanding the limitations of AI, and integrating AI recommendations into their clinical decision-making processes.

Moreover, ethical considerations around **data privacy** and the potential biases in AI algorithms must be addressed to ensure that AI enhances, rather than hinders, equitable healthcare. AI systems must be trained on diverse datasets to avoid perpetuating biases that could lead to disparities in care.

Conclusion

As we conclude this chapter and the book, it is clear that artificial intelligence holds extraordinary promise to redefine the future of healthcare—from enhancing diagnostic precision and personalizing treatment to improving system-wide efficiency and accessibility. The advancements discussed are not speculative; they are already reshaping patient care, clinical workflows, and medical innovation around the globe.

However, the road to responsible and equitable AI adoption is filled with complexities. Ethical considerations, data governance, infrastructure gaps, and the need for robust regulatory frameworks remain pressing concerns. Equally important is ensuring that AI serves as a collaborative partner–augmenting human judgment, not replacing it.

This book has aimed to provide a comprehensive, multi-dimensional understanding of AI in healthcare–its capabilities, limitations, and transformative potential. The future lies in a thoughtful, inclusive approach that blends technological innovation with human empathy, where AI doesn't just serve systems but truly serves people.

Points to Remember

- AI in healthcare is a tool that enhances the work of healthcare providers rather than replacing them. It plays a key role in Clinical Decision Support Systems (CDSS), where it provides real-time, evidence-based recommendations to help doctors make more informed decisions, reducing errors and improving patient outcomes.
- In diagnostics, AI assists in analyzing medical images and patient data, helping doctors detect diseases more accurately, especially in areas like radiology, pathology, and dermatology. It also plays a crucial role in robotic surgery, where AI-driven systems offer real-time guidance, allowing surgeons to perform minimally invasive surgeries with greater precision.
- AI is also transforming personalized medicine by analyzing a patient's unique data–such as genetics and lifestyle factors–to recommend tailored treatments, particularly in cancer care and chronic disease management. In preventive care, AI helps by using predictive analytics to identify patients at risk of developing health issues, allowing for early intervention and proactive care.
- Beyond clinical roles, AI improves administrative efficiency by automating tasks like scheduling, billing, and managing resources. This allows healthcare providers to spend more time focusing on patient care. While AI is powerful in processing data and recognizing patterns, human intuition, empathy, and experience remain essential for clinical decisions.
- However, for AI to be trusted in healthcare, it must be transparent, with healthcare providers understanding how AI reaches its conclusions. Ethical considerations, such as protecting patient privacy, avoiding bias in algorithms, and ensuring proper training for healthcare staff, are also important as AI becomes more integrated into healthcare systems.

Further Readings

For further reading on AI in healthcare, you can explore the following resources:

- **"*Deep Medicine: How Artificial Intelligence Can Make Healthcare Human Again*" *by Eric Topol*:** This book explores the potential of AI to improve healthcare, focusing on how AI can restore the human touch in medical practice by reducing administrative burdens and enhancing diagnostic accuracy.
- **"*Artificial Intelligence in Healthcare*" *by Adam Bohr and Kaveh Memarzadeh (Editors)*:** This textbook provides a comprehensive overview of AI applications in healthcare, covering clinical decision support, imaging, personalized medicine, and the ethical challenges associated with AI integration.
- "*Superintelligence: Paths, Dangers, Strategies*" *by Nick Bostrom*: Although this book focuses on the broader implications of AI, it offers important insights into the ethical considerations and future challenges AI poses, including in the healthcare sector.
- "*Machine Learning for Healthcare Technologies*" *by David A. Clifton (Editor)*: This book provides a detailed look into how machine learning techniques are applied in healthcare technologies, including diagnostics, medical imaging, and patient management.
- "*Artificial Intelligence in Medicine*" *journal (Elsevier)*: This peer-reviewed journal focuses on the use of AI in medical research and clinical practice, offering the latest studies and findings on AI's impact in the healthcare sector.
- "*The Future of Healthcare: Humans and Machines Partnering for Better Outcomes*" *(Deloitte Insights Report)*: This report discusses the future trends in healthcare and how AI and machine learning will drive changes in patient care, administrative processes, and personalized medicine.
- "*AI for Healthcare: Insights and Opportunities*" *by Accenture*: This report explores how AI is revolutionizing healthcare, with a focus on its economic impact, the role of AI in improving outcomes, and the challenges in widespread adoption.
- "*Transforming Healthcare with AI: The Impact on the Workforce and Organizational Structures*" *(McKinsey Report)*: McKinsey's report discusses how AI is transforming healthcare organizations and its implications for workforce structures, patient care models, and healthcare delivery.

Index

A

I

K

L

M

N

R

S

T

U

X